Reinterpreting Revolution in
Twentieth-Century Europe

THEMES IN FOCUS

Published Titles

Jonathan Barry and Christopher Brooks
THE MIDDLING SORT OF PEOPLE: Culture, Society
and Politics in England, 1550–1800

Patrick Collinson and John Craig
THE REFORMATION IN ENGLISH TOWNS, 1500–1640

Moira Donald and Tim Rees
REINTERPRETING REVOLUTION IN TWENTIETH-CENTURY
EUROPE

Christopher Durston and Jacqueline Eales
THE CULTURE OF ENGLISH PURITANISM, 1560–1700

Paul Griffiths, Adam Fox and Steve Hindle
THE EXPERIENCE OF AUTHORITY IN EARLY
MODERN ENGLAND

Tim Harris
POPULAR CULTURE IN ENGLAND, c. 1500–1850

D. Power and N. Standen
FRONTIERS IN QUESTION: EURASIAN BORDERLANDS,
700–1700

R. W. Scribner and Trevor Johnson
POPULAR RELIGION IN GERMANY AND
CENTRAL EUROPE, 1400–1800

Reinterpreting Revolution in Twentieth-Century Europe

Edited by

MOIRA DONALD & TIM REES

REINTERPRETING REVOLUTION IN TWENTIETH-CENTURY EUROPE

Introduction and editorial matter © Moira Donald and Tim Rees;
Chapter 2 © Pamela Pilbeam; Chapter 3 © Moira Donald; Chapter 4 ©
Edward Acton; Chapter 5 © Catherine Merridale; Chapter 6 © Jeremy
Noakes; Chapter 7 © Tim Rees; Chapter 8 © Jonathan Osmond;
Chapter 9 © Richard Sakwa; Chapter 10 © Krishan Kumar 2001

St. Martin's Press, Scholarly and Reference Division,
175 Fifth Avenue, New York, N.Y. 10010

First published in the United States of America in 2001

This book is printed on paper suitable for recycling and
made from fully managed and sustained forest sources.

Printed in China

ISBN 0–312–23622–0   clothbound
ISBN 0–312–23623–9   paperback

Library of Congress Cataloging-in-Publication Data

Reinterpreting revolution in twentieth century Europe / edited by Moira
Donald and Tim Rees.
    p. cm.
    Includes bibliographical references and index.
    ISBN 0–312–23622–0 (cloth)   ISBN 0–312–23623–9 (paper)
    1. Revolutions–Europe. 2. Europe–History–20th century. I. Donald, Moira.
    II. Rees, Tim, 1960–

D424 .R44 2000
303.6′4′0940904–dc21

                                                        00-031129

Contents

Acknowledgements

First and foremost the editors wish to thank the contributors to this book for taking part and for their patience during the process. We are also very grateful to those colleagues at Exeter who attended the series of papers that were the origins of many of the articles in this collection and who offered their comments and support. Finally we want to thank the history editors and staff at the publishers for their efforts in producing the book.

1. The Dynamics and Meaning of Revolution in Twentieth-Century Europe

TIM REES with MOIRA DONALD

The aim of this volume of essays is to examine political revolution in Europe during the twentieth century. The term 'revolution' has been widely applied to developments in areas as diverse as communications, information technology, medicine, science and travel, and indeed revolutions in these areas have arguably been of great significance in shaping European societies last century, but it is politics that is the focus of this present work. Nothing else has raised quite the same passions, or had the same significance, as the struggle to make fundamental and enforced changes to systems of government and the societies in which they are based. We have also limited our discussion to Europe, not because we feel that the revolutionary experiences in East Asia or Latin America, for example, are not significant, but because the global importance of political revolution necessitates some narrowing of scope. Despite confining the analysis of revolution to the European continent, we have still had to be selective for the purposes of a book of this length. Nevertheless, several of the chapters give some sense of the extra-European dimension to revolution and the final piece in the book is wholly devoted to an analysis of European revolutions in a world context.

In inviting contributions to this book we were concerned to reflect the diversity of political revolution. One way in which this has been done is by taking an interdisciplinary approach with authors drawn from the specialisms of history, political science and sociology. We aimed to give the authors as much freedom as possible in choosing the terms within which to explore the subject of revolution. One might also add here that revolution is a term open to multiple definitions, giving rise to huge

1

discussions and a voluminous literature. Accordingly, our greatest desire was for this book to reflect as many facets and meanings of revolution as possible. At the same time, to try and avoid over-eclecticism we did suggest a few guidelines. Firstly, we asked that authors should not provide just a blow-by-blow account of a revolution or revolutions, but that they should consider the broader anatomy of revolutionary political change. What makes a revolution; in what circumstances do revolutions arise? Is it necessary for them to exhibit certain common features? What are revolutions about; what are the motivations and ideas that inspire and guide the participants? What makes for the success or failure of revolution? Secondly, we suggested that the meaning of revolution should play some part in the analysis provided in each essay. To what extent is revolution ultimately elusive and uncontrollable? As John Dunn wrote in the early 1970s:

> Revolution, like the doors of the Temple of Janus, has two faces. One is an elegant, abstract and humanitarian face, an idyllic face, the dream of revolution.... The other is crude, violent and very concrete, rather nightmarish....[1]

Is revolution always driven forward on a tide of optimism, carrying with it great hopes for change and a better future? Is the outcome of revolution always a far cry from the original aims of the revolutionaries and must some degree of disillusionment always result? To a greater or lesser degree, all the contributors have addressed these questions as well as raising many others of their own. The result is that, while each essay stands in its own right, there are a number of themes running through the book on which the authors express different, even opposed, views.

The structure of the book and the subject matter of the essays also reflect this broad approach. Later on in this introduction we outline and discuss the main features of political revolution, referring to the existing literature on the subject, and also drawing together and commenting upon the main themes to be found within this volume. Two overviews taking a particular perspective on revolution provide the opening and closing contributions, the first on the legacy of the nineteenth century for the twentieth and the last placing twentieth-century Europe in a global context of revolution. Between these two is a series of case studies of radical political change. Some examine examples that are conventionally considered as revolutionary, such as Russia in 1917 and Eastern Europe in 1989–91. Others reconsider episodes that are only partially recognised as revolutionary, or which tend to be overlooked, such as Russia in 1905 and the Spanish Civil War. Finally, there are essays that analyse experiences which are not consistently labelled as revolutionary, including Stalin's great turn and Nazism. The intention is to take a fresh look at the apparently familiar, to rediscover the forgotten, and to test the boundaries of what revolution had been last century. But why a new book about revolution in twentieth-century Europe? One simple answer is that the end of the century provides the perfect opportunity to re-examine many of the important concepts that have helped us understand and define political change. And there is no doubt that 'revolution' has played a key part in the way politics in modern Europe has been analysed. Perhaps only wars have rivalled the attention and importance given to revolutions in defining the main periods of European political development and in outlining their characteristics.[2] However, an artificial sense of centennial retrospect means little in itself, and it begs the more difficult question of whether the European revolutions of last century are really important enough to justify a volume to themselves. That our answer to this is 'yes' is the real justification for this book at this time. Indeed, the notion that it is only now possible to re-evaluate the meaning of revolution during last century, and even to think of it as perhaps *the* century of revolution, was uppermost in our thinking when we launched this project. It also forms one of the themes, either explicitly or implicitly, to all the essays in the volume.

The assertion that revolution has been of considerable importance is one that requires some further elaboration. In order to appreciate why there might be some doubt about it, one has first to acknowledge the powerful role played by two revolutionary experiences in providing key paradigms and crucial watersheds defining, but also limiting, our ideas about revolution: those of 1789 in France and of 1917 in Russia. These are the 'classical' and undisputed examples of revolution in the modern era. The period between them has often been seen as defining a great 'age of revolution'. As Pamela Pilbeam shows in her chapter, the 'long' nineteenth century witnessed outbreaks of revolution in 1789, 1848 and 1871 which defined many of the models of revolution with which we are familiar. At the same time, the Russian revolutions of 1917 have often been seen as both the last of this, predominantly French, cycle of revolutions and also a final, definitive revolution itself.[3] The Bolsheviks self-consciously proclaimed themselves as the architects of the only real revolution since the French Revolution. Although both the exclusive claim to revolution and the revolutionary nature of the Russian experience have always been questioned, it is impossible to deny the profound effect that it has had as a model of revolution.

Ironically, the long shadow cast by 1917 has curiously diminished the importance attributed to revolution in twentieth-century Europe when political change has been analysed. Though it could be pointed out that all proponents of revolution have tended to see their particular one as the revolution to end all revolutions, the sense that revolution in Europe reached a definitive climax at the beginning of the century has been exceptionally strong, and felt well beyond the ranks of committed Marxists. Its corollary was an equally forceful assumption that the rest of the century has seen the exhaustion of revolution because of the failure to repeat the Bolshevik experience, except when imposed on Eastern Europe via the bayonets of the Red Army or by Communist resistance movements after the Second World War. The outbreak of the Cold War only served to confirm the identification of Russia as the main model of revolution and to institutionalise the unrepeatable nature of revolutionary change. The revolts of 1956 and 1968 in Hungary and Czechoslovakia, or the student uprisings of the 1960s in Western Europe, only served to reinforce this view because of their failure. Not surprisingly, as Krishan Kumar suggests in his chapter, the majority of commentators saw the baton of revolution being passed from Europe to China, the Caribbean, Central and South America, and Africa. Cold War brought apparent certainty and stability to Europe, at least as long as the Communist regimes remained solidly in place – as most commentators clearly felt they were and would remain so.

It must be recognised that a few dissented, one such being Crane Brinton who wrote in mid-century that:

> The nineteenth century which thought it was about to abolish foreign wars, thought also that it was about to abolish the kind of internal civil war we associate with revolution, and indeed would make revolution unnecessary. Change was still to be the characteristic of our culture, but it was to be orderly, peaceful, gradual change. Our grandfathers' catch phrase, 'evolution, not revolution' now has a faraway sound. We live in the midst of the alarums of war and revolution....[4]

Some writers even foresaw the possibility of anti-Communist revolution, though they tended to see this as a rather remote prospect. Thus John Dunn wrote in the early 1970s that:

> It is *conceivable* in the future, though not in a future which anyone has yet imagined in a very plausible way, that the political systems of those societies [the USA and USSR] too may be destroyed because of

their inability to serve the needs of their societies. But ... both of these states and a large number of their more immediate satellites are too powerful and not oppressive enough for there to be any serious prospect of revolution within an imaginable future.[5]

However, it was only with the largely unexpected overthrow of communism between 1989 and 1991 that our perceptions of revolution could be radically changed. Suddenly, the possibility of profound and rapid political change, of revolution, was a reality once again. And this time it was a revolution, or series of revolutions, which redrew the political map of Eastern Europe in a manner which buried the 'revolutionary' regimes that had seemed so solidly in place there. As Richard Sakwa points out in his contribution on the developments of 1989–91, this was paradoxically an anti-revolutionary revolution. In the wake of the immediate elation produced by the fall of European Communist regimes, some commentators attempted to claim that this, once again, was a revolution to end all revolutions. The 'end of history' was proclaimed and the assertion was made that liberal democracy was now the universal model.[6] Developments in Eastern Europe quickly made these glib predictions redundant, as liberal democracy failed to take root in many areas, and economic collapse and civil war followed. It is because we now know the end of the Soviet story, but at the same time we can see that the possibility of revolution has not ended with it – indeed we recognise that communism was itself vulnerable to revolution – that this book has become possible. More than at any other time since 1917 we are now able to see many varieties of revolution, rather than few, and for us to recognise for Europe the perspicacity of Brinton's comments and to agree with Dunn that 'as far as sheer destructive power is concerned, capacity for upheaval, the twentieth century has been the great century of revolution'.[7]

One important effect of this broader perspective is to make the definition of revolution even more of a matter of debate than it has always been. As a matter of convenience, up to this point we have used rather minimalist terminology to describe revolution as profound and enforced political change. That change needs to be deep, seeking to overturn the existing political order, is certainly at the heart of the modern conception of revolution. In one of his earlier works on the subject Krishan Kumar made the point that revolution is historical in nature, taking its 'meaning and resonance from the fact of its origin in the French revolution'.[8] As Pamela Pilbeam shows in her essay on the nineteenth century, revolution came to mean not just the overthrow of the existing order but its replacement by something different in kind. It follows that after 1789 revolutionaries have sought to recreate the 'feeling that they were attempting something great and unprecedented in the history of mankind' and that a revolutionary movement could be distinguished from others seeking change in so far as it was 'a social movement in which participants are organised to alter drastically or replace totally existing social, economic or political institutions'.[9] The fact that, in practice, the line between reformists and revolutionaries might be blurred does not render this distinction meaningless, what matters is the difference between the intention to modify the existing order and that of replacing it entirely.

That revolution also involves force is perhaps a more moot point. It could be argued that it has not necessarily followed that the aim of transforming the political order has to involve forceful means. Comparisons with other kinds of revolution – agricultural and industrial for instance – would further suggest that open force was not of the essence.[10] However, political revolution surely is distinguished from other kinds of revolution, and from reform, not just in the scope of its aims, but in that it involves an overt and immediate struggle for power. Again it is the French Revolution of 1789 which is the starting point for our modern concept of revolution; incorporating by necessity the attempted overthrow of an existing order. If revolution involves the confrontation of radically different versions of political authority and society, it follows that only a measure of force – though not necessarily of violence – must play a part. As Kumar puts it:

> The revolution lasts as long as the monopoly of force is broken, and the organisation of social groups is anarchistic. It ends, or is defeated, when one or a number of groups emerges and effectively reconstitutes the sovereign power of the state.[11]

This breaking of the power of the existing order, and the struggle to create a new one, also suggests that revolution involves sudden, not gradual, change. By definition revolution is not evolution, it marks a sudden break with the past. When we think of revolution, we also think of speed, of the acceleration of events. Revolution is dramatic and passionate, with high stakes involved for the contending parties.

While this basic conception of revolution might serve as the starting point for a definition, clearly it is inadequate in and of itself. As usual, the devil is in the detail. Particularly if one accepts that there can be no single dominant model of revolution, the real problem is degree. Exactly what constitutes a true alternative to an existing order? What range of elements are needed for us to recognise that a revolution is taking place?

Must revolutionary actors show particular ideological traits, act in a certain manner or even be aware that they are involved in a revolution? Must a revolution succeed for it to be a revolution, and how does one judge 'success'? Above all, what differences can be encompassed by revolution? In addition to these questions of definition, there is the problem of explanation. Why have revolutions occurred? What determines their course and outcome? Not surprisingly, it is in these sort of areas that both the existing literature and the contributors to the present volume display their greatest disagreement. One can perceive two overall approaches that correspond, in part, to a division between social scientists and historians.[12] Following the influential study by Theda Skocpol, *States and Social Revolution*, the former have tended to offer a structural and comparative approach, often seeking a theory of revolution and usually taking a global perspective. For instance, in a recent work James de Frozo suggests the existence of four main theories of revolution: Marxist, systems, modernisation and structural.[13] The emphasis is on discovering what a revolution is and examining its constituent parts. In contrast, historians have been more concerned with the processes of revolution, usually focusing on a particular example. The how and why of revolution are privileged here over questions of categorisation and the comparison of characteristics. The origins of revolution, the way it develops and its outcome is decided, and the role of revolutionary actors, are the main concerns of the historical approach.

The fact that each of these approaches tends to grapple with only one set of the questions raised by revolution suggests the limitations of any over-arching view of this complex political phenomenon. That there are also no clear-cut answers to any of these questions only reinforces the lesson that revolutions are intangible, not one thing but many things. Whatever approach one takes, sudden political change is chaotic and often unpredictable, with new developments and events almost taking on a life of their own. Even so, the whole idea of revolution involves movement from one state of being to another. Almost all studies, including the essays here, reflect this by breaking revolutions into different phases or constituent parts. Not surprisingly, the questions addressed and the approach taken tend to influence the distinctions drawn and the conclusions reached about them.

In what follows we attempt to combine these different elements, in order to examine them in more detail and also to assess the contributions of the different essays in this book. Under a series of broadly defined phases/stages of revolution, we look at different questions and approaches.

Revolutionary situations

In his study of European revolutions Charles Tilly makes a useful distinction between revolutionary situations and revolutionary outcomes. The first of these is a vital prerequisite of revolution, involving a breakdown in authority that allows a challenge to the existing order, which may lead to the actual transfer of power, but does not always do so. In outlining this division Tilly also expands the scope of revolution by taking the view that the existence of a revolutionary situation is sufficient to define the existence of a revolution, even if it does not lead to a revolutionary outcome.[14] This is obviously a contentious point, illustrated in the present volume in one of its aspects by a division between those essays that consider attempted revolutions and those that consider 'completed' ones. It is a problem the wider implications of which we will return to later. Even so, the need to explore the origins of revolution within an existing political order is universally accepted as an important stage in any revolutionary process.

The difficulty that is immediately raised is how we recognise the existence of a revolutionary situation and understand its development. This is by no means as straightforward as it might seem. As the essay by Pamela Pilbeam on the nineteenth century shows – supported in different ways by Edward Acton on Russia in 1917 and Krishan Kumar on the revolutionary idea – there is a very strong 'classical' image of the origins of revolution. This involves the existence of contending social and political blocs, representing the existing regime and revolutionary challengers to it. A revolutionary situation is produced when the forces of the existing order are so weakened that the opportunity for its overthrow appears. The origins of revolution lie in great part, therefore, within the status quo, and its breakdown is the mechanism by which a revolutionary situation is produced. Most often, and indeed always so in the case of the structuralist model, the existing order is conceived of as an established state and system of government – such as that of the absolutist monarchy in France or Tsarism in Russia – which faces a revolutionary threat from elements of a discontented populace. The 'old order' can be weakened in a number of different ways: by a failure to legitimise the state because of its social bases, its policies or repressive actions; by the impact of economic, political or military catastrophes; by the activities of a revolutionary opposition; and by divisions among the regime's supporters that undermine its power and authority, leading to defections to the revolutionary camp and a collapse of state institutions of control.[15] Once the monopoly of force is broken, the revolution begins.

This understanding of how a revolutionary situation is produced clearly has a great deal of validity. However, what many of the studies in this volume illustrate as well are some of the limitations to this 'classical' conception. While the Revolution of 1905 in Russia and the overthrow of Communist regimes in 1989–91 fit the pattern well, albeit with quite different versions of existing regimes, the other case studies do not. This is because the nature of the status quo that revolutions seek to replace is not always conceived in such a clear-cut fashion as might be thought. As Acton shows for Russia in 1917 – reinterpreting a supposedly 'classical' revolution – along with Noakes and Rees for Germany and Spain in the 1930s respectively, revolutions occurred here in reaction to no fixed existing 'old order' but rather to a 'new order' that was itself revolutionary. In Russia, the fall of Tsarism in February 1917 produced a regime which was itself overthrown in October 1917. In many analyses this is glossed over by underplaying the importance of February as a revolution, seeing it instead as a mere stepping-stone to the 'real' thing in October. Even if one was to accept this as a valid interpretation, the origins of the revolutionary situation and its nature are still made more complex. Similarly, the Nazi takeover in Germany and the revolutionary episodes of the Spanish Civil War came not as reactions to the long-established orders of the Second Reich and Restoration Regime, but to their replacements in the form of the Weimar and Second republics. For the Nazis, Weimar was an illegitimate 'revolutionary regime' and in the case of Spain, Rees argues explicitly that this was a revolution that came out of revolution. In these examples one set of revolutionaries came to embody, sometimes very briefly, a status quo that was challenged by other sets of revolutionaries.

An even more convoluted revolutionary situation was produced in the case of the Soviet Union under Stalin. Merridale's essay examining the 'great turn' shows how the status quo and the challenge to it were both represented within the regime, which already proclaimed itself as revolutionary in nature. Stalinist Russia also challenges some of our ideas about the need for regimes to suffer a breakdown before a revolutionary situation exists. No weakening of the state's control occurred, instead it was from within the state itself that revolution was unleashed. The Civil War in Spain was also an unusual form of state breakdown, in that the revolutionary situation was produced by a reactionary military coup, aimed at restoring a version of the status quo predating the Republic, which only half-succeeded. It was the ensuing power vacuum that then allowed revolution to spread.

This suggests that if our conception of the existing order and its breakdown can be problematic, then so can our understanding of the forces of revolution seeking to overthrow that order. For example, rather than 'outsiders' threatening to replace regime 'insiders', the proponents of the Stalinist new order were members of the state elites acting against wider society. As such, they also represented no organised revolutionary bloc or mass movement – often seen as a vital characteristic of revolution in the modern era[16] – but rather they formed 'a revolution without footsoldiers' as Merridale terms it. In fact, most accounts of revolution, including the essays collected here, acknowledge the often inchoate and disorganised nature of revolutionary forces. More often than not, a revolutionary threat comes from no single source but from a variety of different groups. This was true of Russia in 1905, 1917 and 1991 for instance. Nor is it possible to see a fixed social basis to revolutionary forces. Since the nineteenth century Marxists have often proclaimed that the industrial working class would be the locus of revolutionary activity. However, the messy reality of revolution has not proved this to be a universal truth. Even in self-proclaimed proletarian revolutions, such as October 1917, the numbers of workers involved was small, in a Russia dominated by rural peoples. In response to this, and other case studies from outside of Europe, Theda Skocpol has gone as far as suggesting that revolution has only been possible in countries which are agrarian rather than urban in nature.[17] In fact, taken together, the case studies in this book show that just about every section of whatever society can have the potential for revolutionary activity – if one accepts that a variety of revolutionary ideologies can exist.

The importance of revolutionary ideals in trying to analyse the phenomenon of revolution is difficult to underestimate. More than the existence of people or movements dedicated to changing the political and social order, it is the nature of the new order they wish to see in existence that makes them revolutionary. As already stated, what constitutes a revolutionary ideology, and the extent to which ideas actually matter in revolutions, are moot points. As Pamela Pilbeam shows, in the nineteenth century revolutions involved a wide range of ideas including anarchism, liberalism and socialism. In the twentieth century, a Marxist conception of revolution (whose nature has itself been a matter of some debate between Marxists) would lead one to conclude that very few revolutionary situations have earned that label. However, the commentators on revolution in this book largely accept that a variety of ideas as great or greater than those of the previous century can be said to be revolutionary. What matters, it can be argued, is whether they have presented a significant alternative to the status quo. This is obviously not a hard and fast test. Language and mentality might be important as well: revolutionary ideologies are those ideas espoused by people who believe themselves to be revolutionaries, as Rees argues for Spain in the 1930s. Nor are they necessarily the monopoly of the political left.[18] The essays by Noakes and Rees, for instance, analyse revolutionary movements based on the radical, ultra-nationalist and racial right. Others demonstrate the importance of a range of ideas – from anarchism, democratic liberalism, through varieties of Marxist socialism – as possible ideologies for revolutionary forces.

Equally, it has been possible for one set of ideas to be revolutionary in some circumstances, depending on the order they are in conflict with, and part of the status quo in others. This is evident in the case of liberal democracy – normally seen as 'centrist' in nature – which in our examples was a part of the revolutionary ideal in Russia in 1905, February 1917 and 1991, in Spain in 1931, and in Eastern Europe in 1989. However, in Germany in 1933 or Spain in 1936, it formed the basis of the status quo and was overtaken by other revolutionary ideals. Similar contrasts can be found with Bolshevik-style Marxism, which was a revolutionary ideal in 1917 but had become part of a threatened status quo by the end of the twentieth century. Evidently revolutionary ideologies are relative rather than absolute in their natures, and greatly dependent as sets of ideas on the circumstances in which they are to be found. In a recent analysis, Mark Katz has suggested that revolutions run in ideological waves, with Marxism-Leninism in the ascendant after the First World War and liberal democracy so in the 1980s and 1990s. Fred Halliday also sees revolutions as specifically international in scope, with revolutionaries having a universalist conception that leads them to seek to export their ideas.[19] However, as many of our examples show, this might underestimate the complex mixture of ideologies espoused during any particular revolutionary situation. Without downgrading the importance of choice on the part of revolutionary actors, it is perhaps possible to argue that it is the nature of the existing order that greatly determines the ideas of its opponents. In a sense, regimes tend to get the revolutionary oppositions they deserve.

Perhaps the most contentious question about ideology is what importance it has had in fomenting and guiding revolution. Many studies have suggested that material factors, particularly economic interests, have played a more crucial underlying role in the production of revolutionary situations. According to this view, revolutionary ideas are peripheral, and, at best, the preserve of revolutionary elites, with little direct impact on the 'masses'. Historians, in particular, have frequently been very taken with a 'view from below' that has largely downgraded ideological concerns. The contributions in this book suggest a more cautious reaction to this problem. All take ideas seriously as a key element in revolution. Ideological differences are seen to matter in the shaping of revolution. Most accept, either explicitly or implicitly, that their detailed exposition may have been generally confined to revolutionary elites but this does not mean that 'ordinary' men and women have been incapable of grasping the subtleties of ideological debate or have therefore responded only to more basic stimuli. At the same time, none of the authors here – including those whose essays are wholly dedicated to the exploration of ideas – would deny that ideas can be separated in any meaningful way from issues of self-interest. If nothing else, ideology articulates interests and serves to bind together social groups and organisations. Ultimately, however, the degree to which action depends upon a consciousness of ideas is virtually impossible to delineate precisely. Maybe all that can be said is that it has clearly been a characteristic of revolutionary situations that they have been accompanied by a great interest in ideas, and that they have at least *seemed* to matter.

Struggles for power

The role of ideology and leadership in revolutions has broader implications when one considers the next 'stage' in an unfolding revolution following the breakdown of an existing political order: the open struggle for power. That a revolutionary situation leads inexorably to such a contest might be said to be intrinsic to any understanding of revolution. However, it has sometimes been claimed that a revolutionary situation has existed but no attempt to seize power has actually occurred. Such arguments have tended to come from the perspective of the political left. A good example is that of Italy (and indeed most of Europe outside of the Russian Empire) after the First World War. Here, it has been suggested, the opportunity for revolution existed in the unrest that seriously weakened the Liberal State, but that the Socialist Party failed to seize the opportunity to overthrow it. Such an analysis clearly has a strong element of counter-factual reasoning and closely follows the arguments of the Communist International which was formed in 1919 to create Bolshevik-style parties that would fulfil their self-assumed 'proper' historical role. According to this view, revolutions (or potential revolutions) were, in effect, stillborn because of a lack of will on the part of Socialist leaders and their failure to realise that the opportunity for revolution actually existed. Ironically, of course, by the end of its life in 1943 the Comintern itself had completely failed in its task of promoting revolution – outside the rather peculiar case of Mongolia![20] It is, of course, impossible to prove conclusively the validity of such arguments – themselves the basis for many sectarian discussions among the twentieth-century political left. Our examples do not explore this aspect of revolution; instead we have chosen to examine situations where a struggle for power has actually taken place.

Once again, we have strong 'classical' images from the nineteenth century of what such a contest can be like. Conflict between two camps, the defenders and opponents of the existing order, is usually assumed. The emphasis has frequently been on naked violence between the contending groups as they grapple for power in a form of civil war. As Pamela Pilbeam's essay illustrates, the weapons of nineteenth-century revolutionaries included the erection of barricades, revolutionary riots, strikes and armed insurrection. In response, the forces of counter-revolution have deployed their own means of violence, usually utilising military or paramilitary methods in the defence of the existing order. It is a powerful and enduring image of revolutionary struggle. During the twentieth century we have also had just such a dominating revolutionary power struggle of this kind, complete with a key event (one might say myth) in the form of the storming of the Winter Palace by Bolshevik forces in October 1917. Others of our examples also fit, at least in part, this image of revolutionary and counter-revolutionary conflict: Russia in 1905, the Spanish Civil War, and many of the struggles of 1989–91 in Eastern Europe and the USSR.

While confirming some aspects of the dominant image, our case studies also suggest that a more nuanced view of the struggle for power needs to be taken. The first area where considerable variation has existed is in the nature of revolutionary struggles. In some instances, for example, conflict was virtually non-existent or severely curtailed, as the existing order proved to be too weak to effectively resist. The mere threat of force, or only a minimal application of it, was sufficient to complete a total collapse. As Noakes shows, the Nazis were effectively handed power (as were the Fascists in Italy) in Germany, rather than having to struggle openly to get it. Moves to consolidate Nazi rule did involve the suppression of political alternatives, but this hardly amounted to a classic 'seizure of power'. Similarly, many of the

Communist regimes of Eastern Europe were in such a state of decay by 1989 that they largely capitulated in the face of opposition with no serious attempt at defence. Such instances show that a struggle for power is not just a matter of the willingness of revolutionaries to engage in a seizure of power, but also requires the defenders of the old order to join the dance.

Even where there has been a serious struggle for power, this has often not involved a clash between two well-defined blocs. A striking example is that of Stalinist Russia, where the struggle to redefine the nature of Soviet power and society took place within the confines of the regime. In many respects conflict took place between different groups and organisations that were competing for control within the USSR. More often than not, the revolutionary bloc turns out to be at least as divided as united during the struggle for power. In this sense the 1905 Revolution, with its different and competing strands, was a foretaste of the Civil War after 1917, when the Bolsheviks consolidated their revolution over the bodies of not just the counter-revolutionary Whites but also over those of other revolutionary forces with quite different agendas from theirs. An even more complex competition for power occurred during the Spanish Civil War, where the dichotomy of revolutionaries versus reactionaries broke down completely with opposed versions of revolution competing within and between both sides in the war. So common is some kind of division, that one could argue that it is effectively the norm, and only the benefit of retrospect has given some struggles any different appearance. Far from being a controlled clash between blocs (a view much better seen in retrospect), revolutionary struggles have generally been chaotic affairs in which the contending parties battle on more than one front simultaneously.

The second point of contention concerns the means of force used to pursue power struggles. Again we can see from the case studies that military violence – while certainly part of the equation in just about every case – has not been the only weapon used in revolutionary struggles. The clearest cases where it has been the dominating feature are civil wars (Russia 1917–21, Spain 1936–39) and in counter-revolutions, like that which followed the Russian Revolution of 1905, and in attempted counter-revolutions such as occurred in Romania in 1989. Perhaps the most violent use of revolutionary coercion, closely linked to military force, has come from the state. Stalinist Russia and Nazi Germany provide us with the two clearest examples of such 'revolutions from above', where the Soviet new order and Hitler's racial projects were imposed by party dictatorships using forms of state terror. In other instances we find a repertoire of forceful means to contest power, including strikes, attacks on property, boycotts and demonstrations. Most have involved a battle to define the strength of popular opinion – a key feature for sustaining or removing states in the twentieth century, which have increasingly relied on a strong measure of consent for their operation and survival. Another element to this has been the importance of language and symbolism in political conflicts. As Pamela Pilbeam shows, this was already present in nineteenth-century revolutions, but it became a vital feature of those of the twentieth. Propaganda and its dissemination have played a key role in the battle for hearts and minds which has been part of revolutionary struggles. Control of and access to the expanding means of mass communication – print, radio, film, television, the Internet – have often been crucial. Likewise rival rituals and symbols have often figured prominently in revolutionary struggles. Flags, anthems and uniforms have defined political movements and regimes. Statues, buildings and street names have been important components in the struggle for 'symbolic domination' of society – perhaps most clearly seen last century when the Berlin Wall fell in 1989.

Revolutionary outcomes

The struggle for power determines whether revolutions ultimately succeed or fail, and powerfully shapes the form of any new revolutionary political and social order. However, the nature of success or failure is notoriously difficult to judge when it comes to revolutions. Many successful revolutions have been claimed but how many have actually been achieved? A revolutionary outcome occurs, according to Tilly, if a transfer of power into the hands of revolutionaries takes place and they hold that power, in a significant portion of a state, for at least a month.[21] This arbitrary time limit does, as he recognises, broaden the scope of a successful revolution. Too much so, according to other analysts who insist that a full transformation of the political and social order has to be achieved for there to be a revolutionary outcome. An even harder test is applied in the essay in this volume by Krishan Kumar, who argues that in the absence of a complete transformation there has been no revolution to speak of at all. For this reason – like Theda Skocpol, but in contrast to most of the other contributors to this book – he argues that Europe has ceased to be a centre of revolution in the twentieth century. In an earlier work on the subject he also pointed out another problem of revolution:

The persistent failure of revolutions to fulfill themselves, to make secure the conditions of freedom when once they have achieved the dissolution of sovereign power, enables us to see why political revolution has been so rare and fleeting a thing....[22]

This might be said to be the final test of a successful revolution: does its result live up to the expectations of its protagonists and is it truly a break with the past?

The problems of examining revolutionary outcomes are well illustrated by the contributions to this book. Our 'classical' conceptions are again strong. The old order is trampled into dust, with new leaders, institutions and social groups in command. Yet, even in the supposedly great age of the nineteenth century, as Pilbeam shows, the results of revolutions were often elusive and impermanent. It is all too easy to appreciate the reply attributed to Chairman Mao (among others) in response to a question about the effects of the French Revolution: 'It's too early to tell.'

The situation is no simpler for the twentieth century; Edward Acton's comparison of Russia in 1917 and 1991 explodes any lingering myth that the Bolshevik experience was somehow definitive. As we have seen, claims to having achieved a revolution have if anything multiplied during the century, to cover virtually the whole of the political spectrum. Perhaps those of the political extremes seem the clearest examples of revolutionary transformation: fascism, along with radical socialism, communism and anarchism. Radical Falangists in Spain and the Nazis in Germany, as well as Fascists in Italy, saw themselves as having created new ultra-nationalist and racial, political and social orders. Likewise, Anarchists, Communists (both Bolshevik and others) and radical Socialists in a variety of countries and situations have proclaimed the triumph of their brands of revolution.

What is more striking and contentious is the extent to which liberal democracy – theoretically in the political centre – has figured as a revolutionary outcome, to the extent that it could in some ways be claimed as the most successful form of revolution of the last century. This depends, once again, upon a claim to revolutionary status based not on intrinsic ideology but upon the clash of opposites: did democracy replace a very different type of regime? The most obvious examples of just such changes are those of February 1917 in Russia, and 1989–91 in Eastern Europe and the former USSR. However, the same could be said for many of the regimes that emerged after the First World War. Some of the changes were quite marked from what went before: Weimar

Germany, the Austrian Republic, the Portuguese Republic and the Spanish Second Republic for instance. Even countries such as Britain, France, Belgium and the Netherlands, which had fairly liberal regimes before 1918, were not liberal democracies on the pattern that only became established after that date, though here, however, the move to full democracy was more a case of evolution than revolution. Nineteenth-century liberals (and most Liberal parties) were wary of full democracy, if not downright hostile to it.[23] The banner of democracy, in the modern sense, was carried mainly by the Social Democratic movement as part of its socialist ideology. Therefore, liberal democracy is a true product of the twentieth century, not the nineteenth. Arguably what obscured the claims of liberal democrats to have achieved revolutions was the conviction that some other kind of revolutionary regime *should* have been the outcome of change. Thus the German Revolution of 1918 was a failed revolution if the expectation was of a Bolshevik-style regime rather than a liberal democratic one. For similar reasons, the achievements of the 1905 and February 1917 revolutions in Russia are easily glossed over by the assumption that the 'real' revolution was yet to come.

Not surprisingly those who proclaim themselves revolutionaries also claim, once they are in power, that they are fulfilling the ostensible aims of the revolution. However, it is equally as axiomatic that the reality of revolution is often quite different from its original aims. In terms of our case studies, it was certainly evident that, with the partial exception of 1905, significant shifts in leadership took place with revolution. At first glance, the USSR under Stalin would appear to have been an exception. However, while Stalin himself remained as supreme leader, beneath him great changes in personnel took place as the Terror claimed all the old Bolsheviks and many functionaries of the regime. Whether a real break with the past took place has, of course, been a matter of great debate: Stalin himself always claimed to be following in the path of Lenin. Moreover, the realities of both Leninist and Stalinist rule – no matter what the claims made for them – could hardly be said to have matched the utopian visions of the pre-revolutionary Bolsheviks. Similar doubts could also be applied to all the other revolutions discussed in this book. It is certainly true that in every instance, dissenting voices doubting the true value of revolution can be found. Thus disillusioned Falangists in Spain quickly came to question whether the Franco regime really represented the national syndicalist state they had envisaged. Nazi Germany also failed in some degree to match the expectations of many party supporters, though in its racial campaign it all too horrifically fulfilled and even went beyond what had been promised. In the same way, the fall of communism in 1989–91 has not led in the eyes of many of the supporters of change to the kind of regimes they had hoped for.

If it is true that all revolutions tend to raise a level of expectation which cannot possibly be achieved in reality, it is also clear that the extent to which they let their supporters down also varies greatly. Unified Germany and most post-Communist regimes in Eastern Europe might not be the paradises that some hoped for, but they have not yet devoured themselves in quite the fratricidal manner of the Spanish Civil War or Russia after 1917. It seems also to be the case that no complete break with the past is really possible. Even in revolution, present reality remains partially rooted in the past. This is not to say, therefore, that there has never been a real revolution in Europe, but rather to suggest as many of our contributors do that the pass mark cannot be 100 per cent. Political revolutions do not end politics, they place it in a new context. Compromises and competition are the result, and some jettisoning of erstwhile supporters and ideological baggage inevitably takes place.

In this introductory chapter, we have tended to have avoided definitive statements about revolution, stressing instead its ambiguous and relative nature. This is perhaps an appropriate place to be a little more definite about one lesson drawn from the twentieth-century experience of revolution in Europe. While it can always be debated as to whether great ages of revolution have taken place, what the twentieth century has shown is that revolution itself cannot ever be pronounced dead. It is something that is an established fact of the modern world. As the essays in this book show, revolution is something in a constant state of reinvention and reinterpretation. By its very nature it is surprising and unexpected and, therefore, will always remain a possible, if not always probable, development. Accordingly, there is no reason to suppose that the twenty-first century will not prove to be as revolutionary as those which have preceded it.[24]

2. Chasing Rainbows: the Nineteenth-Century Revolutionary Legacy

PAMELA PILBEAM

It is no flight of fancy to compare rainbows and revolution; both are elusive, will-o'-the-wisp, transient. Revolutions fit this definition both as process and as philosophy, even before historians start to unravel them. After the turmoil which followed the French Revolution of 1789, the nineteenth century experienced a plethora of revolutions from the smaller skirmishes of the 1820s and early 1830s to the major upheavals of 1848, terminating in the Paris Commune of 1871. The memory and effects of the 1789 Revolution dominated concepts of revolution for much of the century, stimulating liberal/constitutional objectives and nationalist ambitions. The experiences of the 1790s and responses to economic change in the following century also helped to shape the socio-economic aspirations of those involved in revolution.

This chapter will compare what contemporaries thought revolution signified with the verdict of historians and in particular will reflect on recent reappraisals.[1] Why did nineteenth-century revolutions occur? How important were memory, myth, tradition and physical symbols of earlier revolution in producing and moulding later upheavals? Who were the revolutionaries and what were their expectations? How near did they get to the rainbow's end? Why was it that insurrection was rarer in the second half of the century when revolutionary philosophies and rhetoric were much more pronounced?

Today revolution implies little more than change of some sort. It may be used to describe events in Eastern Europe, the appointment of a new manager of the England football team or an uplift bra. In the nineteenth century it was invoked in totally contradictory senses sometimes indicating a return to a starting point, sometimes a dramatic launch into the unknown. It might mean returning to first principles, which was how the American colonists defended their defiance of the British government, or a violent onslaught on an established regime and the setting up of a replacement reforming government, as in France in the 1790s. If the challenge was repulsed contemporaries might refer to the sequence of events as an insurrection, a revolt, a riot, a rising, an episode of popular effervescence, a conspiracy or even a criminal event, depending on which side of the barricades the commentator stood. Historians have added further imprecision by using revolution to describe all manner of change, economic, social, cultural and political. This chapter will focus on political and socio-economic phenomena and will expect any self-respecting revolution to involve some violence and at least to alter the personnel of central government.

Contradictory definitions reflect the political orientation of the commentator. There were three basic strands to nineteenth-century concepts of revolution, ranging from the vigorous rejection of right-wingers, the tempered acceptance of the moderate conservative/liberal *juste milieu* and the welcoming enthusiasm of some radicals. Thinkers and politicians on the extreme right, including French ultra-royalists like Joseph de Maistre, believed that revolutions were part of social degeneration and collapse, signalling a threat to the traditional authority of monarch, Church and landed titled elites. In part, 1789 was the result of economic, in part of moral, change. Materialism, disregard of spiritual authority and community values underlay right-wing explanations of the revolution in the 1790s and throughout the following century. In 1796 de Maistre was convinced that Satan had a role in bringing about the French Revolution.[2] During the nineteenth century this apocalyptic view of revolution as an extension of the Book of Revelation was refined by writers like Drumont in the 1880s who asserted that the Jewish community was particularly blameworthy. The right never saw revolutions as accidents, but as manifestations of the Anti-Christ.

Those more moderate contemporaries who gained power in the 1790s and in subsequent upheavals were less inclined to look for long-term causes. They saw revolution as the work of man, the product of error, accident or ill-judged government policy. They were inclined to deplore the violence of revolution, but appreciated its potential to rationalise, secularise and centralise the state. The conservative liberal Alexis de Tocqueville argued that the Great Revolution was less the product of the sins of the *ancien régime* than the reaction of those threatened by the reforming activities of Louis XVI's ministers.[3] Revolutions, in his view, were produced by those who resisted change, rather than the reverse, which definition at least fits the idea of revolution being a return to your starting point. De Tocqueville was a gloomy outsider in political life.

Those liberals who gained power after violent upheaval had a different view. Guizot and his fellow liberals argued that the 1830 Revolution was set off by the reactionary policies of Charles X,[4] but they would say that, wouldn't they? Revolutions are like traffic accidents, a case of two peaceable elements in inexplicable collision. Liberal contemporaries saw revolution as unavoidable and dangerous, but also as a confirmation that men controlled their own destiny.[5]

For a time of revolution, the nineteenth century is remarkably lacking in individuals, even among radicals, who admitted to being insurrectionaries or to thinking revolution desirable. Robespierre and fellow Jacobins were the mirror-image of de Maistre, believing that, in virtuous republican hands, the revolution would purify and produce a just society, but they did not want to live in a situation of constant upheaval. Their more radical contemporary, Babeuf, argued that revolution, led by a small group of far-seeing individuals, was the only route to a better society. Marx pushed man out of the driving seat. He stressed that revolution was the only significant motor of change and that its pace was determined by immutable economic laws, leading progressively from aristocratic feudalism to the proletarian state via bourgeois capitalism. The intervention of the individual in this process was as irrelevant to Marx as it was to de Maistre.

Marx, and even more rigidly his acolytes, fitted nineteenth-century revolutions into a neat pattern: 1789 signalled the beginnings of the bourgeois takeover, 1830 gave power to the wealthy financial bourgeoisie (two bankers as chief ministers in France within a few months of the revolution); in 1848 came the turn of the less rich middle class, while the June Days (1848) and the Paris Commune (1871) were samples of the proletarian revolution.[6] The Italian Risorgimento was defined by Gramsci as a bourgeois affair, the liberal leaders in 1848 in the German states were middle class. Revolutions had become class wars and tidied into a rational continuum.

The French began to systematise the memory of 1789 in the early decades of the Third Republic partly to prove that their political system was the final stage in revolutionary change. The celebration of the centenary of 1789 provided the opportunity. A professor of the history of the revolution was appointed; and a periodical to document its stages was inaugurated. The documents of the revolutionary period were classified in the National Archives by Aulard and his associates to emphasise the virtues of the centralised, bureaucratic state; 1789 was idealised as a completed revolution of the 'people', its violence for the moment sanctified and bowdlerised. The classic history of republicanism written in the Third Republic (and still in print) was so keen to dismiss the contribution of revolution that it stopped at 1870, making no mention of the 1871 Commune.[7]

Meanwhile Socialist political parties in all Western European countries asserted that revolution was far from over. Following the logic of Marx in *Das Kapital* they claimed that the peaks and troughs of economic growth and crisis which typified Europe through the nineteenth century demonstrated the inescapable decline of capitalism towards proletarian revolution. In the meantime they set to work to try to become majority parties in the national assemblies of their respective countries. The revolutions of 1917 in Russia and 1949 in China made the Marxist explanation of history irrefutable to those on the left, particularly those who preferred not to notice that neither Russia nor China had reached the overblown monopoly capitalism which Marx had argued would be the essential progenitor of proletarian revolution. Both revolutions made nonsense of the theory that political change via revolution would be the product of faceless, uncontrollable economic forces. Revolution once more became the stuff of chance, accidents, conspiracies and the machinations of ambitious individuals. In the inter-war years the left and its historians chose to cleave to their doctrine of messianic progress. The right also lost its dread of the masses and created its own 'revolutionary' fascist initiative to bolster up the state and defend and 'control' capitalism.

In 1944 the liberal revolution found its most eloquent champion with the publication of Namier's *1848: the Revolution of the Intellectuals*. Namier happily accepted that the events of that year were middle-class revolutions, but economic and social issues were dismissed in one paragraph on page 4. 'It was a fight between reason and unreason, between freedom and unfreedom.' By the 1950s liberal, together with left- and right-wing interpretations of revolution were successively discredited, although Sir Lewis Namier is still in print!

By the 1990s theorists were as well versed in the uncertainties and relativities of Heisenberg and Einstein as in the optimism of Marx and Darwin. Revolution is no longer a tale of continent-wide similarities, economic imperatives and emergent class consciousness. A fascination with the specific and particular circumstances of individual revolutions is no longer antiquarianism.[8] Every self-respecting insurrection has a gender angle.[9] Regional investigations have been profitably explored, particularly in France.[10] 'Years' of revolution have given way to more long-term analyses.[11] Historians are inclined to explain revolution not principally by the exploration of long- or even short-term socio-economic factors, but by a temporary interruption in the equilibrium of the state, stimulated by the accident of personality or war – the product of human error. Historians are again inclined to stress the role of the Enlightenment rather than bread prices in 1789. We seem to have gone full-circle back to de Tocqueville; it is not by chance that he is the favourite of the doyen of revisionist historians, François Furet.[12]

What was the legacy of 1789? The Great Revolution was the prelude to a quarter of a century of political experimentation and expedients. The middle-class leaders who gathered to turn the Third Estate into a National Assembly in June 1789 hoped to follow the precepts of the *philosophes* and create a constitutional, decentralised monarchy in which the rule of reason would replace traditional privilege. A variety of factors including their own disagreements and jealousies, the scale of popular protest, the growth of counter-revolutionary sentiments, the decision to embark on a European war and the huge cost of trying to bring about radical change, meant that expediency triumphed over philosophy. The main political heritage of the revolutionary years was confusion and diversity. The French ranged from constitutional monarchy to military dictatorship via a republic, toyed with the idea of democratic representation and slipped into a narrow oligarchy. Hoping to create liberal institutions, they became immersed in a period of Terror. In 1814, thanks to Bonapartist propaganda, the revolution signified violence and anarchy.

The actual political inheritance consisted of a well-intentioned Declaration of the Rights of Man and of the Citizen and the creation, ironically, of the fiercely centralised institutions of all kinds, from administrative to educational, which constitute the modern French state. Napoleon claimed paternity for these and for the Codes of Law, but they should rightly be seen as the revolutionary legacy. That France overran most of Europe in these years meant that they were stamped on conquered territory and local elites came to value them. French prefectoral systems and codes of law remained in place in some Italian states and the Rhineland through the nineteenth century. But the model of an elitist constitutional monarchy which Italians and Germans among others tried to imitate in 1848 was that of the Bourbon Restoration and of Louis-Philippe, not the revolution. Subsequent French revolutions, in 1830 and in 1848, seemed to act as a spur to insurrection elsewhere, particularly in the Belgian and Polish provinces and the Italian and German lands.[13] The French experiments with revolutionary communes in 1870–1 found no echoes elsewhere at the time, although their memory and mythology were to become ingredients in Bolshevik theory.

The French provided more than the ideas and institutions of revolution, they also offered potent visual and musical symbols. The present generation of historians, perhaps because of the domination of the media in our lives, constantly reminds us that the recollection of the past is not limited to the written word, but reflected in symbols, music and other artefacts. If the revolutionary momentum of the 1790s resembled nothing more logical than Russian roulette, revolutionary intent and process owed much to the retelling of history. In nineteenth-century Europe the language and concepts of political change were predominantly French, rooted in the writings of the *philosophes* as well as in the Great Revolution. The events of 1789 and the 1790s were fundamental to the remembrance and re-enactment of revolution, partly because of their chronological scope, and partly because French armies overran more of Europe than any one power had done since the days of Charlemagne. In France subsequent aspirants for political change consciously imitated the processes and adopted the symbols of the 1790s. Although French conquest had been far from welcome, the idea that the French Revolution had a Europe-wide resonance persisted.

In the nineteenth century the symbolism of revolution was French. Two flags stood sentinel; the tricolour being specifically French, the red flag increasingly international. The tricolour flag was concocted in the 1790s to represent the revolution. It was adopted successively by Napoleon and Louis-Philippe. Although this latter designation lost the tricolour some of its revolutionary odour, Louis Blanc's argument that a red flag had been the standard of the Gauls during the Hundred Years War and should be the symbol of the Second Republic was unconvincing. Following appearances in the more violent moments of the 1790s and early 1830s, the red flag came to symbolise radical, and later, socialist revolution. Partisans always asserted that it symbolised the blood of the nation and patriotic unity, but the 1790s left the red flag with the opposite aura of divisive violent class war. The tricolour was the middle-class revolutionary standard, the red flag that of the worker. The latter was the symbol of the 'social' republic between 1848 and 1851 and again in the Paris Commune of 1871. The Communard experience helped to turn it into the international flag of the workers' revolution.

The red Phrygian liberty cap, reminiscent of the headgear of freed slaves in the Roman Empire, was another favourite French revolutionary symbol of the 1790s. Like the red flag its lawless and extreme connotations persisted, especially in official memory. In 1830 the rather conservative liberals who made Louis-Philippe king were keen to mothball Phrygian caps, especially when adorning newly planted liberty trees.

The cap fared no better after the 1848 Revolution. Whereas the seal of the First Republic pictured a female figure carrying a pike surmounted by a Phrygian cap, the female on the seal of the Second Republic sports innocuous headgear representing the sun's rays, similar to that later affixed to the Statue of Liberty in America. The Phrygian cap continued to cause so much alarm that in 1876 a large statue wearing one erected in Dijon to commemorate the repulsing of the Prussian invader was destroyed.

Revolution was always female. In the 1790s well-built and scantily clad young ladies marched in procession representing either the whole revolution or some appealing feature such as Justice or Virtue. Stone, bronze or canvas provided less eye-catching substitutes and the name Marianne (the equivalent of Tracey today) was soon synonymous with revolution. Nineteenth-century Mariannes remained ambiguous. Delacroix chose a stirring semi-naked lady, adorned with Phrygian cap, to stand astride his revolutionary barricade painted weeks after the 1830 Revolution. She was exhibited in the Salon of 1831, and then bought by the government for the nation and spent the next 17 years gathering dust in the basement of the Louvre.[14] Delacroix's descendants must regret that they cannot draw royalties when *Liberty Guiding the People* is endlessly repeated on book covers today.

In the months after the February Revolution, 1848, a competition was held to find a symbol for the Republic. Almost all the entries were female, but there were few symbols of the radical revolution of the 1790s decorating this timid crew and the attempt to represent the republican revolution led to so much discord that no winner was chosen from paintings of the 20 finalists.[15] Daumier never completed his impressive and majestic entry. Those judging the section of the competition devoted to statues managed to make a decision; the one chosen, executed by Soitoux, was neglectful of traditional revolutionary symbolism. True the female figure is dressed in classical robes and leans on a laurel coronet, which itself rests on a bundle of fasces, but none of the radical symbols is present.[16] The experiences of 1848 had made revolution afraid of itself.

The revolutionary tradition was passionately sustained in song, with equally divisive consequences. The 'Marseillaise', written by Rouget de l'Isle as a marching song for the army of the Rhine in 1792 and adopted as the national anthem in 1795, was only one of a number of stirring patriotic and radical songs of the 1790s; the 'Ça Ira', written in 1790 with anti-aristocratic verses added in 1793, and the 'Carmagnole' were equally appreciated. All were subsequently suppressed as subversive, giving way to tedious Bonapartist marching music. Police reports never failed to shiver at the sound of the 'Ça Ira' in the years before 1848. The 1848 Revolution reinstated the 'Marseillaise'. The Russian Populist Peter Lavrov published new words for a 'Workers' Marseillaise' in his London newspaper *Vpered* (Forward), founded in 1873. This was to become popular before and after the 1905 Revolution in Russia.

> We go to our imprisoned brothers,
> To the hungry people we'll go.
> We'll deal damnation to the scoundrels
> And summon the people to struggle.
> Arise, revolt, toiling masses!
> Arise 'gainst the foe, ye hungry folk!
> Ring out the call of peoples' vengeance!

The Paris Commune of 1871 inspired the two most popular revolutionary songs of the next century. 'The Red Flag', based on a Communard tune, was written in 1881 by the Polish poet, B. Chervinsky:

> Down with tyrants! Off with fetters!
> No more oppression, slavish chains.
> We will show the earth a new road,
> Labour shall be the world's master.

The 'Internationale' was written by Eugène Pottier, a French poet and revolutionary while he was a fugitive in the aftermath of the Paris Commune. He published it along with other revolutionary songs in 1887. The tune was added within a year by Pierre Degeyter, a composer and lathe-operator and sung at a meeting of the International Working Men's Association in Lille. It achieved an immediate and lasting popularity.

> Arise, ye by a curse downtrodden,
> The earth's hungry and enslaved!
> Our outraged soul cries out
> And is ready to fight to the death.
> The world of violence we will destroy
> Down to its core, and then
> Our new world we will build up,
> He who has been naught, he shall be all.[17]

Who fought for, and who gained from, nineteenth-century revolutions? Contemporary paintings, lithographs and other illustrations of insurrection show 'the popular classes' of both sexes at war with the army of the current establishment. Records of dead, wounded and arrested combatants emphasise that it was artisans, not the middle classes, who were prepared to man the barricades. These were skilled men, often with some education, including tailors, weavers, hatters, printers, cabinetmakers and metalworkers. Although it was the urban revolt which always tipped the balance to produce a new regime, the countryside was often in ferment. Wine-producers and small-scale farmers rioted, attacking tax offices, bakers and merchants.[18]

As socialists like Cabet and Blanc never failed to remind their readers, revolution once made was smuggled away by politically ambitious members of the elite. Those who took control were not a new aspiring elite, but part of a traditional one, many of whom were landowners, who had often acquired church or *émigré* land during the 1790s, usually with the compensation the revolution paid them for giving up venal offices. They were professional men, often lawyers, sometimes academics, writers or doctors. Many were in government service. In the years after Napoleon's defeat, radical ferment within the elite centred on dismissed Bonapartist officials and army officers, both in France and the Italian states. They argued for checks on restored rulers, the writing of constitutions, partly in defence of their own careers. The leaders of the United Diet which fought with Frederick William IV about railway development in 1847 were his own bureaucrats. They wanted to circumscribe autocracy, develop consultative and representative assemblies and above all were worried about their own professional future. Successive Prussian governments had made it more difficult for lawyers to enter the judiciary and had reduced promotion prospects.[19] This was not entirely a bourgeois movement. Those who took charge of revolution might be a mixture of a noble and bourgeois elite, sometimes with newish titles. Revolutionary leaders might be entirely blue-blooded, as in Magyar and Polish rebellions, or great-nephews of former emperors, like Louis-Napoleon, might successfully insert themselves.

Fighters and shapers might have very different, even opposing, revolutionary objectives. The educated, comfortably off, politically ambitious men who profited from revolution, and commentators and historians who recounted the events, tended to define their objectives and the consequences of revolution using such terms as 'liberal', 'national' and, less frequently, 'social'. What did these concepts mean, what did they contribute to revolution and to what degree were they shared by the 'popular classes' on the barricades?

Was liberalism a call to arms? The term had no more precise a meaning in the nineteenth century than in our own. Benjamin Constant, a leading figure among those who came to be called liberal in the 1820s, defined it in 1819 as a series of 'rights' by which society was defined: the right to live within a recognisable system of agreed laws; to express opinions, choose a way of earning a living; to travel freely; to meet in association with others; follow a chosen religion; and have some say in government. He contrasted the indirect and small role each individual could expect to play in modern representative government with ancient Greece and its potential for direct democracy.[20] He failed to mention that the representative system set up in France in 1814 followed the British bicameral system rather than any of the experiments of the 1790s.

Liberal aspirations for wider electorates and the reduction of autocracy which figure among the demands of critics of autocracy and among revolutionary achievements can easily be interpreted as a selfish clawing for control by a wealthy elite. In 1827 Guizot, who had been banned from lecturing at the Sorbonne for several years, opened a series of lectures on civilisation in Europe, defining the principles of civilisation as 'justice, legality, publicity, liberty'.[21] The revolution contributed, once the upheavals were over, to the creation of 'a social state, which has as its basis discussion and publicity, that is to say, on the empire of public reason, on the empire of doctrines, of convictions common to all members of society'.[22]

In what ways did early nineteenth-century liberals think that liberty was a product of the revolution? Much had to be set aside that was outrageously illiberal about the 1790s before its liberal facets could be discerned. French administration, the organisation of justice, the Codes of Law, the restructuring of the Church would be claimed as the triumph of reason and liberty and offered for imitation. It is immediately apparent that the French liberals of the 1820s–1840s had a definition of liberty not unlike that of the ancient Greeks whose history had dominated their education and whom they much admired. Liberty meant freedom exclusively for wealthy males. Only those judged economically 'independent' qualified. This was measured by the amount of direct tax paid. Thus in the years of the constitutional monarchy (1814–48), 90 000 qualified as voters up to 1830 and at the most 240 000 before the 1848 Revolution. When a Landtag was created in Prussia after the 1848 Revolution, one-third of the deputies were elected by the richest 4 per cent of the voters, who paid one-third of the direct taxes. A further 13 per cent of comfortably off male citizens elected another third of the deputies, leaving the vast majority of taxpayers the right to vote for only one-third. The Piedmontese constitution, decreed by Victor Emmanuel after the 1848 revolutions, was modelled on that demolished in France in the same year and called into being a tiny electorate of adult males who paid 40 liras or more in tax annually. The same elitist system was used in united Italy from 1860.

Guizot and his colleagues argued that a certain level of income guaranteed independence, that rich voters would not be seduced by bribes. Wealth was also an indicator of education; the poor could not pay the 1000 francs or so for secondary schooling. Educated voters would be able to discern the public interest and not be consumed by private concerns and ambitions. This definition of elitist liberal politics was hard to justify, particularly as a product of revolutionary endeavour. What level of tax contribution safeguarded a man's independent judgement, 300 francs a year, as decreed in 1814, or 200 francs (post-1830) or 100 francs the level at which those with *capacité* (members of learned societies, etc.) voted after the July Days? It was transparently obvious to more radical politicians in the 1840s who argued in Banquet Campaigns and the press for a larger electorate that Guizot and his ministers were primarily concerned with keeping their jobs. The assertion that wealth guaranteed independence was scarcely sustainable when 40 per cent of the Chamber of Deputies were office-holders. The broadly held assumption, before the 1848 Revolution blew it to the winds, was that the poorer the voter, the more radical his preferences.

The revolutions of the 1820s, 1830 and 1848 are usually labelled 'liberal'. However their leaders rarely sought violent change and habitually yearned for very limited, self-interested liberty and were terrified of the insurrectionary aspect of revolution. It is not difficult to categorise what those who profited from these revolutions wanted. The model was either France, not the France of the 1790s, but of the 1820s, or, in the case of Spain, the resurrection of the Spanish constitution of 1812. Both the French constitutional charter of 1814 and the Spanish model conformed to Constant's ideas. They set up a framework for non-arbitrary, constitutional government, providing bicameral parliamentary structures alongside the traditional hereditary ruling house. Neither was strictly a parliamentary system; in neither was it specifically stated that the king should choose ministers pleasing to Parliament and there was no constitutional mechanism through which deputies could put pressure on the king either to appoint or to dismiss a group of ministers.

In effect neither Charles X of France in 1830 nor William I of Prussia in 1862 could govern constitutionally unless their governments satisfied the liberal majorities in the elected assemblies. In both instances the conflict reached a crisis; in 1830 Charles X's attempt to override the liberal majority resulted in his revolutionary overthrow; in 1862 William successfully challenged the large, but quarrelsome and fragmented liberal majority, and appointed his choice of chancellor, Bismarck. In 1830 insurgent Parisian artisans egged on reluctant liberals to defy the king, while in 1862 Prussian liberals were neither willing, nor able to seek popular backing. Indeed the liberal-dominated Landtag inspired so little popular confidence that participation in elections was only around 30 per cent.[23] In the years 1820–48 the creation and preservation of parliaments run by and for a wealthy elite had apparently seemed worth dying for to working people. By 1862 Berlin artisans were no longer willing to fight for the political pretensions of the rich.

If there was a growing distrust of the political ambitions of the liberal elite, so also was there for liberal claims for individual rights. Liberals stressed religious freedom, which, when honoured, as in France after the 1789 Revolution, offered opportunities in public life for other faiths as well as a guaranteed salary for all clergy. However the selling-off of the lands of the Catholic Church, in France in the 1790s, Spain after 1830 and Italy, both during the revolutionary years and after unification in the 1860s, only benefited the rich. For the poor it was a liberal freedom to starve because the state was slow to take over the charitable, medical and educational roles the Church had fulfilled (however badly). Clergy often found ways of continuing to collect an equivalent of the tithe, although they no longer honoured some of the obligations for which it was levied. The attack on the Church may have been revolutionary; so also was its defence, fought by the poor in counter-revolution, particularly in western France.

Likewise, and ironically, the revolutionary onslaught on feudalism profited the better-off. From the late eighteenth century feudal dues were gradually eliminated. The revolutionaries of 1789 issued a much-publicised abolition, but landlords' agents merely raised rents. The other side of 'de-feudalisation' was an attack on communal rights and the selling-off of common land, habitually to the wealthier members of the community. Liberal 'modernisation' of this kind was associated with revolution, but in reality it provoked sustained popular resistance and unrest throughout much of the century. The protection of communal traditions formed the background for all of the revolutionary outbursts of the Risorgimento in the Italian peninsula.[24]

Liberals proclaimed the freedom of the individual to associate and to make public his views. The right of association and the freedom of the press were frequently discussed in French parliaments during the constitutional monarchy. Along with other liberal 'rights' already mentioned they were written into the 1814 constitutional charter and formed part of the liberal platform during the 1820s. However, once in power men like Guizot and Thiers found it expedient to strengthen laws against public meetings (1831), against societies (1834) and against the press, culminating in the September laws of 1835.

Most expressive of the very limited nature of nineteenth-century liberalism were economic and commercial stratagems. Liberal policies did not mean the espousal of free international trade with the exception of about 20 years in mid-century. Indeed until the 1850s there was no distinction in the commercial policies of those who thought of themselves as liberals and more conservative politicians. It was widely believed among the elite that tariff barriers within a state held back economic growth; however, in times of dearth the poor engaged in extensive 'revolutionary' protest against the movement of grain, accusing merchants of profiteering. Tariff barriers were removed in Prussia after 1818. From 1834 the Prussian government initiated a series of trade treaties with other German states, the *Zollverein*, which by 1854 incorporated all except Austria and a couple of free cities in a free-trade area, with high protective tariffs to keep out foreign goods. Charles Balbo urged the adoption of a similar strategy within the Italian peninsula. The firm conviction that high external tariffs were vital, especially to keep out British manufactures, were shared by ruling elites everywhere.

Free-trade notions became associated with liberalism first in Britain and were implemented as a French initiative from the late 1850s for a generation. *Laissez-faire* strategies were also associated widely with liberal and conservative alike for the liberal economic recipe for a successful economy. Minimum restraints on producers and the least state intervention, pleased all property-owners who demanded effective military protection for their businesses and other property. Liberals argued that, free to develop without state intervention, the perceived evils of capitalism would be 'ironed out'. Bismarck secured the support of Prussian and other German liberals in the late 1860s when he offered a basket of such liberal goodies as common currencies and weights and measures.

Thus there was little that was distinctive in the economic thinking of liberals and certainly very little that was revolutionary. The reverse was true; popular insurrection was directed against liberals. Artisans protested about a wide range of changes in a variety of trades which led to increased production, at the cost of their own livelihood. Country-dwellers fought constantly, and unsuccessfully in the German and Italian states, against the dilution and abolition of the communal system. Ironically, liberal notables often profited from this unrest.

To what extent were nationalist aspirations expressed in revolutionary form? In the first half of the century liberal and national ideas were usually linked. Later liberal historians, describing the 1848 revolutions, especially in the Italian and German states, sadly reflected on the contradictions between the two which became apparent. In the Frankfurt Parliament, when the elected constitution-makers, most of them experienced bureaucrats, clashed with other national groups as well as with artisans, they were rudely dispersed by the armies of Prussia and Austria. At the beginning of the twentieth century Trevelyan rather too optimistically, given the prolonged civil war which ensued, described Garibaldi's landing in southern Italy in 1860 as an act of national liberation.[25] French revolutionaries, above all the Abbé Sieyès, taught Europeans that a nation was the sum of all its free and equal male citizens. Nations should govern themselves by written constitutions and not tolerate autocracy. Within three years the French armies were set on nearly a quarter of a century of war, launched initially ostensibly to liberate the peoples of Europe from despotism. Whether being overrun actually inspired a nationalist spirit in sympathy with the conqueror, or the reverse, the French liberal idea of constitutional nationalism had an influence in Europe, certainly until 1848.

Aspiring educated wealthy elites delighted in defining themselves as leaders of a national group using historic, cultural and linguistic criteria dear to themselves. Nationality was part of the Romantic reinvention of the past. Much about it was far from revolutionary. The cultural nationalism of Czechs and others within the Austrian Empire, encouraged by Metternich, included the composition of dictionaries, poetry, history, music and the creation of folklore museums. Cultural traditions often had to be reinvented. Italian, spoken only by the Tuscan educated elite, had to be learned by the rest of the peninsula. National sentiments was sometimes encouraged by the Great Powers to further their own ambitions against Napoleon. The rediscovery of the Greek nation fitted Great Power rivalries as much as Byronic stanzas; there was virtually no native Greek nationalism in the 1820s. There was some international reserve when the Belgians rose against their union with the Netherlands made at Vienna, until it was clear that a Belgian nation-state would not challenge the balance of power on the continent. There were murmurs of sympathy for the Poles in 1831, but no real questioning of Russian suzerainty.

In the early 1800s the German writers Fichte and Herder warned of the dangers of linking the idea of the *Volk* with political unification given the division of German lands into independent states, the major of which housed substantial non-German populations. The Italian patriot and idealist, Mazzini, set up a Young Italy as the first stage in his dreams of a Young Europe. In 1848 was witnessed the first full exposure of the complexities of revolutionary nationalism and the dichotomy of nationalism was exposed as a liberal and liberating doctrine. Europe was no more neatly divided into 'national' groups in 1848 than in the present and then as now the conflicting demands of states prevailed over nationality. Palacky, who earlier had written a history of the Czech people in German at the behest of the Bohemian Diet and was one of the organisers of the Bohemian Museum in Prague, led a movement for Czech linguistic and political autonomy when the Frankfurt Parliament tried to persuade Czechs to attend their German constituent assembly. Likewise the Poles of East Prussia proclaimed their historic right to links with Russian Poles rather than a federal Germany.[26] In the Hungarian provinces of the Austrian Empire Croats and Serbs found themselves in conflict with rival Magyars angry over attempts to Germanise and centralise their lands on Vienna. After 1848 nationalism became a theme, not of liberal revolution, but of power politics. The issue changed from liberation to domination. Nationalism ceased to be a creed of the left and became a dogma of the state and of the right, wrapping intolerance and racism around itself.

Were nineteenth-century revolutions really class wars? Were they the social revolutions ultras deplored and socialists predicted? From the early nineteenth century observers of all political persuasions were convinced that 1789 had brought the middle class to power, which to them meant professional men and government servants. Aristocratic monarchists wrung their hands at the eclipsing of the traditional landed nobility, liberals welcomed the demise of irrational privilege and the birth of a society which offered opportunities to men of intelligence and initiative. Socialists like Louis Blanc in the 1840s were critical that 1789 had laid the ground for a takeover by a selfish entrepreneurial middle class. The French Revolution actually hampered rather than assisted such economic change.[27] In recent years debunkers of Marxist theory have enjoyed disproving what few Marxists ever claimed root and branch, that 1789 was a capitalist bourgeois revolution. Revisionist historians have observed the absence of a specific social agenda, other than the attack on the Church. The tenacity of the nobility in retaining economic power and rebuilding political influence in the nineteenth century revealed the very limited 'social' character of the revolution.[28]

Social revolution had another face. Waves of peasant revolt against feudal dues accompanied the calling of the Estates-General. Urban rioting signalled the presence of serious harvest failures, food shortages and a commercial crisis. Traditionally, the poor would protest in such times and expect some redress. The 1790s were different because of the scale of France's economic difficulties and because revolutionary rhetoric encouraged the poor to expect more than the political leaders were prepared to deliver. Civil and foreign war added to France's economic crisis and made poverty much worse. Revolution had seemed to offer hope to the underprivileged, with talk of liberty, equality and citizenship. The Jacobins tried to fix maximum prices for basic foodstuffs. But successive revolutionary governments struggled to contain the popular violence which was a feature of a sense of deprivation and disappointment.

In 1796 Babeuf, a former feudal lawyer turned economic egalitarian, argued that the fighting power of the dispossessed 'people' should be mobilised using the wisdom and energy of a 'vanguard' party. A temporary dictatorship would be accompanied by the sequestration of property and its equal redistribution to all. He argued that without such a social revolution, political change would always fail. Babeuf's 'conspiracy of the Equals' of 1796 was stillborn, betrayed by a government agent who had joined the group. Babeuf and other leaders were guillotined before they could test their hypothesis that workers were 'natural' revolutionaries.

The dual notion that the 'people' were always potential revolutionaries and that revolution could be manufactured to order by tiny secret conspiracies underlay the formation of some of the secret societies like the *carbonari* cells in Italy and France in the early 1820s. In 1828 Buonarroti, one of Babeuf's conspirators, published an account of the 1796 plot[29] and after the 1830 Revolution was welcomed by Parisian radicals as the guru of a revived republican movement. Disappointed by the lack of reform after the 1830 Revolution, radicals, in part inspired by babouvist revolutionary ideas, organised secret republican clubs, the Friends of the People, the Rights of Man and others which looked for political and social reform. Their members were supposed to drill and arm themselves. Terrified for their own security, the Orleanists forced most clubs to disband (1834–5). The most fervent believers in synthetic revolution were Auguste Blanqui, Barbès and Bernard who continued to conspire, creating, successively the secret societies, the Seasons and the Family.

In 1839 the Family tried to seize power in Paris with an 1000-strong secret society of artisans, whose attempt to take the Prefecture of Police and the Hôtel de Ville, would, they believed, gain the immediate support of the entire neighbouring artisan district. Their total failure and consequent long imprisonment did not lessen faith in, and fear of, the revolutionary power of the masses. Blanqui was a revolutionary socialist, a rare breed at that time. He wanted revolution, not only to eliminate monarchy, but also to create an egalitarian social order.[30] Economic change gave new intensity, and more apparent credibility, to the notion that the 'popular classes' were always potentially insurrectionary. Alterations in the organisation and financing of traditional craft industries were producing proto-capitalism which reduced the independence of the craftsman. Most of Blanqui's followers were skilled artisans who felt that changes in production were depriving them of a future. Although there was constant, underlying rural unrest, defending communal customs and rights, combating tariff policies and so on, it was disruption in capital cities which resulted in decisive political change. Revolutions always occurred during one of the almost tenyearly cyclical depressions, when harvest failure, financial, commercial and industrial recession coincided, although every period of economic difficulty did not lead to revolution.

Social commentators criticised the selfishness and materialism of capitalism. Talk of class war became common. However most early socialists suggested alternative economic structures to capitalist competition rather than revolution. They were more concerned with educational, moral and spiritual issues than violence. Most socialists were far more interested in setting up worker or retail co-operatives than in turning the world upside down. But property-owning political elites heard phrases such as 'property is theft', knew that Cabet, with his 100 000 Icarian artisan followers, dreamt of abolishing private property and were convinced that socialism meant upheaval.

If early socialists did not issue a call to revolt, the writings of Cabet, Blanc and others aroused expectations of change among their supporters. Literacy among artisans, particularly groups such as silkworkers, was high.[31] Newspapers written by and for artisans were beginning to appear, including *L'Atelier* and Cabet's *Le Populaire*. A handful of memoirs of working people survive[32] and we know something of worker associations.[33] However the preponderance of evidence, paintings, cartoons, novels, poems, government reports and trials, reflect working people through the distorting mirror of middle-class attitudes.[34]

The evidence provided by police records and court cases indicates that working people became involved in revolutionary activity for specific and particular motives. Tailors, shoemakers and silkweavers were concerned to arrest the erosion of their skills and trade, to check the growth of 'ready-made' tailoring, the financial control of craftsmen by merchants, the increased employment of cheaper female and/or foreign labour. Violence was one tool, but so was the formation of worker self-help associations. Violence was not an end; artisans were trying to influence government, not take it over. There was widespread popular protest in rural areas, sometimes linked to artisan issues, but more frequently it involved peasant attempts to prevent the free circulation of foodstuffs, particularly grain, or to check the erosion of communal traditions, especially the gathering of wood in communal forests. The rapid rise in the price of timber in the early nineteenth century made communally owned forests attractive to both the state and the better-off members of the rural community. During the century infringement of increasingly draconian forest laws was the most frequent cause of popular disturbance leading to arrest in Germany.

In the first half of the century popular revolt was thus preoccupied with the defence of traditional and specific rights. Artisans and peasants were not class warriors. Up until 1848 they expected governments to listen, appealing to somewhat romanticised notions of an abandoned 'moral economy'. Nor did they usually protest most violently when economic circumstances were at their worst, when food was most scarce or expensive, but at a stage when recovery was occurring,[35] though not fast enough to satisfy expectations.

The grievances of artisans and peasants were at the heart of all revolutionary outbursts in nineteenth-century Europe. Without them there would have been no revolution. However until 1848 those who manned the barricades assumed that the political elites could be made to listen and help. The experiences of 1848 altered perceptions. The June Days, when Parisian artisans vainly fought against government troops in defence of the right to work, made the notion of 'class war' sustainable, even though we know that the men who defeated the insurgents were from the same social background.[36] Subsequent government repression, including that of the risings after the coup of December 1851, heightened the sense of alienation. Less important at the time, but of significance later, Marx and Engels published *The Communist Manifesto*. The formation of the International Working Men's Association in 1868 urged the international solidarity of the proletariat. Its leaders quarrelled, the organisation fell apart, to be replaced by a Second International, which while not much more harmonious, managed to subsist. The idea of the brotherhood of all workers may have alarmed governments, but its practical implications were few.

The Paris Commune of 1871 was proclaimed, somewhat belatedly by Marx in a famous pamphlet, a civil war for France and the first workers' state. It was to become a symbol for later revolutionaries. In reality the rebellion in Paris in March 1871 was a product of the crass ineptness of Thiers' attempt to bully Paris back to 'normal' after a five-month siege and defeat by the Prussians.[37] The decision to form a commune was an imitation of a previous German invasion in 1792. Over a third of those elected to the 1871 Commune were working men, but this was less a sign of ideological motivation than a reflection of the social composition of the capital after the siege when those with somewhere more comfortable to live than Paris had left the city. There were socialist elements of various hues. The Commune, despite its defiant and precarious position, embarked upon a range of social reforms, such as the abolition of night work for bakers. However the two Marxist revolutionary socialist communards did not command much of a following. The communards challenged Thiers' right to give them orders, but they expected to be offered a negotiated settlement. Thiers and the elected Parliament regarded the communards as rebels to be fought and killed not pacified by compromise. It was the slaughter of Bloody Week, when the troops finally marched on the capital and shot those who had surrendered and were prisoners which made the Commune the successor to the June Days and the long-enduring symbol of proletarian revolutionary struggle.

Given the divisions among participants and leaders, why did any revolution succeed, even ephemerally? Although popular unrest was the motor of all revolutions, there were a number of times when it was not enough. In France alone one may list the abortive conspiracies of 1817–22, June 1832 in Paris, November 1831 and April 1834 in Lyon and May 1839 in Paris. Popular violence alone was not enough to make a revolution. Nor were elite grievance and criticism of a regime sufficient to bring it down. It was the coincidence of the two that was decisive. Revolution owed far more to the collapse of confidence of the existing regime than to subversion by its critics. Revolution is explained more by negatives than positives. Charles X and Louis-Philippe lost France when the regiments ordered to hold the capital deserted. On 18 March 1848 Frederick William IV withdrew his unbeaten troops from Berlin, ostensibly to avoid bloodshed.

The geography of the nineteenth-century city was crucial to insurrection. Revolution was urban and a successful revolution needed a capital city as its base. Cities were growing rapidly; Paris doubled in size in the first half of the century. Growth was unplanned, uncomfortable and relatively uncontrolled, especially when, as it was with most capitals, they were leading centres of industry as well as government. It should be no surprise that such cities were volatile; government and the homes of the elite, artisan workshops and dwellings and the national press with its politically conscious journalists and printers all lived on top of each other. The narrow streets were easily defended, but almost impossible to attack. Barricades in key streets could topple a regime.

If the difficulty of controlling urban centres tipped demonstration over into revolution around 1848, the decline in insurrectionary upheaval later in the century can be related to the resolution of the problem of how to police and feed a large city. The building of railways and the proliferation of the telegraph were to make the problem of containing a rapidly growing population much easier. Thus 1848 was the last year of widespread revolution. In the next harvest crisis, roughly ten years on, both troops and food could easily be moved around to check unrest. A generation later and Europe's repeated food shortages triggered by simple harvest failure were over. Grain could be imported from both Russia and the Prairie provinces. The Paris Commune survived from March to May 1871 only because disruption at the end of the war with Prussia delayed the massing of sufficient troops to defeat it. Until the disasters of the First World War stimulated new problems, large-scale food shortages and resultant popular unrest were over.

The third negative factor in explaining why revolutions succeeded was the dichotomy between the increased role of government and the absence of commensurate force to sustain that function. Police, armies, civil militia were sometimes too small or in the wrong place; in 1830 a large contingent of the French army was conquering Algeria not defending the capital. In addition, loyalty to the revolutionary traditions of the 1790s often challenged or subverted what should have been the forces of order. Bonapartist sympathies remained strong in the French army during the Restoration, and in Italy and Spain and Portugal officers and men who had prospered during the Revolutionary Wars were pushed aside in the years after 1814.[38] It was no accident that army officers were often leaders in secret societies, such as the *carbonari* and *adelfia*. The civil militia, in France the National Guard, retained both philosophical and personal sympathies with the Great Revolution. Habitually in the years after 1814, its officers were retired members of Bonaparte's armies. During the Restoration and July Monarchy this numerous (at least on paper) organisation could be relied on to take the side of insurgents.[39] In the Italian states the old Bonapartist militia regrouped behind Garibaldi and Mazzini and represented the radical wing of the

Risorgimento. In Prussia the reserve army or Landwehr occupied a similar position of independence, so much so that in 1858 the Regent, William, proposed that it should be taken over by the regular army.[40] Given all these circumstances it is not entirely surprising that regimes were often far from stable in the first half of the nineteenth century. The motives of soldiers, junior officers and national guardsmen who took the side of rebels might have been influenced by issues other than high politics. Garrison life in the prolonged peace which followed the lengthy Revolutionary Wars was both tedious and expensive for soldiers whose wages were poor.

Later in the century these disruptive civil militias, which had contributed much to the defiance of the establishment, were brought under control. The French National Guard was disbanded after the defeat of the Paris Commune. In Prussia the Landwehr was brought under the control of the regular army and the former recalcitrant bourgeois who had struggled to maintain its autonomy then vied to secure commissions in the subservient Landwehr. The government of united Italy merged the revolutionary militia into the regular army and pensioned Garibaldi.

Socialists continued to express themselves through a revolutionary rhetoric and the International Working Men's Association apparently had a considerable following at the turn of the century. But what mileage could be expected from revolution in these years? None of the revolutions of the nineteenth century had succeeded. Fighters and shapers never shared common objectives. Liberal and national ambitions were in mutual conflict. The high point of revolutionary success, the declaration of a democratic republic in France in February 1848, was followed by the June Days and the election of Louis-Napoleon as president in December. Revolution did not have a good track record.

Meanwhile established rulers were learning a 'stick and carrot' routine to control the radical urges of their educated critics. In Prussia civil servants who had led the liberal movement in 1848 were variously dismissed, threatened or promoted. Legal training and subsequent job prospects were expanded too. Elitist parliamentary systems to the taste of liberals were set up in Prussia and Piedmont. The notables continued to rule, both under Louis-Napoleon and the Third Republic.

If narrow electorates pleased liberals, emasculated universal suffrage helped to conciliate socialists. Bismarck adopted a democratic system for elections to the Reichstag in 1871. From 1871 onwards socialist representation in elected assemblies increased rapidly, to make them the most numerous (if not always the most united) element in the French and Italian parliaments by 1914 and the largest (and united) group in the

German assembly. Governments went further. In the 1880s Bismarck introduced imperial social insurance schemes, to provide sickness benefit and old age pensions. Free compulsory education for all became the norm. Those who had fought earlier in the century because they thought they were not being considered by governments, could no longer claim to be totally excluded. Trades unions were legalised, although strikes were repressed by military force and the mobilisation of persistent participants. The failure (often violent) of the numerous strikes in these years was a further indication that governments were in control. The socialists might be the masters of revolutionary rhetoric, but looking back, at the turn of the century the future seemed to lie with parliaments. Did contemporaries see it that way? Socialist internationalism and revolutionary language carried considerable resonance. One of the best known popular writers of the time, the American socialist, Jack London, gave a lecture entitled 'Revolution' two days before Bloody Sunday, 1905. He talked of an army of 7 million men, 'fighting with all their might for the conquest of the wealth of the world and for the complete overthrow of existing society'. There were many within the governing elites of the European states who believed him.

3. Russia, 1905: the Forgotten Revolution

MOIRA DONALD

In 1988 the eminent American historian of Russia, Abraham Ascher, published the first volume of a two-volume history of the Russian Revolution of 1905. In the introduction he observed that: 'The individuals who participated in the mass movements of 1905 did not believe that they were merely preparing the way for the real event at some future date. They were trying to bring about far-reaching changes there and then.'[1] Ascher's work was published almost on the eve of the momentous events which were to lead to the collapse of Soviet power in the third great revolution experienced in twentieth-century Russia. As Ascher rightly pointed out in his history of the 1905 Revolution, until the publication of his own work there was no comprehensive scholarly account of 1905 in English and few Western historians had chosen to make 1905 their field of study in contrast to the multitude of monographs and journal articles on the 1917 revolutions. Soviet interest in the events of 1905 had always been high, but was inevitably coloured by Lenin's declaration in *Left-wing Communism* that 1905 had been the dress rehearsal for 1917. East or West, in the decades following the Bolshevik Revolution it seemed impossible to escape this view. Until, that is, the events of 1989–91 stopped the historical trajectory as abruptly as it had begun. Suddenly it was possible to believe that Russia could have, and historically might have, followed an alternative path of development. If the 1917 Bolshevik Revolution might cease to be regarded as inevitable, then might not its precursor cease to be viewed as just the appetiser, the herald of greater things to come? Might 1905 not at last be taken seriously as a major historical event in its own right? Inevitably the collapse of Soviet power immediately affected analyses of the 1917 Revolution. Two leading scholars in this field, Edward Acton and Richard Sakwa, put forward their analyses of the 1917–1989/91 continuum in the present volume. But there appears to have been less interest than one might expect in revising interpretations of 1905. The phrase 'the twentieth-century Russian revolutions' frequently appears to exclude that first major upheaval of the century. Is this because it failed, in the sense that the Romanov dynasty was not at that stage overthrown? Or is it rather because the events of February–October 1917 still loom so large in historical perspective that the earlier revolution pales in comparison? In this chapter I shall present the view that the revolutionary events of 1905 in Russia will one day be seen not merely as having led the way towards 1917, but as a revolution worthy of inclusion in the annals of great revolutions alongside those of 1789, 1917 and 1989–91.

Let us then take the other European crises which have in modern history been termed revolutions: 1789, 1830, 1848, 1905, 1917, 1918/19, 1989/91. The Russian Revolution of 1905 was not the only one within this group to have fallen short of a total transformation of the political regime. The revolutions of 1848 provide the most immediate parallel in so far as (other than in France) they did not result in an end to the previous ruling group. Yet 1848 has always been hailed as the 'year of revolution' despite its apparent short-term failure. Similarly, the 1905 Revolution has always been defined as a revolution by contemporary commentators and modern analysts. It was a momentous period in Russian history, but one that has always stood in the shadow of 1917. Lenin's description of it as a dress rehearsal has captured the popular (and indeed the scholarly) mind to such an extent that it is difficult not to see the participants in some way practising or preparing for the main event at a later date. But that is merely history's sleight of hand. For to those involved in the events of 1905 in Russia there was no doubt in their minds that they were experiencing the real thing, that revolution was occurring in Russia, and that the Romanov dynasty might not survive the upheavals of that year. Although I can only summarise here the main events of 1905 briefly, following this with a comparison with 1917 and an assessment of how 1905 fits into typologies of revolution, it is my hope that the reader will view these events with fresh eyes, seeing 1905 as a major revolution in itself, rather than the prelude to the class act.

Summary of events

The 1905 Revolution was sparked by the events of Bloody Sunday, 9 January 1905, but of course the underlying strains and tensions had built up during decades of economic growth accompanied by political stagnation. The war with Japan which broke out on 26 January 1904 was both a military and a political mistake. The war resulted in a series of humiliating defeats for the Tsarist forces, and greatly increased liberal and intellectual dissatisfaction with the regime. The liberal opposition became radicalised in the autumn of 1904, as *zemstvo* assemblies in St Petersburg , Moscow and the provinces called for political change. The Union of Liberation, drawing on French historical precedent, organised a banquet campaign in which the call came for reform from above, and in some cases, resolutions were passed demanding the convocation of a constituent assembly. Despite the signs of growing political unrest from every stratum of Russian society, the Tsar, ignoring advice from his Minister of Internal Affairs, Prince Sviatopolk-Mirsky, issued a decree which promised only limited future change and at the same time denounced liberal activity as anti-patriotic. At the same time, workers in St Petersburg went on strike demanding the reinstatement of four of their colleagues who had been dismissed from the Putilov armaments factory. By 7 January 1905 approximately 100 000 people (two-thirds of the Petrograd workforce) were on strike. Into this atmosphere of rising tension and frustration, the Tsarist government provided the spark which lit the tinderbox with their Bloody Sunday action, firing on a peaceful hymn-singing procession which marched on the Winter Palace to present a petition to the Tsar. Hundreds of marchers were killed or injured, and as news spread of the massacre the Empire found itself thrown into revolutionary turmoil. On 10 January, St Petersburg was gripped by a general strike, and there were strikes also in Moscow, the Baltic provinces, Lodz and Warsaw. In both Riga and Warsaw there was further bloodshed when soldiers fired at peaceful crowds. Ascher has estimated that during January 1905 about 414 000 people within the Russian Empire participated in strike action.[2] Workers added their voices to the articulate liberal opposition, and as one contemporary commentator noted, after Bloody Sunday, 'the Russian Revolution ceased to be the preserve of the conscious upper stratum and began to spread throughout the country, turning into a deeply rooted spontaneous movement'.[3]

If it was clear to people in Russia that a revolution had begun, what was the outside world's assessment of events in the Empire? The foreign socialist press immediately declared Russia to be in a state of revolution. Karl Kautsky, the leading intellectual of European social democracy, and the editor of the influential journal, *Die Neue Zeit*, even berated his Russian comrades for being in danger of missing the revolution because of their involvement in the internal party conflict in the Russian party. Rosa Luxemburg published an influential pamphlet in which she described the events in Russia in 1905 as being evidence of Russia at last catching up with the West, experiencing its 1848 half a century after the rest of Europe.

Indeed the only person who seemed not to believe that Russia was in the throes of a powerful revolutionary struggle was the Tsar himself, Nicholas II. In February 1905 several of the Tsar's ministers were urging him to make concessions, although the new Governor-General of St Petersburg, General Trepov, disagreed and encouraged Nicholas to take a firm stand. In the face of pressure, from among others, the new Minister of the Interior, A. G. Bulygin, to announce conciliatory measures, Nicholas apparently said to Bulygin, 'One would think that you are afraid a revolution will break out.' To which Bulygin replied, 'Your Majesty, the revolution has already begun.'[4] Lacking a clear sense of direction, or indeed any real sense of the extent of opposition within all sections of society, the Tsar introduced half-hearted measures and promises which only served to whet the appetite of those demanding reform. In an Imperial Manifesto published on 18 February 1905 the Tsar asked for suggestions on how to improve the state and the state of the people. This led to a tremendous petition campaign which far from pouring oil on troubled waters merely acted as a vehicle for the opposition movement. The Tsar's attempt to satisfy the workers, the creation of the Shidlovskii Commission, was also a mistake. The Commission was to include workers' representatives as well as members of the government and the employers. Not surprisingly, the workers' representatives put forward radical conditions which the Tsar was unwilling to meet, and the Commission was quickly disbanded just two days after the publication of the Imperial Manifesto. This action led to a further wave of strikes. This ineffectual and frustrating episode of mismanagement in the early months of unrest was to lead to the near breakdown of the whole regime.

The unrest and in particular the strike activity continued through the summer of 1905, peaking in a virtual general strike in the autumn. This began with a walk-out of printers in Moscow on 20 September, followed by street demonstrations in which the printers were joined by students. Other workers then joined them in their actions; the printers in St Petersburg and other cities were first, then the railway workers followed. As Figes reports, by 10 October

virtually the entire railway network had come to a halt. Millions of other workers, bank and office employees, hospital staff, students, lecturers and the actors of the Imperial Theatre in St Petersburg came out in support of what had become in effect a national strike against the autocracy. The cities were brought to a standstill, All transport stopped, telegraph and telephones ceased to work.

This certainly was, in Figes's words, 'the classic example of a spontaneous yet disciplined uprising of the working class'.[5]

The revolution spread to the countryside with rent strikes, violent attacks on the estates of landlords and the formation of peasant unions, co-operatives and agricultural societies. Unrest was clearly widespread. Of 1400 replies to a questionnaire on peasant unrest sent in 1907 by the Imperial Free Economic Society to contacts in 47 of the 50 provinces of European Russia, half bore witness to the existence of local peasant unrest.[6] Moreover reports indicated the broad nature of unrest. Although some evidence pointed to the major role being played by the poorest, landless peasants, others emphasised that both middle and richer peasants were involved in disturbances. Although there was evidence of influence from outside on the rural insurgents, many reports stressed the importance of local factors and the 'traditional' methods and goals of the peasants.[7] That there was not greater communication between the revolutionaries in the countryside and the towns is one of the major reasons for the immediate survival of Tsarism after 1905. As Maureen Perry argues, 'The socio-economic development of Russia in the post-emancipation period was such as to guarantee the simultaneity of revolutionary action by the proletariat and peasantry in 1905; her political and cultural development, however was insufficient to ensure conscious co-ordination between town and countryside, or much awareness of common revolutionary goals.' What changed between 1905 and 1917 was not that the revolutionaries were more successful in bringing together these movements, but that the nature of the opposition they faced had changed. 'In a situation in which the coercive power of the state had already collapsed, as in 1917, this lack of co-ordination mattered little; in 1905, however, it was a fatal weakness.'[8]

One of the features which identifies the events of 1905 as something more than a series of isolated events was the extent of national unrest which became evident over the revolutionary months. Poland was gripped with strikes and violent unrest, and Polish nationalists sought to achieve greater autonomy and liberty through working with Russian constitutionalists during the revolution. Few concessions were made to them by the government and even their supposed allies proved a disappointment. In 1907 the Kadets as well as the Octobrists rejected a demand for Polish autonomy introduced via the Second Duma. During the revolution both the Polish Socialist Party and the Marxist Social Democratic Party of Poland and Lithuania attracted thousands of new members and both groups joined together in calling a general strike. Finnish militancy before and during 1905 resulted in a temporary victory for Finnish autonomy when the Tsar removed the powers of the Governor-General in October 1905 and then agreed to sweeping reform of the Finnish Diet in 1906. This reform made the Diet one of the most democratically elected governing bodies in Europe. However the Diet suffered the same fate as the Dumas in the same period: it was dissolved several times as Tsarism regained its nerve and removed many areas from its jurisdiction until it finally folded after its final meeting in 1911. Many other areas of the Empire experienced anti-Russian unrest during 1905–6 including the Baltic provinces, and the Transcaucasian provinces of Georgia, Armenia and Azerbaijan. If 1905 was indeed Russia's 1848 as contemporary socialists argued, then the role of nationalists in the unrest corresponded closely to the revolutionary influence of the non-German minorities of Austria-Hungary in that earlier wave of revolution.

The reality of the situation was that the government decided to repress the revolution, but for some time did not have the power to carry out its aim. For example, punishment measures for strikers were unenforceable and press censorship was no longer rigidly enforced. Newspapers across the Empire began to report extensively on the crisis that threatened the regime. What saved the regime from complete breakdown was the fact that there was little co-ordination between the strata involved; workers, peasants, nationalists, socialists all operated to different timetables, the Tsar exercised a determination to maintain his power which was founded on ignorance of the precariousness of his position rather than certainty of success, and finally the continued loyalty of the armed forces. Such a united show of disciplined opposition to the regime would have been more than enough to result in complete collapse under other conditions. What is surprising is that Tsarism survived this onslaught – which was undoubtedly of greater magnitude than the unrest which eventually forced the abdication of the Tsar in February 1917.

What then made the difference between survival and collapse? Certainly not adroit political handling of the situation. The Tsar refused to believe the seriousness of the situation, choosing to ignore Witte's advice to make constitutional reforms in October. Instead he called upon his uncle the Grand Duke Nikolai to assume the role of dictator. The Grand Duke agreed with Witte that reform was unavoidable and in a melodramatic gesture threatened to take his own life unless the Tsar agreed to sign Witte's memorandum. Ironically lack of political astuteness at court which could so easily have led to the overthrow of the regime in the end turned out by good fortune (as far as the Romanovs were concerned) to prevent a further decline into anarchy. The pig-headedness of the Tsar in determining to recover power as soon as possible, which in practice meant that he shut down one Duma after another, gave the regime an appearance of an inviolability which it did not necessarily have. One thing which it is possible to learn from the experiences of revolutionary situations which Europe went through in the twentieth century is that as soon as a regime lacks self-belief, as soon as reforms gain a momentum, then the tide turns in the direction of revolution. If an endangered regime shows enough determination, and particularly if it can use an early and decisive show of force, the revolutionary floodgates can be closed.

Another factor which operated in favour of the regime's survival in 1905 was the limited and concrete nature of the demands made by the strikers. They called for a constituent assembly elected by universal suffrage. Once the Tsar agreed to this, and he did agree under the pressure from all sides, the key demand was met. The October Manifesto was received with jubilation. Other more radical demands were not immediately forthcoming. Time was a key issue in shaping the course of events. The general strike was immediately called off. No one tried to radicalise the situation for some weeks. Although the Petrograd Soviet had formed in October it had initially the role of co-ordinating strike action, but it was some weeks before it began to plan to take any more dramatic action. By the time it was preparing, under Trotsky's leadership, to embrace the idea of armed uprising, the government had recovered its nerve. The leaders of the Petrograd Soviet were arrested and the Moscow Soviet decided to take action despite almost complete lack of preparation. As Figes has argued, with just a little more strategic planning the Moscow insurrection might well have succeeded temporarily. But as he admits, given the lack of nationwide support and the collapse of the army mutinies, the authorities were bound to prevail. After a few days in which the situation seemed precariously balanced between revolutionaries and police in Moscow, reinforcements arrived in the shape of a regiment from St Petersburg, and the rebels were shelled into surrender with the loss of a thousand lives, followed by brutal repression. Had this uprising occurred before the Manifesto was published or whilst the general strike was on, the outcome would not have been as predictable.

A crucial facet of the 1905 Revolution which enabled Tsarism to survive the crisis was the loyalty of the armed forces. The famous Potemkin mutiny was an isolated event which arose out of a local incident which was mishandled by the authorities. In 1943 Katherine Chorley published a pathbreaking work entitled *Armies and the Art of Revolution* in which she concluded that the relationship between government and military was the key determinant of revolutionary success. She wrote, 'the rule...emerges clearly that governments of the *status quo* which are in full control of their armed forces and are in a position to use them to full effect have a decisive superiority which no rebel force can overcome'.[9] She went on to argue that revolutions might for this reason be expected in 'the last stages of an unsuccessful war'.[10] However Chorley's conclusions were not that radical. Kautsky predicted in 1902 that if Russia became embroiled in war with Japan, this would weaken the regime sufficiently to open up the possibility of revolution. From his Marxist perspective Kautsky warned then that this was not a desirable outcome, because such a situation would be evidence only of the weakness of the ruling class, not evidence of the strength of the revolutionary class.[11] This opens up a dilemma for revolutionaries. If successful revolution is impossible whilst the status quo government maintains its control over the armed forces, but revolution that occurs on the coat-tails of an unsuccessful war which leaves the government without military backing is undesirable, what hope then for an apposite and successful revolution? With hindsight it is perhaps not surprising that in 1917 Lenin decided to ignore Kautsky's warnings about untimely socialist revolution, exploiting the weakness of the Provisional Government to the full.

Comparison with 1917

How does the situation in 1905 compare with the events of 1917? As the details of 1917 are probably more widely known, I shall just give the barest outline of the sequence of events for the purpose of comparison. First must come the crucial difference between the military conflicts in which the Russian Empire was involved. Although in 1905 the Tsar's prestige was dented by the loss of Port Arthur the previous year, the conflict with Japan was more limited and already over by the outbreak of the 1905 Revolution. By contrast in February 1917 Russia had been involved in a prolonged and increasingly disastrous military campaign against the Central Powers which showed neither any sign of ending, nor of taking an upward turn. Moreover the Tsar himself had taken command of the armed forces in a bold but foolhardy decision made in August 1915. Thus every military defeat reflected on Nicholas personally. The fall of the Romanovs was precipitated by a bread crisis in St Petersburg caused by a breakdown in the transport system. This led to spontaneous demonstrations and popular clashes with police and soldiers. The autocracy repeated its mistake of Bloody Sunday 1905 by shooting on unarmed crowds. As Orlando Figes argues, the Tsar only had himself (and his advisers) to blame for destroying any chance of containing the disorders.[12] Nicholas II ordered the use of military force to quell the unrest. But unlike the 1905 experience, the autocracy misjudged its own strength and the loyalty of the army. Tsarism acted as it had done before, but the troops did not. The crucial difference separating the two events, the earlier revolutionary crisis which the autocracy survived, and the later one which it did not, was the mood and actions of the dispirited troops. The soldiers stationed in Petrograd – many of them teenage conscripts – mutinied and turned the disturbances into full-blown and ultimately successful revolution. It was not just that the army could not be relied upon to put down the disturbances, as Figes points out, the involvement of soldiers in the unrest lent it a greater degree of purpose and organisation.[13] The revolution began on the streets of Petrograd on 23 February. News of events only reached Nicholas on 27 February. By 1 March plans for a counter-revolution had been abandoned and Nicholas was urged by General Alexeev, the Commander-in-Chief of the armed forces, to allow the Duma to form a new government in the belief that this would satisfy the insurgents as the calling of the Constituent Assembly had done 12 years previously. By the following day Alexeev and the other generals were convinced that nothing except the Tsar's abdication would stop the revolution and save the war campaign. Thus the role of the army was crucial in two respects. At the grass roots the unreliability of the troops and their identification with the protesting crowds made it impossible to use force to stem the revolutionary wave. At the other end of the spectrum, the conviction of the Commander-in Chief and the generals that Nicholas must go, was the turning-point in the fate of the regime.

What distinguished February 1917 from 1905 was not the extent of revolutionary activity, but the erosion of political will within the ruling elite, and the erosion of loyalty within that bulwark of the autocracy, the army. Whilst the war played a crucial part in deciding the issue, the memory of 1905 must also have exercised its influence. That events moved so quickly shows that what happened on 23 February 1917 was not so much the outbreak of a new revolution as the final culmination of a longer-term revolution which had begun on Bloody Sunday 1905. Theda Skocpol in her 1979 work, *States and Social Revolutions*, appeared to suggest that 1905 and 1917 were different points in the same revolutionary process. She concurred with Isaac Deutscher's view that in 1917 the revolution 'started again from the points at which it had come to a standstill in 1905.... The "constitutionalist" phase of the revolution had actually been played out before 1917.'[14] Skocpol went so far as to describe the unrest in 1905 as 'seemingly a very Western-style social revolution indeed'. In analysing why this unrest did not bear fruit, she argued that the key factor was the peace treaty signed with Japan in September 1905 which enabled the troops to return home and restore order, crushing the strikes and agrarian revolts.[15]

Typology of revolution

The concept of revolution has been more widely treated by political scientists than historians. It is a subject which received a flurry of interest in the post-1968 generation of the scholarly community which tended to be interested in and influenced by (or reacting against) Marxist ideas.[16] However in recent decades research on revolutions has been rather in the doldrums. No doubt the present volume will form part of a new wave of interest in revolution sparked by the events in Europe and China in the late 1980s and early 1990s. There is not surprisingly little agreement among scholars as to what precisely constitutes a revolution. Crane Brinton in an early study originally published in 1938, *The Anatomy of Revolution*, likened a revolution to a fever. This is his description of the progress of the 'fever':

> In the society during the generation or so before the outbreak of revolution, in the old regime, there will be found signs of the coming disturbance. [...] indications to the very keen diagnostician that a disease is on its way, but not yet sufficiently developed to be the disease. Then comes a time when the full symptoms disclose themselves, and when we can say the fever of revolution has begun. This works up, not regularly but with advances and retreats, to a crisis, frequently accompanied by delirium, the rule of the most violent revolutionists, the Reign of Terror. After the crisis comes a period of convalescence, usually marked by a relapse or two. Finally the fever is over, and the patient is himself again, perhaps in some ways actually strengthened by the experience, immunised at least for a while from a similar attack, but certainly not wholly made over into a new man.[17]

Whilst this description certainly fits the 1917 Revolution, the 1905 Revolution fell short of the full course of the fever because it never reached the stage of rule by the revolutionaries. Instead, Brinton would have categorised 1905 (if he had bothered to examine it) as an abortive revolution by which he meant 'simply the failure of organised groups in revolt'. He includes the European revolutions of 1848 as falling within the abortive group, although he concedes that 'in many countries they helped bring about important and comparatively permanent administrative and constitutional changes'.[18] Brinton's only references to the events of 1905 are that it was a 'kind of dress rehearsal for the great revolution', and that failure in the Russo-Japanese War had 'brought with it a partial collapse of the machinery of internal administration'.[19]

Peter Calvert in his study on revolution published in 1970 shared Brinton's belief that the term 'revolution' might only be used to describe successful attempts at overthrow of government:

Here 'revolution' may be understood throughout as referring to events in which physical force (or the convincing threat of it) has actually been used successfully to overthrow a government or regime. Where such movements have not been successful they are referred to, according to context, as 'rebellions', 'revolts', 'insurrections' or 'uprisings'.[20]

I would argue that none of the alternative labels suggested by Calvert above would adequately describe the events of 1905. Indeed Calvert himself did not apply any of them to the Russian experience. Instead he referred to it as the 'unsuccessful Russian revolution of 1905' and the 'abortive revolution of 1905'.[21] In contrast to Brinton and Calvert, Jean Baechler, writing in 1970, distinguished between 'revolution' (or more precisely revolutionary phenomena) and 'revolutions'. As far as the former is concerned, he took a broad interpretation of the term 'revolution', which he defined as 'any kind of challenge to the social order', subsequently clarified to 'any protest against the social order that has recourse to physical violence on one side and/or the other'.[22] But Baechler, like Brinton and Calvert, applied the label 'revolutions' to specific events only if they were 'protest movements that manage[d] to seize power'. Baechler argued that it is only in exceptional circumstances that considerable sections of the population raise the flag of revolt and go over into opposition. 'Experience has shown that situations in which the dissidents win over the majority are very few...because of this...the established social order reaps an advantage, at the very least, from the neutrality of the majority and usually finds little difficulty in putting down the rising.'[23] Perhaps this is what makes the experience of 1905 so interesting and so unusual. Dissatisfaction was so widespread to make it appear that the majority were won over by the minority – yet in the end the old order was restored. In other words it was possibly the most all-encompassing unsuccessful revolution that the world has seen. Baechler went on to provide us with a clue as to why 1905 was unsuccessful. He argued that if the governing elite which controls the legitimate use of force is united and bent on a show of strength, there is no possibility of successful revolution. He drew from this the conclusion that revolutions can only succeed if the 'governing elite' is disunited. This was true, as Baechler pointed out for both February and October 1917. It is hardly the case though that the 'governing elite' was unanimous in 1905. The vital difference is that they were united in wishing to maintain Tsarism, but divided over the question of whether reform was needed to achieve the regime's survival. Once the Tsar had undertaken the limited reforms requested by the dissidents within the governing elite, the danger passed. The vital difference in 1917 was that many within the elite made up their minds that Nicholas had to go. Once the symbol of authority was removed, the governing elite was irrevocably divided. Baechler shares the view that the army's position in a revolution is fundamental, but he argues that the army's attitude is *always determined within the governing elite.*[24] Where the elite and the army are divided, civil war is a likely outcome of revolution. That the army basically stayed loyal to the Tsar in 1905 is both a reflection of the lack of outright opposition to Nicholas within the elite at that stage and the reason why the groundswell of popular discontent was successfully contained. According to Baechler's typology of political revolutions, intensity of revolution can be roughly gauged according to the following rising scale:

1. *Replacement of the governing body* at the summit of the hierarchy (palace revolution, military *coup d'état* within a military regime).
2. *Replacement of the rules of the political game* without any major changes being perceptible in other sectors of society.
3. *Replacement of the rules of the political game and of the governing elite,* the emergence of new political personnel, drawn from different sections of society or inspired by different aims.
4. *Political and social upheaval:* change of the rules of the political game and the governing elite; upheaval of the scale of values, the hierarchy and the relations between social groups.
5. *Change of civilisation:* a break between past and future at all levels and in all spheres.

Personally I think that level five can be dismissed as unhistorical. The examples Baechler gives of the Meiji, the Chinese and Cuban revolutions do not from the standpoint of 30 years later appear to be quite the total changes in civilisation that Baechler perceived them to be in 1970 (although interestingly the Chinese and Cuban revolutions have proved themselves to be the longest survivors of the twentieth-century revolutions). With that exception stages 1–4 provide a useful typology. The Russian Revolution of 1905, being abortive, would not count in Baechler's scheme of things. Yet when one examines the typology closely, it is only really the first element that is completely absent from the events of 1905. In other words there was a limited change in the rules of the political game, some changes in the governing elite and some extent of political and social upheaval despite the fact that the governing body was not replaced. The top personnel stayed the same but the regime agreed to revolutionise itself from within by agreeing to change from autocracy to what has been termed 'demi-semi quasi constitutional monarchy'. Reformers such as Witte and Stolypin came to the fore, the whole notion of elective assemblies was accepted (with reluctance) and social relations were never to be quite the same again. Popular regard for the Tsar as the 'little Father' was permanently damaged by the events of Bloody Sunday, and quiescent acceptance of autocracy, censorship and lack of political freedom could not be relied upon in the future. Was this not a revolution according to some of Baechler's criteria?

Conclusion

Whether or not academic commentators on revolution regard 1905 as a revolution, it is clear from the accounts of contemporaries that those living through the events had no doubts as to the nature of the events in which they were participating.

Theodore Dan wrote to Kautsky from St Petersburg in October 1905, 'We are living in an intoxicated state here, the revolutionary air is like wine....There is complete freedom of speech and expression. I could have addressed a meeting of more than 6000 workers today. The mood is splendid.'[25]

Trotsky described 1905 as a 'prologue' to the two revolutions of 1917. He laid the blame for the failure of 1905 at the doorstep of the liberals:

The liberals demonstratively backed away from the revolution exactly at the moment when it became clear that to shake Czarism would not be enough, it must be overthrown. This sharp break of the bourgeoisie with the people, in which the bourgeoisie carried with it considerable circles of the democratic intelligentsia made it easier for the monarchy to differentiate within the army, separating out the loyal units, and to make a bloody settlement with the workers and peasants. Although with a few broken ribs, Czarism came out of the experience of 1905 alive and strong enough.[26]

Writing in 1971 Krishan Kumar developed further the idea that 1905 formed part of the wider whole that was the Russian Revolution. He accepted the general view that revolution by definition involves a change or transformation in power, an interruption in the pattern of sovereign rule.[27] However he altered the perspective when he identified revolutions not as single events, but as revolutionary *periods* or epochs. Such periods, he argued, may last decades, or as much as a century. In his view the cataclysmic events usually described by historians as Revolutions with a capital 'R' are 'the *final* stages of the revolution proper, the revolutionary period'.[28] According to this definition the 1917 February Revolution was the moment that the pattern of sovereign rule was permanently interrupted, but that was the culmination of the revolutionary period rather than the beginning of the revolution. The events of 1905 had a far more direct influence on the February Revolution than did the Bolsheviks. As E. H. Carr wrote in 1960, 'the contribution of Lenin and the Bolsheviks to the overthrow of Tsarism was negligible.... Bolshevism succeeded to a vacant throne.'[29] What occurred to turn the revolution which had overthrown the Tsar just six months later into a coup led by the Bolsheviks is another issue. There is some validity to Baechler's explanation that October 1917 can be understood as one of those rare occasions when what he terms 'counter-societies' attract unusually high numbers creating a revolutionary situation. Just as a rare combination of events allowed the dissenters to ride to power with Cromwell, the Bolshevik Revolution can be understood as Baechler contends as 'nothing but a rather banal politico-ideological sect that owed its rise to power to a highly improbable combination of events'.[30]

4. The Parting of Ways: Comparing the Russian Revolutions of 1917 and 1991

EDWARD ACTON

'A legend widely known in Russia,' wrote Alexander Herzen in the mid-nineteenth century,

> tells how a Tsar, suspecting his wife of infidelity, shut her and her son in a barrel and then had the barrel sealed up and thrown into the sea. For many years the barrel floated on the waves.
>
> Nevertheless the Tsarevich grew, and his feet and his head began to press against the ends of the barrel. Every day he became more and more cramped. One day he said to his mother: 'Queen-mother, allow me to stretch to the full length of my limbs.' 'My son, the Tsarevich,' answered the mother, 'beware of doing what you say: the barrel will burst and you will perish in the salt waves.'
>
> The Tsarevich thought in silence for a while; then he spoke again: 'I shall stretch, Mother; better to stretch for once in freedom and perish at once.'

'That legend', Herzen concluded, 'contains our whole history.'[1]

Since Herzen's time, the temptation to view Russian history in terms of deeply rooted continuities generating endlessly recurring patterns has lost none of its power. No country's past has more frequently been interpreted in such terms and recent events have done nothing to break the habit. The dramatic changes unleashed by Gorbachev quickly sent historians back to earlier precedents, the most popular being that of the reforms of Alexander II.[2] Above all, this penchant reflects concern to explain the country's persistent refusal to conform to the perceived Western European norm of constitutional evolution towards democracy.

The explanations advanced range widely – from the belated development of private property,[3] through the weakness of Russia's 'middle class'[4] and the crippling burden imposed on society by the state in its efforts to extract the resources necessary to compete militarily with more advanced Western rivals,[5] to the overriding strength of Russian nationalism[6] and, in apparently sharp contrast, the weakly developed sense of nationhood.[7] But common to each of them is an emphasis on enduring constraints deemed responsible for preventing constitutional development and democratisation.

It is against this background that the following reflections should be read. This essay explores the comparison between the revolution which marked the opening of Russia's 'short twentieth century', the overthrow of Tsarism and of the Provisional Government in 1917, and the upheaval which marked its close, the destruction of both traditional and reformed Communist rule. The case for such a comparison is strengthened by the defining impact of the events of 1917 on the word 'revolution'; by the frequency with which the parallel flickers in and out of commentary on contemporary Russia in support of wildly divergent points of view; and by the fact that participants in the second revolution were themselves so conscious of the precedents set seven decades earlier. The comparison may also serve as a useful counterpart to the burgeoning literature contrasting post-Soviet Russia with successful transitions to democracy elsewhere. For the purpose is not only to reflect on the very real analogy between the two revolutions but also to highlight structural differences too easily obscured precisely because, at one level, the analogy is so compelling.

Three parallels will be examined. The first concerns the process which led to the overthrow of the two *ancien régimes* – Tsarist and Soviet. The two regimes shared a significant measure of common ground. Both presided over a vast territory approaching one-sixth of the earth's surface. Neither rested their claim to legitimacy upon the principle of national sovereignty; both repudiated competitive democracy and narrowly curtailed civil rights. Both witnessed rapid economic and social change. In both cases, popular discontent was fuelled by economic dissatisfaction. Internationally, both confronted hostile Western powers from positions of significant economic and technological disadvantage. And each regime forfeited popular confidence and was abruptly overthrown.

A second parallel matches the failure of the Provisional Government with that of Gorbachev in the period from spring 1989 when he moved towards seeking democratic sanction and legitimation. Both governments sought to distance themselves from the old regimes from which they had arisen; both sponsored a panoply of legislation to entrench civil liberties; and initially both appeared to enjoy widespread public support. But in fact, amidst growing economic crisis, both faced mounting pressure from below which, despite their best efforts, rapidly spilled over the new institutional framework they laboured to erect. The effective power of both governments was rapidly eroded and, while both were reluctant to fall back on force to halt the process, elements within their respective establishments attempted to do so. In each case the result was fiasco and a fatal blow to the government.

A third parallel is that between the regimes which succeeded what turned out to be the transitory governments of Kerensky and Gorbachev. Here, the comparison is between the early years of Bolshevik rule and the Yeltsin/Gaidar phase of post-Soviet Russia.[8] In both cases, the new government signalled a drastic break with the past, far more radical than that undertaken by the Provisional Government or Gorbachev. A new beginning would now be made; economic stability would be restored but on entirely new foundations; confrontation with the more advanced countries of the West would be overcome; and true democracy would replace the 'sham' over which these regimes had presided. In fact, in both cases economic decline and social dislocation accelerated, transforming Russia's foreign relations proved deeply problematic, and popular democracy was placed in jeopardy.

The decline and fall of Tsarism and communism

Described in general terms, the structural crises to which the late-Tsarist and late-Soviet orders were subjected appear closely analogous. The stability of both was eroded by major social change, by economic failure, and by the repercussions of competing against wealthier and economically more advanced international rivals.

To take first the effect of social change: in both societies, economic development generated social groups characterised by levels of skill and education, by a range of aspirations, and by a new consciousness which, so to speak, outgrew the old regime. So far as late-Tsarist Russia is concerned, the emphasis has long been placed on the sense in which this is true of the emergent working class. It was not abject misery and elemental violence which made the working class so dangerous. The gravest threat to the old order came, rather, from those workers who were most skilled, best educated and highest paid. It was they who felt the most acute indignation at the affront to their human dignity they suffered on the factory floor. It was they who developed the most ambitious aspirations, who had the leisure and the modicum of education both to conceptualise their sense of outrage and to organise.[9] While workers are the group on whom most research has focused, attention has also been paid to the peasantry. Here, too, it has been argued that the last pre-revolutionary decades saw a significant measure of change in terms of literacy rates, of contact with a world beyond the village, of consciousness. There was growing evidence of peasant assertiveness and expanding horizons, of declining respect for the Orthodox Church and established authority in general, of increasingly vigorous protest against the arbitrary treatment meted out to peasants by their social superiors – alongside the insistent, unrelenting demand for land.[10] Currently, the social groups attracting most research are the 'middling strata', the growing ranks of professionals (lawyers, doctors, journalists, teachers), of merchants and entrepreneurs, of specialists and white-collar workers employed in commerce, industry and the service sector. They provided the main base for a rapidly maturing commercial press, they sought their own societies and associations, they began to press against a host of restrictions imposed by officialdom. They demanded civil rights and generated a leadership which sought a direct role in political life.[11] Finally, the late-Tsarist period is associated with sustained erosion of the monarchy's firmest social base, the landed nobility – an erosion not only in terms of relative size and wealth but also in cohesion and confidence.[12]

Turning now to late-Soviet society, it is the multi-million 'intelligentsia', the vast ranks of those with higher education, the specialists, the highly qualified personnel in the economy, state institutions and cultural life on which greatest emphasis has been placed. Particular attention has been drawn to the phenomenal pace of urbanisation in the post-war decades. By the time Gorbachev came to power, 180 million Soviet citizens were concentrated in 272 cities and in no less than 23 of these the population exceeded 1 million. This process nurtured a complex network of more or less informal groups and organisations – professional, cultural, recreational, scholarly. Increasingly well educated – and by the 1980s 15 million graduates formed the fastest growing social group in the USSR – this emergent 'civil society' generated mounting pressure for greater autonomy, for a more responsive, flexible and sophisticated political system. A highly qualified and increasingly assertive stratum of experts and specialists, scientists and social scientists, who overlapped with, rather than being rigidly divorced from, the bureaucracy, and who pressed for more space, greater freedom of travel, more information.

These burgeoning new social strata seemed to fit increasingly ill with the formal structures of a one-party state dedicated to Marxism-Leninism. Here, too, society appeared in a sense to have been bursting the bounds of the political order in which it was encased.[13]

What is striking, however, is the difference in the way in which social pressure found political expression. Under Tsarism, it did so outside legal channels, through popular protest in the form of strikes and demonstrations, and through the protest of the radical intelligentsia and the development of illegal and revolutionary organisations – from the Social Democrats and Socialist Revolutionaries to the Liberation Movement. The regime, on the other hand, resisted yielding an inch to new social forces for as long as it possibly could. Nicholas II personified and epitomised an order that was 'structurally and ideologically' incapable of co-operating with and accommodating even the new middle classes, let alone a more demanding peasantry and working class.[14] By contrast, popular protest and illegal pressure remained remarkably modest in the declining years of Communist rule. Despite the courage and heroism of the dissident movement, their organisational coherence and their intellectual impact were no more than faint echoes of their pre-revolutionary forebears.[15] Rather, it was from inside the established order, among social scientists and economists working within orthodox channels, and ultimately through the dynamic intervention of the General Secretary himself, that the pressure for change found expression.[16] Gorbachev strove to expand civil rights, move towards law-bound constitutional government, and broaden political participation. There were many within the Soviet establishment who in fact gave ground with extreme reluctance. But unlike under Tsarism, the leadership itself reflected, at least in part, the increasing sophistication of society.

To highlight this contrast draws attention to the far greater success of the Soviet regime in incorporating new social strata and reflecting, albeit inadequately, changes in the social structure and popular aspirations. It lends little credence to optimistic claims about Tsarism's potential for reform. It suggests, instead, that although Tsarism found many more Western apologists after its fall than has the unlamented Soviet order,[17] of the two political systems it was the Soviet one which had greater capacity for adaptation and survival.

This conclusion is lent qualified support by the role which economic dissatisfaction played in stimulating disaffection and fuelling opposition to the regime. Economic factors constituted an important factor behind peasant protest, working-class strikes and demonstrations, discontent among cossacks and unrest in the Tsarist army. Equally, the Communist

Party of the Soviet Union (CPSU) encountered mounting criticism in its last years for unreliable food supplies, shoddy goods, endless queues, low-quality welfare provision and inadequate housing.

Yet here, too, there is a crucial contrast. In the case of Tsarism, protest was marked even in periods of swift economic growth and a general rise in living standards. In 1916–17, on the eve of the Tsar's fall, it is true, real wages were declining sharply. But the pre-war period had been one of rapidly increasing output and, for a large proportion of the population, improved living standards. Yet here economic growth appeared, if anything, to intensify unrest, especially among the working class – and to swell rather than reduce the ranks of those strata who proved most militant and persistent in their protest.[18] In the late-Soviet case, on the other hand, the evidence is that so long as the regime could maintain economic growth, its stability was not in question. What intensified discontent in its declining years, and especially during the Gorbachev period, was stagnation in output and a decline in living standards.[19] The implication is that, given sustained economic growth, the CPSU had devised a viable long-term formula for holding power, a recipe which enabled it to absorb the challenge of new social groups, to contain and dissipate discontent, and to incorporate a sufficient proportion of the elite – not least among the national minorities – to maintain the status quo. In part, no doubt, this reflected the more vicious, ruthless and sophisticated nature of Soviet repression and the lasting legacy of Stalinist terror. But it also underscores the extent to which the CPSU harnessed economic development and social mobility to its own cause, ensuring a close correlation between career success and party membership, binding the minority national elites to Moscow, creating gradations such as the 'closed' cities and enterprises where the granting of privileges tightened the bond between potentially critical groups and the Soviet order.[20] Indeed, whereas under Tsarism upward social mobility intensified pressure for political change, in the post-Stalin decades it served to stabilise the Soviet political system. Likewise, it was only when this process ground to a virtual halt; when graduates found themselves restricted to posts for which they were grossly over-educated; when access to university for the children of workers and peasants began to close; when men and women on every rung of the social ladder came up against a promotion 'ceiling' that the system became imperilled.

Turning now to the role played by international relations in undermining the two regimes, three aspects of the analogy merit particular attention. In the first place, both regimes sought to compete with economically more developed rivals, with the result that the proportion of

GNP devoted to defence purposes was larger than in the case of their rivals. The economic burden of the European arms race before the First World War and the nuclear arms race after the Second World War distorted the economy and drained resources from the civilian sector.[21] The second point is that competition with more advanced rivals induced both regimes to introduce elements of modernisation which ran counter to and helped to undermine their authoritarian structure. Thus Tsarism was compelled actively to foster industrialisation despite the threat this posed to the traditional order and social base of the regime.[22] It also dictated the introduction of a reserve army system which undermined the army's reliability as an instrument of social control.[23] In the Soviet case, the need to compete technologically pushed the regime towards increasing the autonomy of specialists and professionals and slackening the effective grip of Marxism-Leninism and central control over information.[24] Equally, anxiety at the cost of the arms race and the possibility that the steep rise in arms expenditure under Reagan would enable the USA to steal a march was an important impulse behind Gorbachev's attempt at *perestroika* after 1985.[25] The third point is that both regimes became heavily dependent for their legitimation upon the conviction they carried in claiming to provide security in a hostile world. The foreign spectre played a major role in seeming to justify their repressive nature and obsessive secrecy. Tsarism had played upon the foreign threat since time immemorial, and the Communist regime had done so almost from its inception. The fact that this claim was called into question in the final years of both regimes contributed significantly to their downfall.

Here most striking is the different way in which the two regimes forfeited this source of legitimation. The February Revolution took place when the threat from abroad was at its most acute: the Germans were deep inside the Tsar's territory. Confidence in the regime collapsed, in other words, when the issue critical to its entire ethos, on which its '*raison d'être*, prestige and pride rested'[26] was centre stage, when, other things being equal, there was maximum potential for playing the patriotic card. In the Soviet case, by contrast, the CPSU's legitimacy was destroyed when the foreign spectre was at its most remote. By the mid-1980s, the emotional legacy of the Great Patriotic War, that intense moral indignation and concern for security on which Stalin and his successors had played with such success, was fading along with the generation who fought the war. Moreover, after coming to office in 1985 Gorbachev launched a 'peace offensive' which went far beyond anything attempted in the days of Brezhnev's *détente*. Breaking dramatically with the posture of his predecessors, he froze the deployment of short-range missiles in Europe, unilaterally abandoned nuclear testing, committed the party to seek the destruction of all nuclear weapons by the year 2000, cut the armed forces by 500 000, redeployed Soviet tanks to defensive positions, undertook to withdraw from Afghanistan and, above all, abandoned to their fate the very foundation blocks of post-war Soviet foreign policy, the Communist regimes of Eastern Europe. In short, he undertook a series of international initiatives which conveyed the unmistakable message at home that the 'forces of imperialism' had ceased to imperil Soviet security.[27] Whereas Tsarism was overthrown despite manifest and immediate foreign peril, Communist rule began to crumble when the regime itself signalled the relative insignificance of any military threat from abroad.

The failure of the Provisional Government and of Gorbachev's presidency, 1989–91

The analogy between the Provisional Government and the Gorbachev government of 1989–91 rests upon the widely held notion that the summoning of competitive elections to a new Congress of People's Deputies was 'the decisive turning-point in terms of the transformation of the Soviet system'.[28] It marks the point at which Gorbachev began to shift his claim to legitimacy from his post as General Secretary of the CPSU to that of Chairman of the new Supreme Soviet (the standing body elected by the Congress from among its members). The Prime Minister, N. I. Ryzhkov, was made accountable to the Congress/Supreme Soviet which acquired the power to veto the ministers he proposed. Thus from 1989 onwards, the government sought to distance itself from its roots in one-party rule. The Party Secretariat was drastically reduced in size, scope and influence; the Politburo was displaced as the key decision-making body by a new Presidential Council (later the Council of the Federation); and a commission was set to work to draft a new constitution. In 1990 each of the 15 Union Republics held competitive elections both to its own Supreme Soviet (Congress of Deputies in the Russian case) and to local soviets. The pace of democratisation was reflected in the fact that, unlike in the All-Union elections the year before, no seats were now reserved for the Communist Party and other 'public organisations'. In March 1990 the rupture with the past was underlined when Gorbachev was elected executive President of the USSR by the Congress – and legislation was enacted to guarantee that in future the presidency would itself be filled by direct popular election.[29]

In all this, there were strong echoes of the experience of the Provisional Government of 1917. It, too, had roots in the old regime and was formed by establishment figures, liberal members of the Fourth Duma elected in 1912 under the restricted franchise imposed by Stolypin.[30] Like Gorbachev's transitory government, it became increasingly anxious to identify itself more closely with the new institutions coming into being. In April/May 1917 the Provisional Government buttressed its position by drawing in leading socialist figures from the burgeoning soviets of workers' and soldiers' deputies. It sought to shore up its questionable democratic legitimacy by creating new bodies – Kerensky's State Conference in August and the Provisional Council of the Russian Republic (or Pre-Parliament) in October. It, too, committed itself to the construction of a new constitution, in this case to be settled by a fully democratic Constituent Assembly, and meanwhile summoned fresh local government elections on the basis of universal franchise.

While progressively burning bridges that might lead back to the old order (Kerensky proclaimed a republic in September just as the Gorbachev government had the constitutional guarantee of the party's leading role revoked in March 1990), both governments moved to enshrine the civil rights denied by their predecessors – freedom of the press, speech and association, freedom of conscience and religious organisation, judicial independence and security under the law.[31] And initially both enjoyed widespread popularity. The Provisional Government's formation was greeted with enormous enthusiasm and, following the crisis of confidence in April 1917, reached the height of its popularity when the moderate socialists, who won sweeping victories in all tests of opinion early in the year, joined the cabinet. Gorbachev, too, enjoyed overwhelming support for the democratic reforms which led to the election of the Congress: according to opinion polls carried out in various republican capitals in the spring of 1989, between 81 and 93 per cent approved his election as Chairman of the Supreme Soviet.[32] Indeed, it was in part because they came to take the strength of their support for granted that both governments delayed subjecting themselves to a direct electoral verdict. Kerensky and the moderate socialists long exaggerated the prospects of class co-operation and the unity of all the country's 'vital forces', while the initial enthusiasm for *perestroika* led Gorbachev gravely to underestimate the potential dissent, above all that mobilising behind nationalist goals. Just as the Provisional Government repeatedly postponed elections to the Constituent Assembly so Gorbachev postponed seeking direct popular endorsement for his own leadership.[33]

In fact, support for both began to ebb long before they were finally brought down. Neither government was able to keep pace with or approve the surge of activism from below. 'Civil society' successfully invaded and occupied much of the ground occupied by the state. Both situations witnessed an upsurge in the autonomous activity within society and a profusion of new mass organisations, epitomised in 1917 by a mosaic of workers' and soldiers' soviets and under Gorbachev by popular fronts. In both cases, the government tried to contain and channel the upsurge within established institutions duly reformed and democratised – the *zemstvos* and urban dumas of 1917, the hierarchy of soviets in 1989–91.

The upshot was that neither government succeeded in securing a fresh mandate while in their honeymoon periods, and their honeymoons proved very short. Moreover, both experienced a steep erosion not only of their popularity but also of their ability to impose their will upon society. In 1917 there developed mounting defiance against established authorities of all kinds – against local government, against tax officials and food committees, in schools and universities, against managers, landowners and army officers.[34] Likewise from the latter part of 1989, the authority of the Gorbachev government went into precipitate decline. Newly elected republican legislatures and newly appointed republican governments began to insist on the primacy of their own legislation and to defy the Kremlin on one issue after another, be it by withholding taxation, preventing conscription, or ignoring the instructions of the All-Union economic ministries[35] The most striking feature of the analogy concerns the issue of overt coercion in a situation of collapsing authority. In both cases, the reformist government proved reluctant to resort to force. To do so would have flown in the face of the image that both sought to project – an irreversible break, respectively, with their Tsarist and unreformed Communist predecessors. Moreover, the explosion of autonomous political activity and free political debate over which both governments had presided rendered the reliability of the army highly problematic. Nevertheless, more conservative figures within each establishment resolved upon a reassertion of coercive power. The upshot was the Kornilov affair of August 1917 and the August *putsch* of 1991. In both cases, men appointed by the reformist leaders, Kerensky and Gorbachev, resolved to crush the centres of radicalism. In both cases they failed to carry the legal head of government with them – but believed, or feigned to believe, that they had his support.[36] And in both cases fierce civilian resistance rapidly undermined the will of the troops on which the 'putschists' were relying.

Although Kerensky and Gorbachev alike called for and welcomed resistance, in the aftermath their own prestige went into tailspin. Kerensky had the gravest difficulty piecing together the Third Coalition, while Gorbachev found himself humiliated and denigrated for his close links with the foiled plotters. In September 1917 Lenin began his campaign to goad the Bolshevik Party into leading an uprising against the Provisional Government, while in 1991 Yeltsin combined with leaders of the other Union Republics to dismantle the USSR and abolish its government.

The structural difference between the dramas that merits greatest emphasis concerns the nature of the opposition movement which swept the two governments away. In 1917, the struggle for political power pitting a government under liberal guidance against radical socialists reflected, albeit imperfectly and in a distorted fashion, the extreme social polarisation that had characterised the Russian Empire. Popular support for the far left reflected the specific socio-economic goals of the lower classes. With the fall of the Tsar, the peasantry made abundantly clear their absolute determination to see the transfer of gentry-owned land into the hands of village communes for distribution among peasant households. Under the Provisional Government they became increasingly exasperated by what they saw as prevarication and deliberate delay over land reform. The confrontation between workers and employers was scarcely less direct. Workers bitterly resented arbitrary and degrading treatment at the hands of factory foremen, their pitiful wage-rates, grim working conditions, long hours and total lack of security. During 1917 workers became increasingly united and militant in their determination to secure a government committed to transforming management relations in industry and intervening to halt accelerating inflation, rising unemployment and what they saw as deliberate lockouts by managers. And the gulf separating educated and propertied society from the lower classes was reproduced directly in the armed forces where relations between officers and men reached the point of explosion in the course of the First World War. A fragile compromise between the two built after the February Revolution and resting upon a novel system of elected soldiers' committees was shattered by the fatal decision to tighten discipline for a new offensive in June 1917, thereby provoking wholesale mutiny and mass demands for a hasty end to the war. In short, what underlay the erosion of the Provisional Government's position was a mighty social upheaval which, even before October, had gone a long way towards transforming relations between one class and another, as peasants drove landlords from the countryside, workers undermined the managerial authority and property rights of industrialists, and rank-and-file soldiers destroyed the traditional army.[37]

By contrast with this, the struggle for power in 1991 barely corresponded at all to divisions between one social stratum and another. This time the salient division was not social but national. It was the drive for national sovereignty that galvanised the opposition movements which swept the Gorbachev government away. True, nationalist rejection of Gorbachev's government was fuelled in virtually every case by protest against the same catalogue of grievances: against Communist rule; against the monstrous crimes of Stalin's day; against the oppressive and anti-democratic features of the one-party state under his successors; against *nomenklatura* privilege; against the environmental havoc wreaked by the command economy; against what came to be seen as the USSR's comprehensive economic failure when every month brought a clearer picture of superior living standards in the West and every week brought further evidence that Gorbachev's attempt to reform the economic system had only accelerated decline. But to reject all this was not to identify specific socio-economic goals. Though public attitudes towards the notion of a market economy became much more favourable under Gorbachev's transitory government, this was combined with widespread rejection of privatising large industry, sanctioning unemployment and deregulating prices. Late in 1990 a majority expected transition to such an economy to worsen the plight of most people, and according to some polls a majority admitted they did not know what a market was.[38] The protest movement of 1917 had made clear above all that Russia's future would be in some form 'socialist', that is committed to collective control over all forms of power including economic power, while its national configuration remained open to question. By contrast, the opposition movement of 1991 ensured the break-up of the USSR along national lines but it left opaque the socio-economic path that each would follow.

Post-revolutionary government: Bolshevik (1917–21), Yeltsin/Gaidar (1991–93)

The final analogy to be considered here concerns the regimes which came to power following the overthrow of the Provisional Government and the Gorbachev administration. This is more controversial ground at a time when Lenin's stock has sunk to a new low while Yeltsin is widely portrayed as a good democrat at heart. Moreover, brutal and bloody though some of the actions of the early Yeltsin government were, they pale into insignificance when compared to the horrendous carnage, terror and destruction of the civil war which Lenin fought. Nevertheless, the parallels are worth acknowledging. Both signalled a far more radical break with the past than had the transitory governments of Kerensky and Gorbachev. The Bolsheviks swept away the institutional, legal and social framework they inherited. They scrapped the ephemeral national representative bodies set up by the Provisional Government as well as rural *zemstvos* and urban dumas. They abolished the organisations – and the titles – of nobility and merchants. They separated the Church from the state and imposed severe restrictions upon it. They disbanded the old army and replaced the established legal and judicial system by revolutionary courts. And at the same time as dismantling the superstructure of the traditional establishment, they set about erasing the symbols, the rhetoric and the culture of the old regime. They tore down the Tsar's twin-headed eagle, which had merely been uncrowned by the Provisional Government, and in its place raised the hammer and sickle, the twin symbol of worker and peasant power.

Three-quarters of a century later, the Gaidar government was scarcely less determined to erase the memory, the relics, the social order of the regime that it repudiated. The 'reformers' who took power in Russia as the USSR crumbled away banned the Communist Party outright, consigning to oblivion the structure on which the political system and the social framework had rested. They demolished the symbols of the Soviet era, its monuments, its nomenclature; they repudiated its textbooks, its novels, its films, its very language. This time the hammer and sickle were scrapped and the crowned twin-headed eagle restored. The names of squares and streets, towns and cities, including Leningrad itself, reverted to their pre-revolutionary form. The bureaucracy was to be remoulded in accordance with Western models and the school and university curriculum was to be comprehensively overhauled and 'retooled' with Western texts and techniques and teachers retrained.

Both governments expected to enjoy overwhelming popular support in carrying through a thoroughgoing revolution. The transitory regimes they replaced, after all, had been comprehensively repudiated. There was strong evidence, especially in urban Russia, of a massive rise in the popularity of the Bolsheviks in 1917 and of Yeltsin in 1991. It was not difficult to place a gloss on the Constituent Assembly elections of November 1917, where the Bolsheviks had won less than 25 per cent of the vote. After all, Socialist parties had won an overwhelming victory; many of those who gave the Social Revolutionaries (SRs) their majority were surely signalling their support for the Left SRs who were moving into alliance with the Bolsheviks; and in any case Lenin took the view that popular support for soviet power rendered the assembly an anachronism.[39] Nor was it difficult for Yeltsin and his allies to dismiss the March 1991 referendum, in which 71 per cent within the RSFSR (76 per cent in the USSR) voted in favour of preserving the USSR on a 'renewed' basis between sovereign republics. After all, the proposition put before the electorate was ambiguous; at the very same time, in virtual contradiction, almost the same proportion voted in favour of a directly elected president of the Russian Federation; in June Yeltsin won a sweeping victory in the election for the new post; and the August *putsch* radically altered the whole political context.[40] Both governments expected and were ready to take drastic action against die-hard resistance and any attempt to organise a renewed *putsch* by defenders of the old order. But both were confident of mass support for the socio-economic and diplomatic revolution on which they were determined. Accordingly both boldly proclaimed their commitment to democracy and their intention to enshrine popular sovereignty in a new constitution.

In reality, the measures which the two governments resorted to once in power proved incompatible with democracy. In both cases, they were driven in part by determination to render any restoration of the old regime impossible and in part by the desperate economic crisis they inherited. But in neither had the approach they adopted received conscious democratic endorsement – the one was obscured by enthusiasm for 'peace, bread, land and soviet power' and general endorsement of socialism, the other by enthusiasm for the demolition of Communist rule, the establishment of a specifically Russian state, and general endorsement of a shift towards a market economy. Rather than reflecting popular will, the manner in which they chose to tackle the crisis reflected the specific ideological baggage with which they took office – the one drawing upon Marxism, the other upon Western economists of the Chicago school. In the case of the Bolsheviks, their fundamental premise was that economic development based upon the market, private enterprise, the profit motive and economic individualism had reached a cul-de-sac. Not only had it been responsible for Russia's involvement in the carnage of the First World War but it had proved unable to cope with the economic dislocation brought on by the war. Capitalism had demonstrated beyond dispute that it was incapable of resolving its inherent contradictions. The way forward lay in public ownership, planned production and distribution according to need.[41] In the case of the Gaidar government, the fundamental premise was the exact reverse. Central planning and public ownership, it was now believed, was the root cause of Russia's economic plight. Not only had the commitment to such an economy poisoned the country's relations with the developed world, it had proved inherently incapable of competing with the dynamic growth rates of capitalism. The only way forward lay in wholesale privatisation, the abolition of price controls, a massive reduction in government expenditure, and a free market.[42]

In fact, neither government had any comprehensive programme for transition and both fell far short of the goals they set themselves. The Bolsheviks adopted the policies that came to be known as 'war communism' in an *ad hoc* fashion, and those policies were frustrated at every turn. Illegal trade abounded, the peasantry showed no inclination to move towards collective farming, and despite the nationalisation of industry the decline in output accelerated.[43] Moreover, far from triggering a world revolution which would put an end to the old diplomatic/military order and transform the country's relations with the West, the Bolsheviks found themselves at loggerheads with virtually all their neighbours. Gaidar's 'shock therapy', likewise, was composed of *ad hoc* measures pointing in the general direction of the capitalist utopia, rather than a coherent overall package, and it too failed to achieve many of its aims. The freeing of most prices (January 1992) without tight control of the budget and money supply sent inflation soaring to new heights thereby wildly distorting the signals sent out by the emergent market; agricultural workers on state and collective farms showed limited interest in private farming; and the programme of industrial privatisation failed to break up many of the monopolies or halt the decline in output.[44] And here, too, the anticipated transformation in foreign relations proved deeply problematic and the aid from the IMF and Western governments unexpectedly meagre.

Nevertheless, in both cases the attempt to recast the entire economic structure provoked widespread opposition not only among the minority who championed the old order or regretted the fall of the transitory government, but among vast sections of those who in 1917 had welcomed soviet power and in 1991 hailed Yeltsin's ascendancy and Russian national sovereignty. The Bolsheviks ran up not only against property-owners and industrialists but also against a growing proportion of workers, disillusioned by industrial decline and increasingly harsh disciplinary measures, and the great bulk of the peasantry, who experienced forcible grain requisitioning as an alien assault. Gaidar ran up not only against those members of the *nomenklatura* who could not adapt to the new conditions, as well as military leaders, industrial managers and local government officials, but also against the tens of millions whose jobs, income, security, welfare provision, pensions and status were thrown into jeopardy by accelerating industrial decline, the lottery of privatisation, rising unemployment, virtual hyper-inflation and a drastic fall in real expenditure by the state. Moreover, both 'experiments' were associated with an attempt at cultural revolution which clashed with the most deeply rooted mores. Alongside their assault upon the market, the Bolsheviks attacked religion, the family and peasant autonomy.[45] Seven decades later the Gaidar government championed economic individualism and the market ethic among a people whose cultural heritage, both high and low, had for centuries been steeped in countervailing values and who had long been accustomed to guaranteed employment and (modest) welfare provision. And to make matters worse, 'shock therapy' was accompanied by a policy of international conciliation which seemed to fly in the face of Russian dignity and the national interest.[46]

Neither government was overthrown. Each found a measure of support among its protégés. Lenin was supported by those relatively well-educated and politically committed workers and peasants recruited into and promoted through the ranks of the party, the Red Army, and the swelling soviet apparatus after 1917.[47] Gaidar was supported by the beneficiaries of privatisation after 1991, notably small traders and a substantial proportion of the old *nomenklatura* who were best placed by virtue of wealth, contacts and political influence to take advantage of the process. Each benefited, too, from the limited political appeal of their most strident opponents – be it the White Generals confronting Lenin or the leaders of the Russian Supreme Soviet, headed by Rutskoi and Khasbulatov, who challenged Gaidar's government. And in both cases, the failure of political change to improve the quality of life tended to breed apathy, disillusionment and a search for individual strategies of survival rather than generating alternative programmes capable of mobilising coherent social constituencies.[48]

Nevertheless, both governments found it necessary to cut one democratic corner after another. The supremely democratic ideal enshrined in the new Constitution of 1918 was flagrantly flouted. Authoritarian relationships were re-established over the peasantry, in industry, in the new Red Army. Lenin's dream that all public officials should be elected and paid a normal worker's wage receded to the horizon. The Cheka became firmly entrenched as a nationwide police force free from any form of democratic control. Opposition activists were hounded by the police and their activities narrowly circumscribed, and as soviet elections became less and less frequent and meaningful and soviets at every level were subordinated to the corresponding party committee, popular participation in politics declined and democratic decision-making was reduced to a mere charade.[49]

The Yeltsin–Gaidar government, though hailed across the Western world as the champion of democracy, delayed two years before introducing a new constitution.[50] Meanwhile, Yeltsin postponed fresh local and parliamentary elections and instead of seeking to entrench democratic institutions, relied upon emergency presidential powers and the appointment of special 'presidential representatives' to impose his will. By the summer of 1993 opinion polls suggested that support for government policy had fallen below 10 per cent. Yet when the Supreme Soviet (elected in March 1990) obstructed the government and its policy of 'shock therapy' he confronted it head on, high-handedly proclaimed its dissolution and in October 1993, faced with continued defiance, resorted to force and the arrest of its leaders. Only then did he summon fresh elections (December 1993) and, with television, the radio and most of the press in the hands of his supporters, stage a plebiscite over a new constitution carefully crafted to maximise presidential authority. As in Lenin's Russia, political participation and faith in democratic procedures underwent precipitate decline and the very words 'democracy' and 'democrat' took on ever more negative connotations in popular speech. Thus when at last voters were given the opportunity to pass a verdict on Gaidar and his policies, a mere 55 per cent bothered to vote at all, and Gaidar's party scraped only 15.4 per cent – less than 9 per cent of the electorate as a whole.

Were the analogy considered here extrapolated into the future, it would point to a short period of relative tranquillity followed by a resumed and supremely authoritarian dose of 'shock therapy'. It would suggest that the exit from government of Gaidar and virtually all those most enthralled by the Chicago school, following the election of 1993, has inaugurated only a brief period of compromise analogous to that of the New Economic Policy (NEP), and that the post-Soviet regime can be expected in due course to launch a renewed assault, matching Stalin's 'revolution from above' in its disregard for democracy, this time designed to smash the remaining 'socialist' obstacles to a free-market utopia. While such a scenario is not impossible, the structural contrasts point elsewhere. In the first place, the doctrinaire commitment to unfettered capitalism of the immediate post-Soviet period had far shallower roots than did the anti-market ethos of 'war communism'. Gaidar's successors found it much easier to abandon the short road to utopia than did the Bolshevik leadership when coming to terms with NEP. Second, the market project depends in a way that Stalin's project manifestly did not upon inspiring confidence in international institutions, foreign governments, bankers and investors: the penalty for too overt a disregard for civil liberties and at least some democratic forms would be high. Third, whereas popular (primarily peasant) opposition to 'war communism' stopped it dead in its tracks, the millions of humble victims of 'shock therapy' lacked both the social cohesion and the economic leverage to mount equivalent resistance. Here the effective opposition to the utopian experiment came, rather, from elements within the military, managerial, political and cultural elites. Given the variety of different, often conflicting motives of these elites, it remains an open question how far they will carry their resistance to marketisation. But whereas the resumption of the Bolshevik project at the end of the 1920s involved overt mass coercion, a resumption at more measured pace of marketisation need not necessarily do so. And whereas NEP manifestly failed to bend the peasantry to the Bolshevik will, it is possible to envisage a prolonged process of milder 'therapy' which succeeds in subjecting post-Soviet society to the dictates of the market.

Conclusion

The comparison between the 1917 and 1991 revolutions highlights a common tragedy. Both brought to power governments inspired by economic ideals which led them to adopt policies conflicting directly with the wishes and interests of vast sections of the population. The result was to place democracy in jeopardy. Yet the comparison also suggests that the legacy of the USSR and the Gorbachev government provides less inhospitable soil for democracy than did that of Tsarism and the Provisional Government. True, even a gradual marketisation will take a heavy toll upon superfluous workers in heavy industry, peasants on collective and state farms, employees in health and education and public services, intellectuals, students and pensioners. The form of democracy that sanctions such a process may be impoverished and do little to empower citizens or consolidate legal constraints on the executive; it may flout civil rights; and it may be marked by widespread political apathy and perilously low levels of participation. Yet it need not involve the authoritarian resurrection that Herzen's fable foretells.

5. Stalin's Great Turn: a Revolution without Footsoldiers?

CATHERINE MERRIDALE

Most of the revolutions discussed in this volume involved complete changes of regime, the more or less violent overthrow of an established government by revolutionaries dedicated to far-reaching political and, usually, economic and social change. By these criteria, Stalin's so-called 'great turn' of 1929–32 is not at first an obvious candidate for the title of revolution. The Soviet Union's leadership was not overthrown, and the political programme to which Lenin's revolution of 1917 had been dedicated was ostensibly continued. But the speed and scope of change in the three years in question defy most other definitions. Contemporaries referred to the period as the 'great break' (*velikii perelom*); historians have spoken of 'cultural revolution', 'revolution from above', the turning point.

Because there was no change of leadership, confusion arises not merely about the extent of the transformation but also about the impulse which drove it. At the time, Soviet propaganda spoke of the organic link between the people and their leader, of Stalin's ability to interpret and then implement the best interests of the Soviet revolution. There was little talk of the state or of revolution from above – a concept which makes no sense if the leader is merely the servant of his people. Subsequently, however, the idea of a state-led revolution, or even an assault by the Party leadership upon the Soviet people, has come to dominate historical discussion of the first Five Year Plan. The notion of state-directed revolution from above has nearly always been employed by critics of the changes.[1] Even those who admired the more heroic aspects of the economic transformation conceded that they had been won in the teeth of enormous suffering and the loss of millions of lives. Revolution from

73

above became a more or less pejorative way of describing the costly process of industrialisation, the elimination of the ancient system of peasant farming and the final consolidation of Communist Party rule. The idea is so important for the understanding of one of the most influential revolutionary regimes in twentieth-century history that it deserves inclusion in any anthology about revolution.

If the limited nature of the changes, and specifically, the continuity of regime, raise questions about Stalinism's revolutionary credentials, the question of revolutionary agency – revolution 'from above' – is even more controversial. Some would argue that such a transformation does not qualify as a revolution at all. As one theorist put it, 'social revolutions are rapid, basic transformations of a society's state and class structures; and they are accompanied and in part carried through by class-based revolts from below'.[2] Without the element of pressure from below, the process can appear as a coup, a set of far-reaching reforms, a state-led campaign of modernisation. These are not merely semantic distinctions, and certainly were not for historians of the left in the 1960s and 1970s. The socialist credentials of the Soviet system, the heir to Stalin's great turn, depended, in part, on the discovery of evidence of revolution from below. For a whole generation of historians, then, the discussion of Stalinism necessarily involved two major questions: the nature of the transformation (revolution, counter-revolution, coup) and the agency by which it was effected. In this essay, I shall examine both issues before turning to the wider question of how Stalinism and the whole issue of revolution in Stalinist Russia may be approached in the post-Soviet era.

Stalin's great turn, initiated in 1929, involved change in every sphere of life and affected every Soviet citizen. The innovations, moreover, were not accidental or random, but were initiated in pursuit of a clear ideology of revolution. The most conspicuous change was the collectivisation of agriculture.[3] The campaign lasted for just over two years. Private agriculture was not entirely eradicated from the USSR, but there were very few private farmers left in the so-called grain-surplus regions after 1931, and many who resisted collectivisation had been deported to the north and east. The human costs – the devastation of individual lives, the overturning of cherished expectations for old age or family life, the loss of accustomed routines and property, the slaughter of livestock, the intervention of seemingly inexperienced outsiders – all these were serious enough. For some who remained on the collectives, however, the ultimate price was even higher; death from starvation or disease in the famine which struck Ukraine, Kazakhstan and southern Russia in 1932–3, killing an estimated 10 million people.[4]

It would be splitting hairs to deny that upheaval on this scale was revolutionary. On Theda Skocpol's definition of revolution as a fundamental revision of the relationship between state and society and also of social relations,[5] collectivisation comfortably qualifies. It also had a far-reaching political as well as an economic purpose: to force the 'bourgeois' peasant into rural 'factories', to create a rural 'proletariat' and to facilitate the latter's incorporation into the Communist political system. As Karl Bauman, the future secretary of the Moscow Party organisation, put it in 1927, 'there cannot be two socialisms; one for the countryside and one for the towns'.[6] In the process, a whole social class disappeared within a matter of months, although it is difficult to say what replaced it, for the next few years were to see massive movements of population, individual mobility between countryside and burgeoning industrial cities, while those who remained in the villages were not transformed into rural proletarians, or even into willing collective farmers, within a generation. Indisputably, however, the state had asserted itself over the peasantry at last, transforming itself in the process, closing its inner ranks against criticism, and plunging irrevocably into the stream of change for fear that any reversal, or even a pause, might threaten its stability.

Collectivisation was accompanied by other changes of almost equal significance. The elimination of private trade, for example, fundamentally altered urban life, and resulted in the deportation or ruination of a large number of small business people, part-time craftspeople and what the Soviets inelegantly called 'former people' (minor members of the old aristocracy, priests, members of professions whose contribution was no longer recognised), some of whom had survived up to that point on their wits and the last scraps of the family silver.[7] The other innovation, rapid industrialisation, ripped apart the fabric of Tsarist manufacturing and ushered in a period of frenetic industrial activity. Entirely new cities were planned and eventually built, existing factories were gutted and rebuilt or razed and reconstituted, resources were exploited at record rates to raise capital for more building, more tools, better machinery.[8] The process was accompanied by a training programme intended to produce engineers and technicians to run the new enterprises within two or three years.[9] If the tangible achievements of the first Five Year Plan for industry were limited, visible more in the upheaval they created than in attained levels of sustainable output, at least the commitment was solid to increase production at any cost, to concentrate on industrialisation, to catch up with the West, as Stalin put it, within ten years 'or we shall go under'.

Doubters and critics of this optimistic programme were well advised to remain silent. Those who did not, and indeed some who merely refrained from praising its achievements, found themselves the object of concentrated political pressure, and in some cases, such as that of the Industrial Party, the victims of trumped up criminal charges.[10] For some, the charges carried the death penalty, and in certain instances, even at this early stage in the development of the Stalinist system, the threat was carried out. Stalin's great turn, then, involved political as well as economic and social upheavals. These included a transformation of the Communist Party's political style – a greater intolerance towards dissent, a cruder campaigning language, a focus on practical goals – as well as some personnel changes.[11] Among the latter, at the elite level, the old *émigrés* within the Bolshevik Party, the comrades who had shared Lenin's exile or lived out the last years of Tsarism in the cafes and hostels of France and Austria, were ousted at last. The victory of Stalin and his close associates represented a turn towards that section of the party which identified itself as Russian, had spent little or no time abroad, and was committed to the idea of building a strong state within the USSR rather than to the Leninist-Trotskyist utopia of world socialism.[12]

The political changes may be described as a shift in emphasis. The party's Russian wing had always been influential; the power of individuals like Stalin, Molotov and Kaganovich had been growing since the mid-1920s. Moreover, intolerance had long characterised intra-party debates, and the anathematising of supposed 'oppositionists' had become almost routine. But the shift of 1929–32, arguably, was so decisive and rapid that it, too, amounted to a revolution in Soviet political life. The cosmopolitan, discursive Bolshevism of Trotsky and Kamenev was gone for ever from the political scene.[13] In its place the crude, boorish and over-simplifying ideology of Stalinism had arrived to stamp its imprint on every aspect of Soviet cultural and political endeavour.

If Stalin's great turn was not a classic revolution, therefore, its claim to bring revolutionary change is almost beyond dispute. Far more controversy surrounds the interpretation which is placed on the events – whether they are seen, for example, as an episode in the construction of a socialist state or as the final consolidation of a vicious monopolistic dictatorship. These questions have been reopened since the collapse of the Communist system in 1991. But before we examine the recent debate, it is important to establish the ground from which it sprang.

The original interpretation of the great turn, put forward by the Soviets themselves and mentioned briefly earlier, saw Stalin as the heir of Lenin. According to the established Soviet line, Stalin's task in 1929 was to carry forward and complete the work the first leader of the Soviet people had begun.[14] Thus, Stalin took a country of peasant smallholders and transformed it into an industrial giant. He even overcame the idiocy of rural life, creating modern, large-scale farms free from the oppression of landlessness, small-scale hired labour and the lonely drudgery of poor peasant existence. Significantly, too, the industrial basis for a proletarian socialist society was laid in this period, and consciously planned cities were built to combine efficient production and civilised urban living. The USSR also became one of the world's leading military powers. The foundations for its victory over fascism, which represented a victory for the entire free world, were laid during this crucial phase of socialist transformation.

There are elements of truth in this narrative. It suggests that the great turn was not a discrete revolution, but part of what Antonio Gramsci would have seen as a revolutionary process,[15] a 20-year-long transformation of old Russia into the modern USSR. In the past, and especially in the 1960s when the search for 'socialism with a human face' was under way in Eastern Europe, some left-wing critics of Stalin argued that he broke with Leninism, employing violence and coercion where Lenin might have used subtler means.[16] For these commentators, Stalinism contained more than an element of counter-revolution. The official Soviet line denied any such suggestion, and recent archival evidence suggests that it was largely correct to do so. Lenin was neither mild nor patient, and the violence he was prepared to use, for example against priests, boded ill for later oppositionists or recalcitrant social groups. As he put it, 'no revolutionary government can do without the death penalty, and the essence of the question is only against what class will the weapon of the death penalty be directed.'[17] Religious protesters of the city of Shua were clearly on the wrong side of this class divide, for in 1922, he called for them to be punished 'so brutally that they will remember it for decades to come'.[18] The wider question of what Lenin might have done if he had lived is impossible to answer, and complicated by the fact that his mind was clouded in his last two years by the sclerosis which eventually killed him.[19] Crude though Stalin was, however, and literalist about the grosser aims of class war, what he sought to achieve, as the Soviet account suggests, was hardly contrary to Lenin's teaching.

Where the official Soviet account was obviously misleading was in its unashamed understatement of the costs involved in Stalin's great turn, its ignorance of the fact of resistance and its bald overestimate of its achievements. In view of these shortcomings, and also bearing in mind their origin in propaganda, it is striking that the Soviet meta-narrative about progress and economic transformation should have largely set the research agenda for historians across the political spectrum from the 1930s onwards.

The second school of interpretation, then, although largely hostile to Stalin, in fact took its cue from the Soviets' own account of themselves. The classic interpretation of Stalinism as revolution from above was given, in fact, by Robert Tucker, who would certainly not consider himself to be an apologist for communism or a supporter of Stalin. Tucker saw Stalinism as one of a long series of transformatory episodes in Russia's quest for modernisation.[20] There was a good deal of criticism of Stalinism and of Stalin personally in Tucker's work – he singled out the terror, for example, as an example of the cruelty which has traditionally accompanied attempts at modernisation in Russian history – but where he was broadly in line with the Stalinist school was in emphasising, as do most historians of the Soviet Union, the teleology of industrialisation. The idea that there was a forward momentum in Soviet history, that it was defined by economic change, and that Stalinism was a crucial phase of it, was not challenged.

A great deal of excellent historical work, including a range of economic histories of Soviet industrialisation, has been written with the idea of modernisation, of progress, somewhere in the background. Most historians are sharply and accurately critical of the excesses and mistakes involved.[21] But for members of this tendency, the primary focus remains the idea of development, and the organisational thread running through their work follows the line of economic growth and teleological planning. Stalinism, then, is seen as a revolution from above, one which laid the foundations of a modern industrial society. By emphasising this aspect, the undercurrent of development economics, historians tacitly accept many Soviet statements about the meaning of the period, however critical of its costs they may be.

The final line of interpretation, at least until recently, was represented by the totalitarian school. Historians writing in this tradition were among the most openly hostile to the Stalinist project.[22] Their model of it, indeed, was largely elaborated during the Cold War. Writing in the 1950s, historians such as Merle Fainsod saw the establishment of the Stalinist regime as the imposition of a murderous dictatorship upon the Soviet people. Fainsod in particular was prepared to accept that state power had its limitations, that control was not absolute.[23] But the underlying idea – of a single-person dictatorship backed up by modern technology and powerful propaganda – took the revolution from above model to its extreme. The study of the Stalinist system became, on this reading, a matter of examining the elite to see how power was exercised. Society, after all, was shattered – atomised – by the assaults of collectivisation and mass terror, and by 1932 was no longer a significant actor in the political process. If the Soviet people were to be studied at all, it was as victims of this dictatorship – Ukrainians dying in the 1933 famine, officials and technicians swept away in the purge, young men whose lives were recklessly thrown away in the early months of the Great Patriotic War. Hostile to the Soviet Union though they were, however, there was one sense in which even totalitarian theorists subscribed to Stalinist rhetoric. Even those who perceived, as Fainsod did, the gaps in central control and the inconsistencies in policy, regarded the Soviet Union as a Great Power. Cold War history was predicated on the idea that the Soviet Union was a formidable enemy, and that it was Stalin's revolution from above which had laid the foundations for this strength.

This historiographical review has necessarily been simplified. But even if there had been space for a longer discussion, many of the basic points would not have changed. Soviet history was profoundly affected by the simplicity of the Soviets' own propaganda. In addition, historians of any nationality were bound by the relatively simple language and limited scope of their source material. As long as the archives of the Communist Party and state apparatus were closed, historians relied on the limited range of published sources. This limitation also partly explained the dominance of the Soviets' own official picture of themselves. But the other factor influencing the debate was the importance of Soviet history and of understandings of Stalinism for political and ideological struggles taking place outside Russia, notably in the United States of America. Only this over-charging of the discussion can account for the viciousness with which a fourth group of historians, the so-called revisionists, were received when their work began to appear in the late 1970s. In view of the anger which they attracted, it is surprising to find that the 'revisionists' did not exist as a school.[24] It is difficult to generalise about their conclusions. But at its simplest, the impact of much of their research was to question the 'atomisation' of society and to ask, tentatively, whether evidence could be found for support for Stalin's revolution from below, from the people, as well as from the elite. They did not suggest that the masses turned out in force in the countryside to collectivise themselves, or that there was always enthusiasm for the extremer aspects of mass terror. But they did seek to identify certain groups in Soviet society who might have had something to gain from the change of policy, and they tried to show how, in what they saw as the chaotic conditions of the great turn, such pressure could be converted into the political actions which helped to shape its final outcome.

Although they were accused of 'whitewashing' the Stalinist regime,[25] shifting the blame on to the mass of the population, the impact of this aspect of their work, properly interpreted, in fact appears bleak. For, as historians of Nazi Germany discovered when they, too, found evidence of 'collaboration', the idea that thousands of people could have colluded with and even helped to create policies which brought suffering and death to millions is hardly a matter of historical whitewash.[26] The claim that ordinary people supported aspects of Stalinism does not reduce the burden of Stalin's personal culpability, or the extent of the atrocities committed. The argument only becomes distorted if the claim is made that popular support was in some way an indicator of the morality or altruism of Stalinist policies, as if the people were better arbiters of justice than their leaders. But while Soviet propagandists, in their gross simplicity, may have used the idea of a popular mandate in that way, no historian need be so naive. Evidence of revolution from below of itself neither exonerates nor condemns the policies in question.

As more evidence is unearthed, post-glasnost, of the full impact of Stalin's purges and of the misery inflicted through repressive social and nationality policies throughout the Soviet period, the idea of collective responsibility, which is a consequence of accepting the model of revolution from below, has become increasingly sensitive within Russia. A debate which took shape in the shadow-boxing between right and left in the West in the 1970s has become a live political issue in the rebuilding of post-Soviet consciousness within Russia. As in post-Nazi Germany, but at a lag of two generations, questions have been asked about individual and collective guilt. Inevitably, the challenge is evaded wherever possible. The commonest response is to direct attention to the country's continuing crisis, to say that history is a diversion. Alternatively, those who write about Stalinism are tempted to adopt the totalitarian model as a way of ensuring that any historical blame remains firmly with the leadership.[27] If society was atomised, if the state was all-powerful, there cannot be collective responsibility and the post-Soviet person can get on with life with a clear conscience.[28]

It was through debates about collaboration and responsibility, therefore, that the question of revolution from below acquired a new resonance in the 1990s. In the former Soviet Union as in the West, historians became keen to discover what ordinary people thought of Stalin's great turn, how they contributed, what political views they held in the face of so much propaganda. And with access to important archives now almost guaranteed, those who studied the elite could explore the concept of 'leadership' more thoroughly, to look for factions and debates where previously the press presented them with an impenetrable united front. It was tempting, as the archives opened, to suggest that at last historians might find answers to their questions, that the evidence for 'revolution from below', for example, might be waiting in the thousands of manila files which they could now read. A scramble for documents followed. Archives came alive to the clatter of portable computers. But when the dust settled, survivors were forced to agree that certain types of evidence were still lacking; public opinion surveys, for example, or diaries and memoirs which told the uncensored truth. What the historians of the 1990s have found, in short, is that the most important historical questions are not susceptible to simple answers.

A number of new strands of interpretation have emerged. Not all rely on 'new' facts. Many have been provoked by new approaches to history, often initiated outside the sphere of Soviet studies. Before turning to these, however, we should deal with the extent of the available evidence for revolution from below. As I have already suggested, a good deal of this focuses on the Communist Party rather than society as a whole, but it nonetheless challenges traditional images of central control and smooth channels of decision-making.

Serious historians have long understood that government under Stalin was far from simple. Although recent archival discoveries confirm that one-man rule could be absolute on specific occasions, refuting for ever the suggestion that Stalin was unaware of the political murders of the 1930s, for example, most decisions were more complex than the signing of a death warrant. Where priorities had to be fixed or scarce resources assigned, tension between different interests, even within the elite, could lead to genuine faction-fighting. Even within the charmed circle of hand-picked officialdom, the *nomenklatura*, recognisable interest-based alliances were formed and dissolved in the 1930s. Moreover, the elite was itself isolated from society; isolated, at times, even from its own rank and file. As early as 1920 the elite had begun to be cushioned from day-to-day reality, protected by special rations, chauffeur-driven cars (which had to be stored nearer and nearer to the Kremlin itself to avoid assassination attempts and vandalism[29]) and foreign medical experts and treatment.

A glance at almost any set of documents from the 1930s takes this picture still further, showing how isolated even Stalin had become from solid information about conditions in the localities.[30] Information was distorted, reports written to conceal the truth, interests and friends protected by silence or lies. Day-to-day decision-making was clearly compromised by this, but so was the formulation of strategy. If Stalin's revolution of 1928 came from above, therefore, it was at best a blindfold leap in the dark.[31] The leap, moreover, was not uncontentious. The leadership, even in the 1930s, was not monolithic, and real debates continued.[32] True, the big ideological issues of the 1920s ceased to be open to question after 1929, and a good deal of the wrangling after that date was about resources and priorities rather than political goals, but the idea that Stalin presided over a united team no longer fits the evidence.

One or two rungs down the ladder from the Kremlin mandarins were the regional and metropolitan party officials. These, too, were in turmoil throughout the early Stalin period. Technically they were in close contact with Stalin and his officials on a daily basis, but the interruptions and misinterpretations involved in this dialogue left them with a great deal of responsibility for the formulation of policy. The directives they received were often contradictory. Local secretaries had no choice but to prioritise, decide between options and fill in the yawning gaps in their instructions. An example can be drawn from the Moscow region itself, where the party's first secretary, Karl Bauman, presided over a distortedly extreme campaign for the rapid collectivisation of agriculture in 1929–30.[33] His initiative, although at first tacitly sanctioned by Stalin, proved so costly in terms of economic disruption and peasant hostility that it was abandoned on Molotov's orders in March 1930. But up to that point, the Moscow party secretary had been able to design and carry out a policy far in excess of the official plan. The effect on peasants in the Moscow region, and also on village schoolteachers, retired professionals, the innocent rural population of a large area around Moscow, was catastrophic.[34] Villages 'collectivised' by force were 'decollectivised' days later. Elderly ex-doctors or minor administrators of the old regime were condemned as *kulaks*, only to be rescued at the eleventh hour. Collectivisation in the Moscow region aroused violent resistance.[35] A more measured campaign, while hardly gentle, at least might have avoided the worst excesses. Was Bauman's initiative, and the many others like it, revolution from above or below? The expression is largely meaningless. Perhaps it is better to speak instead of hand-to-mouth decision-making on the spot, local conspiracies, and rank disorganisation.

Turning now to the other half of the debate, society, the 'below' of revisionist history, the material coming out of Soviet archives again presents us with a much more complex and contradictory story than before. Crucially, it has at last become possible to document resistance to Stalin's policies at virtually all levels. Debate within the party elite has already been mentioned. But there were also criticisms from the factory floor and more serious opposition – even armed uprising – in the countryside, at least until 1930. Organised resistance was very difficult to sustain after that; the secret police were active in every workplace and no large conspiracy has so far come to light. But small groups undoubtedly continued to form and dissolve, spurred by poor food, dangerous working conditions, incompetent foremen.[36] In rural areas more organised opposition focused around religious groups, especially dissenters such as Seventh Day Adventists and Baptists.[37] Where published sources say virtually nothing about this kind of opposition, secret police reports and Party memoranda, however elliptical, make the story clear.

After so many years of censorship and official complacency, it is understandable that scholars should be eager for evidence of resistance to Stalin's revolution. But what of the other side of the story, the evidence of support? It is here that the problem of collusion and collective responsibility arises, here that the material becomes most sensitive. Unless the totalitarian model is to be taken to an absurd extreme, however, the creation of the Stalinist system must be seen as the work of tens of thousands of hands. What is more difficult is to distinguish between the relatively few conscious Stalinists, the committed ideologues of the cultural revolution, and the huge number of people caught up in changes which they hardly began to comprehend. Revolution from below does not necessarily imply a conscious programme. Many contributed to the shaping of the great turn without accepting, possibly without even knowing, its precepts. It is the mentality of these people which has intrigued the latest generation of social historians, and which remains, for all their efforts, a largely unknown quantity.

Committed ideologues, surprisingly, are also difficult to identify. Stephen Kotkin, writing about the people of Magnitogorsk, rightly criticised historians who sought to divide the population into 'believers' and 'disbelievers', supporters and opponents. 'Elements of "belief" and "disbelief" ', he wrote,

appear to have coexisted within everyone, along with a certain residual resentment…. Even in the case of the category of 'true believers' it is necessary to think in terms of a shifting compromise, of rigidity and the search for slack, of daily negotiation and compromise within certain well-defined but not inviolate limits. Those limits were defined by recognition of the basic righteousness of socialism – always as contrasted with capitalism – a proposition that few people did or could have rejected, whatever resentment or ill-will toward the Soviet regime they harbored.[38]

Initiating the great turn was not quite the same thing as supporting or tolerating the high Stalinism of the 1930s. The revolutionary moment of 1929 had a drama which carried even relatively lukewarm supporters along in the short term, and many of the future costs of the decision were yet to become apparent.[39] But mixed motives of the kind Kotkin described nonetheless predominated over blind enthusiasm. Skilled workers, for example, were a potential source of support for the Stalinist option at the beginning of the first Five Year Plan. Most were committed to industrialisation. In part, this was a matter of protecting jobs, but it was also an ideological issue; industrial workers of the late 1920s had seen the 1917 Revolution, and their belief in socialism, even if it did not coincide fully with Stalin's, at least embraced the idea of advanced industry and material progress. Many also supported collectivisation, often in the belief that they were about to bring civilisation and prosperity to the countryside. Finally, overriding considerations about food supply, and for the more literate, about the potential threat of war, led many to believe that a combination of industrial investment and a more coherent grain policy was essential. Its long-term implications, at this stage, were not spelled out for them. But as one contemporary recalled, two words, bread and war, were on everyone's lips at the end of 1928.[40]

But this set of preoccupations did not fit squarely into the programme which the political elite was preparing. For example, many skilled workers also held land in the villages where their families originated.[41] Retiring to the country was a popular dream, even if dream was all it would ever be. So the idea of 'squeezing the *kulak*', forcing the peasants into collectives, imposing urban values on the ancient village, had limited appeal. The gap between city and village was not as wide as the party elite supposed. In the case of one of Moscow's leading factories, it was only after the peasants attacked and killed several volunteer collectivisers that altruism turned to hatred and a version of class war.[42] By 1930, Elekrozavod workers were as keen to repress and punish the peasants as they had been eager to help them in 1928. This revanchism led them to commit excesses beyond the minimum needed to drive the peasants into collectives. Here was revolution from below, though hardly the kind which revolutionaries might celebrate.

A close study of the urban population of any large city suggests that 'workers' were no more homogeneous a group in 1928–30 than they had been in 1917. Mentalities change when people arrive in an urban setting; village lads did not retain their peasant outlook and loyalties intact.[43] But those who had recently arrived, and seasonal workers who returned to the village regularly, had little reason to sympathise with an assault on the peasantry, however positively it was portrayed in the press. Their affinity with older, hereditary workers was even more limited.[44] Strain between generations and between individuals of different backgrounds divided urban society more deeply in the 1920s and 1930s than would be the case after the war. And these strains and fissures led to the formation of strange alliances, the exploitation of official demands for local, short-term ends. What appeared to be support for a campaign against specialists who resisted the plan, for example, might easily have been a cloak for the removal of oppressive foremen whose attitude towards new arrivals had alienated a close-knit group from neighbouring villages.[45] Once again, this was revolution from below, but it was not part of a concerted programme of long-term reform.

In the countryside, the picture was also more complicated than official histories have allowed. Both Lenin and Stalin had claimed that the poorer peasants had a good deal to gain from collectivisation. In the event, however, few actively supported it. The villages opposed city intervention in general, and the taking of grain, with all the memories it stirred, in particular. Resistance was widespread, violence commonplace. Not everyone resented the so-called *kulak*; in many cases the peasant community as a whole resisted the incursion of city-based plenipotentiaries. Identifying the wealthier members of the village was a hit and miss affair. Where it was done on the basis of records of hiring labour, for example, it could strike the most vulnerable and least resented of the population; the elderly, widows, people whose infirmities made extra help essential.[46] In March 1930 a temporary pause was signalled by Stalin's article, 'Dizzy with Success', itself recognition of the limits of forced revolution from above. But by 1931 the majority of peasants were members of collectives, and thousands had lost their homes to join the stream of *kulaks* heading for exile.

Even in the countryside, however, there were individuals prepared to take advantage of the opportunities which chaos provided. The mentality involved had been shaped by decades of hardship. Less than a generation before, after all, in 1921, the only way many survived was by eating roots, dead flesh, or even, in extreme cases, by cannibalism.[47] The individuals who profited from the upheaval of collectivisation often did so by seizing land or other property for themselves. De-kulakisation offered opportunities for the private settling of scores, the appropriation of long-coveted goods. Even the famine of 1932–3, whose effects were so devastating that none could be said to have lived through it without harm, provided opportunities for limited personal gain. In some cases, for example, when whole villages were wiped out and no record remained of their former inhabitants, pillaging, and later, opportunistic resettlement, were inevitable.[48] At the time much of this was explained away in a rhetoric of expropriation and socialist construction. But many paid lip service to these concepts, and indeed furthered the processes of the great turn, for reasons which neither Marx nor Lenin would have recognised.

Finally on this theme, the exploitation of local conflicts cannot be ignored. One of the problems with the two-dimensional model of revolution from above or below is that it fails to consider lateral tensions, especially those between different ethnic or religious groups. And yet the archives testify to the role these played during the great turn, with mini-pogroms taking place in some localities, and witch hunts against religious believers, sectarians, Muslims or priests a matter of daily report.[49]

The so-called revolution from below, then, turns out to be an even more confused and unconscious a phenomenon as the coup from above. The whole picture was further complicated by the deliberate falsifying of information, the lies and exaggerations with which local officials attempted to protect themselves. Lying had become endemic by 1930, to the extent that only the direct intervention of the GPU, itself a compromised institution, could establish the true condition of a local organisation, farm or factory. Competition between institutions for resources or favours made all this more complex still. 'Above' was divided against itself, while 'below' was in turmoil throughout the period. At any moment, moreover, local alliances of mutual protection could be formed between them. As if the Soviet Union's very collapse had not made the point, it now becomes clear that Stalin's great turn was not simply the seminal moment in the establishment of a major dictatorship. The process was much more confused and fractured than the revolution from above model implied, and the result, the modern Soviet Union, was neither as economically successful nor as politically secure as might have been supposed.

Local case studies are one of the best ways of exploring the details of the transformation, and a number of excellent ones have appeared in the past few years.[50] Many focus on the workplace, usually the factory or construction site, one of the most important centres of collective activity during the first Five Year Plan. Thousands of documents have been read, in some cases including the crucial reports of secret police officials working at the grass-roots level.[51] The work has been rewarding and important, but it leaves unanswered its own initial question. We cannot know, in detail, what ordinary people thought, and we cannot quantify resistance and support.[52] There will never be a posthumous election campaign for Stalin.

Perhaps, then, the question itself requires review. Few other groups of historians would have been asked to quantify support for a regime in this way, they have too many other questions to answer, and they have worked for years within the limitations of their sources. The two-dimensional world of Soviet political studies has constrained the debate about Russia, arguably, for long enough. As I have made clear, there have been good reasons for its hold on the field, but the time may have come to ask whether we need to continue our search for collaborators and opponents in quite such a narrow way.

One obvious alternative, and a fruitful one, has been to study the language of ordinary Soviet citizens, what remains of their mental world, without focusing exclusively on the question of support or opposition.[53] For it is unquestionably true that Russian workers occupied a different linguistic and mental space from the leadership. In some cases, they appropriated its jargon, and even its ugly acronyms. But in others, a separate culture held sway, parallel with but not entirely subordinate to that of the printed newspapers and propaganda films.[54] Recovering this, discovering the Soviet person in his or her own language, is difficult but crucial for an appreciation of what the great turn and its consequences meant. For some critics of the approach, it can seem that the vital questions are getting ignored. If the most important fact of Stalinism, for example, is regarded as its dictatorial cruelty, then the examination of jokes, graffiti, the slang with which workers described their bosses and the labour process, may seem an indulgent diversion.[55] But accounts of popular cultures and languages need not amount to history with the politics left out. The Soviet Union was a society permeated at every level by politics; culture itself was a target for political transformation. Social history, in the Soviet case, is itself the history of a political project, the scope and limits of change, the reception of policy, responses to some of the most intrusive political interventions ever made.

On the other hand, the history of Soviet people has an importance of its own, divorced from familiar debates about socialism and Stalinism. Contemporary Russians have little sense of their cultural identity. In the first place, much that was Russian was subsumed under the mantle of Soviet power. 'Soviet' culture, though easily seen as an entirely artificial product of propaganda and social engineering, in fact was grafted on to deep Russian roots. But there is little understanding of the processes and compromises involved. The temptation has therefore been for modern Russians to discard the heritage of the past 70 years in its entirety, to idealise an obscure and reactionary Tsarist fantasy. The rediscovery of the paths linking pre-revolutionary Russia with the modern Soviet state, the reappropriation of the Soviet era, is crucial to the reintegration of Russian national identity. It will involve asking questions which go far beyond the two-dimensional 'above' and 'below' model. And it is likely to take time, for a range of historical techniques will need to be employed, and the answers are unlikely to be simple or schematic. But it is a process which could bring the twentieth-century history of Russia into the realm of mainstream historical discourse at last, restoring, if it is successful, the sense that Russia is a society like any other, if one which has endured a particularly traumatic past.

The alternative to this process of integration is that Russians may continue to regard themselves as a special case. Expressions such as 'experiment', 'guinea pigs', 'catastrophe' justifiably echo through the conversation of those who currently attempt to describe the Soviet experience in Moscow and St Petersburg. But this sense of exceptionalism does not allow for reconciliation. It throws the historian back on to the familiar questions: what went wrong, who was to blame, who colluded, and what should we do with them? Projected backwards on to the whole of Russian history, it may also suggest that Russians are somehow doomed to undergo periods of crisis and revolution from above.[56]

Far more fruitful than either of these positions is one which attempts to understand the processes of the Soviet transformation despite their complexity. We need to consider more seriously the parts of the story which do not fit along the teleological narrative thread. The study of politics and society may be combined, transcending the antagonism between those who focus on the state – the revolution from 'above' school – and those who wish to focus on support 'from below'. The picture then becomes multidimensional. And it might begin to answer the sorts of question which historians of other societies, less bound by the explicit ideological claims of their subject, have been asking for decades.

What are these questions? Many will only arise from the problems and demands of contemporary Russian life. The dialogue between history and politics has been restored in Russia now, and it is again legitimate to ask about the origins of social as well as political or economic phenomena. Historians in Russia and the West are writing about morality and etiquette, the history of the family, suicide and despair, sport and the hunt.[57] They are also looking for the deeper roots, in pre-revolutionary society and culture, of anti-Semitism, patriarchy, the acceptance of authoritarianism. Because the whole discourse of Soviet history is in turmoil, it is difficult to generalise now about 'schools', political lines of interpretation. It is harder, too, to decide which type of argument, for now, is the more politically correct (even – naturally – depending on one's definition of correctness). But this is a far healthier situation, I would contend, than one in which the history of an entire century in the life of the largest country in the world could be reduced to a geometrical diagram with arrows pointing up and down, signifying the flow of one set of ideas either from above or from below.

6.   The Nazi Revolution

JEREMY NOAKES

The question of Nazism and revolution has generated a large literature that has raised major issues about the nature of Nazism and its impact on German politics and society.[1] However, in order to fit in with the comparative focus of this volume, this chapter will consider the Nazi revolution primarily in terms of the Nazi takeover or 'seizure' of power during the years 1933–34 with only a few final reflections on what one might call 'the revolution in power' which continued until 1945.[2]

The Nazi revolutionary agenda

From his earliest days as a political activist in Munich Hitler believed that he was engaged on a revolutionary project.[3] 'We are not improvers but revolutionary reformers', he wrote on 17 July 1922 and, a few days later, he told a Munich audience: 'Let there be no doubt: we Nazis are not a second Gironde.'[4] By the time he was writing *Mein Kampf* in his Landsberg prison cell in 1924, Hitler had developed a more or less coherent view of what he understood a revolution to be and the kind of revolution he wanted to bring about.

He developed his notion of revolution to some extent in contradistinction to the German Revolution of November 1918, which he referred to in a speech in Passau on 20 June 1923 as 'the so-called revolution, which was not a revolution because basically the same system remained in place…a true revolution should have dealt with all those elements which plunged us into disaster'.[5] In his view a true revolution required a 'great idea' and he saw his own project in the historical context of other revolutions, which he regarded as true revolutions precisely because they had such an 'idea', as he put it in *Mein Kampf*:

The fact of having a new great idea to show was the secret of the success of the French Revolution; the Russian Revolution owes its victory to the idea and only through the idea did Italian Fascism achieve the power to subject a people in the most beneficial way to the most comprehensive creative renewal.[6]

Again, in a speech to 'old fighters' on 19 March 1934, he reiterated the point: 'The victory of a party is a change of government; the victory of a world view [*Weltanschauung*] is a revolution, which transforms the conditions of a nation profoundly and in its essence.'[7]

In effect Hitler's 'world view' represented a rejection of the core values of Western civilisation based on the Christian–humanist tradition.[8] Its central theme was a racist and above all anti-Semitic form of Social Darwinism, which, according to Hitler, simply reflected the 'laws of nature'. The central proposition was that human life, like animal life, was a struggle for the survival of the fittest. The key unit of human organisation was the nation, which was based essentially on ethnicity or 'blood'. The struggle for survival took the form of a conflict between nations to control the resources of the earth, which were necessary for survival. A nation could not remain permanently at peace nor could it stay in equilibrium. It had either to expand or to decline and, in the end, fall victim to another more vigorous nation.

Individual human beings acquired their identity and significance as members of a nation and in terms of their contribution to the nation, which was the source of all values. On 23 February 1937, in the context of a discussion with Hitler about the iniquitous nature of Christianity, the Propaganda Minister, Joseph Goebbels, noted in his diary: 'The Führer says his great work has been: "I have taught the world once more to differentiate between means and ends. The end is the life of the nation, everything else is simply means." '[9] Nations in turn formed the components of a race. Hitler believed that human beings were organised in a hierarchy of races, a hierarchy determined by their relative cultural value. The so-called Aryan race was at the top, with the other races in descending order with the Jewish race at the bottom. The Aryan race was composed of different nations of whom the Germans had the greatest claim to predominance on the basis of their superior creative abilities.

If the Aryans were at the top of the racial hierarchy because they were the only truly creative race, the Jews, at the other end of the scale, were a particularly pernicious race. For, although they lacked all creativity themselves, they were extremely effective at exploiting the creative abilities and efforts of other races and nations. They battened on to other nations like parasites and their ultimate aim was to gain control of the world. If they succeeded, this would represent the death of culture and civilisation. For, in Hitler's eyes, the Jews lacked the gift of creativity; they were essentially barren.

Applying these ideas to Germany, Hitler's starting point was Germany's defeat in 1918 and the revolution which had followed it. He believed that these events represented the culmination of a state of racial and moral decay that had been developing for centuries. It was a consequence of allowing the Jews and their values to acquire growing influence in the state and society: notions of *liberalism* which, as he saw it, meant the self-interest of individuals taking precedence over the interests of the nation, the 'national community'; *democracy*, or as he saw it, the granting of power to all citizens irrespective of their gifts and merits and so producing the lowest common denominator, the triumph of mediocrity preventing the emergence of great leader figures; *Marxist socialism*, again as he saw it, encouraging a levelling down and, above all, internationalism rather than nationalism – the idea that the German working class had more in common with the working class of other countries than it did with the German upper and middle classes. And, he argued, this socialist internationalism had encouraged pacifism, thereby sapping the moral strength of the nation, weakening its determination to fight in the eternal struggle between races and nations.

In the eyes of Hitler these political ideologies – liberalism, democracy, Marxist socialism, internationalism and pacifism – were like poisons or parasites in the nation's bloodstream implanted by the Jews so that they could take over the body politic. Faced with what he believed was the terminal decline of the German nation, Hitler wanted to bring about its rebirth. He believed that the only cure for a sick German body politic was a drastic purge, expunging the poisonous ideologies that were sapping the nation's strength and, above all, eliminating the Jews who were the prime cause of Germany's problems. Once the purge had been carried out, the task of infusing new blood could be achieved through the indoctrination of the Nazi 'world view': the emphasis on the importance of racial purity, above all through anti-Semitism; improving the nation's health and efficiency through eugenic and social measures; encouraging a commitment to serve the national community and give priority to its needs before the interests of the individual or his or her family; and the development of a martial spirit glorifying military values: physical courage, loyalty and obedience. Starting with German youth they would create a new man who would enable the German nation to compete successfully in the struggle for survival.

These ideas were not unique to Hitler; in various forms they were commonplaces of the discourse of the extreme right in Germany during the post-war period, and in the case of eugenics were even part of a more mainstream project to improve the 'national body'. What was unique was their formulation into the agenda of a political movement which, by acquiring total power, had the chance to realise them. From the very beginning of his political career Hitler considered the key to Germany's revival was the recovery of its will to power; everything else was secondary.

Before 1933, however, the Nazis did little to prepare detailed plans for a takeover of power let alone to prepare concrete policies to implement them. However, one sign of the radical nature of Hitler's objectives was his refusal to accept anything short of the post of Reich Chancellor even at the risk of plunging his movement into a potentially lethal crisis. For Hitler politics was always ultimately a matter of all or nothing. Before 1933, however, the focus was on achieving power and then on the elimination of all those elements – individuals, political parties and other organisations – whose values ran counter to the Nazi 'idea'. Hitler distinguished between the initial phase, involving the takeover of power, which was termed by some at the time – but not by Hitler – the 'Nazi Revolution', and what he saw as the true Nazi revolution, a long-term project, though he had few concrete notions about how to achieve it. 'The conquest of power itself is simple', he commented on 6 July 1933 after it had been achieved. 'But the conquest is only secured when the people have been renewed in accordance with the new form.'[10] However before the Nazis could implement a revolutionary agenda they had to secure power and the key to this was the critical state of the Weimar Republic.

The revolutionary situation 1932–33

The Nazi Revolution began with the appointment of Adolf Hitler as Reich Chancellor on 30 January 1933. His appointment represented a desperate attempt to fill a power vacuum in the German state which had existed since the fall of Chancellor Heinrich Brüning at the beginning of May 1932.[11] However, it was by no means inevitable that the political vacuum caused by the collapse of parliamentary democracy should be filled by the Nazis. Indeed, at the time of Hitler's appointment as Chancellor the Nazi Party was undergoing a severe crisis which threatened its very existence. At the same time, the representatives of the German elites who appointed him were despairing of finding a solution to the problem of how to consolidate a regime of the right. It was their failure to do so that had created a vacuum into which the Nazis were able to move. Hitler's appointment represented their fourth attempt in less than three years to find an alternative to the Weimar model of parliamentary democracy, following the disintegration of the coalition government of the Social Democrat (SPD) Chancellor, Hermann Müller, in March 1930. As Hans Mommsen has put it: 'Weimar democracy did not break down because of Hitler, but rather Hitler was the final consequence of its breakdown.'[12]

On the surface, the fall of Müller's government, which initiated the end of parliamentary democracy in Germany, had resulted from the inability of two of its leading components – the SPD and the German People's Party (DVP) – to agree on how the increased burden on the unemployment benefit system resulting from the depression, which had begun in 1929, should be financed. The SPD argued that the employers should pay, the DVP that the employees should do so. However, in fact, the collapse of the Müller government was the result of two distinct developments.

In the first place, it was the culmination of a systemic crisis, a crisis above all of legitimacy. Not only was there a lack of a strong democratic tradition in Germany with liberal democracy being seen by many as essentially un-German. But, even more important, the Weimar political system had failed to establish its competence. It had shown itself incapable of delivering the goods to the German people in terms of political stability, economic prosperity and social peace. This problem was exacerbated by the burden of expectations placed on the state by the German people.[13] In part this reflected the extent to which the pre-1914 German state was far more involved in social and economic matters – for example, through tariff and social insurance legislation – than in comparable European states. These expectations had been greatly increased since 1918, for the so-called 'Weimar compromise', which had emerged from the Revolution of 1918, involved the assumption that the state would actively intervene to ensure full employment, stable prices, fair wage settlements and effective social welfare provision. Elaborate structures – e.g. for wage arbitration – had been erected to ensure this. But the result was not only to create unrealistic popular expectations of the state's role but to politicise directly whole areas of social activity. The failure to meet these expectations further undermined the democratic system's legitimacy, particularly since many compared it unfavourably with the imperial regime of pre-war Germany, which now appeared in a golden light.

Specifically, the crisis resulted from the polarisation and fragmentation, which had already characterised German politics before the First World War, but which had greatly increased since 1919.[14] Political divisions became deeper and more embittered as the serious economic problems of Weimar fed directly into the political system in the form of distributional conflicts, particularly after the depression began to bite in 1929–30. With the economic cake shrinking, each economic interest and each section of the community fought to maintain its own slice in what had become a zero-sum game. The government, to which people looked to resolve these conflicts, was itself racked by division, since the various interests were closely allied with political parties and so the conflicts were carried directly into the cabinet itself making coalition government increasingly impossible. The disagreement between the SPD and DVP over the financing of unemployment benefits, which destroyed the Müller government in March 1930, was a classic example of such a conflict. For at issue was the question of which social and economic groups should pay the main costs of the depression.

The fall of the Müller government, however, was not simply the product of a systemic crisis, the culmination of years of political instability and the consequence of distributional conflicts exacerbated by economic crisis paralysing the system. It was also the result of a determined attempt by representatives of various elites to destroy parliamentary democracy and replace it with a more authoritarian form of government. The initiative had been taken by General von Schleicher who had become convinced that the army could not fulfil its ambition of German rearmament within a regime in which the Social Democrats played a significant role. He was supported by senior civil servants who resented what they saw as the chaotic and disorderly nature of parliamentary democracy. They disliked what they regarded as its excessive 'pluralism', which resulted in the state becoming the plaything of organised interests pursuing selfish goals at the expense of the general interest, of which they saw themselves as the true embodiment.

This desire to replace Weimar democracy with a more authoritarian regime was shared by the two economic elites – big business and landowners, particularly the heavily indebted Junker landowners of East Elbian Prussia. Big business was concerned about the extent to which the democratic system enabled labour interests to exert political pressure to achieve high wages at the expense of profits and a generous welfare system through high taxation. The Junker landowners, on the other hand, were concerned to secure high tariffs and large subsidies from the government to protect their uneconomic estates from the effects of agricultural depression and resented the way in which the democratic system facilitated the expression of consumer interests. The main concern of these elites was to ensure that the SPD should be permanently kept out of the government.

The enemies of the SPD had been unable to strike while the new reparations agreement, the Young Plan, was being negotiated during 1929 because they needed to secure the Socialists' support. But, the moment it had passed through the Reichstag Schleicher and his allies were able to prepare for the replacement of Müller by Heinrich Brüning of the Catholic Centre Party with the full support of the conservative Reich President, Field Marshal von Hindenburg. Thus the conflict between the SPD and the DVP within the coalition was as much a pretext as the cause for the demise of the Grand Coalition and the end of full parliamentary democracy in Germany.

The paralysis of the Reichstag, which followed the fall of Müller and which was increased by the success of the Nazis and Communists in the election of September 1930, ensured that power became concentrated in the hands of the right-wing camarilla round the Reich President, who represented the views and interests of the German elites. The political parties were increasingly marginalised. Nevertheless, the question of popular support remained crucial to the attempt to consolidate a regime of the right. In this respect the Brüning government represented a transitional phase from parliamentary democracy to dictatorship. Although Brüning relied on the emergency powers of the President to rule by decree, he also depended on the toleration of the Reichstag, including the SPD. It was this that eventually led to his dismissal, since the camarilla's objective was above all to eliminate the influence of the SPD.

The fall of Brüning at the beginning of May 1932 represented the end of parliamentary democracy in Germany. The problem was that the right was united only in its hostility to the SPD and to parliamentary democracy; it could not agree on an alternative. Brüning's successor was Franz von Papen (May–November 1932), whose project for a 'new state' envisaged the imposition of an authoritarian dictatorship on the mass of the population. This, however, was vetoed by the army in the shape of the Defence Minister, General von Schleicher, who feared a civil war which the Army would be powerless to control and which would leave Germany weak and vulnerable. Schleicher himself (December

1932–January 1933) tried to secure mass support by winning the trade unions away from from the SPD and a section of the Nazi Party away from Hitler through wooing the head of the Party's organisation, Gregor Strasser, but failed on both counts. Hitler's appointment as Reich Chancellor represented, therefore, the last desperate attempt to secure mass support for a regime of the right by incorporating the 'healthy national(ist) elements' of the Nazi movement. It would be a regime dominated by the traditional elites and avoid what was seen as the worse alternative, namely a return to a parliamentary regime and the renewed influence of the left that would follow.

The Nazi takeover of power in 1933

On 30 January 1933, Adolf Hitler was the head of a coalition cabinet in which only two other members were Nazis, his party lacked a majority in Parliament, and in order to govern he was dependent on a Reich President using emergency powers under article 48 of the Weimar Constitution. Yet, on 24 March 1933, the new Reich Minister for Popular Enlightenment and Propaganda, Dr Joseph Goebbels, could note in his diary: 'We are now masters of the Reich constitutionally as well.'[15] In less than eight weeks the Nazis had succeeded in securing a position which it had taken Hitler's Italian counterpart, Benito Mussolini, nearly three years to achieve. How did this come about?[16]

Although, at the time of Hitler's appointment as Reich Chancellor, the Nazis' power was apparently quite severely circumscribed, the fact was that the democratic regime had already been hollowed out by a period of nearly three years in which the Reichstag had been marginalised by a government ruling under a state of emergency. Thus, during the years 1930–33, laws passed by the Reichstag had increasingly been replaced by government decrees issued by the Reich President under article 48 of the Weimar Constitution. In 1932, for example, there were 60 emergency decrees compared with only five laws passed by the Reichstag. The democratic forces were already on the defensive. Since the breakdown of parliamentary government in March 1930, the political parties had been increasingly confined to the periphery of politics, while power and influence were concentrated in the hands of the President and his entourage, the bureaucracy and right-wing pressure groups. The demoralisation of the democratic parties had been reinforced by the election results between 1930 and 1933, which – with the exception of the Catholic Centre – had shown a continuing and in some cases drastic decline in support. After Hitler's appointment they found themselves confronted with a dynamic Nazi Party proclaiming its determination to solve the national crisis and lead Germany to a better future.

The Nazis benefited greatly from the fact that Hitler's government could initially be seen as just another in a succession of presidential governments. Indeed, initially, many expected it to last no longer than its two immediate predecessors: a matter of months if not weeks. Few expected a Nazi revolution. During their first weeks in office, the Nazi leadership set out to reinforce this image of continuity by calling the new cabinet a 'government of national concentration' uniting all patriotic Germans. At the same time, they were careful to give the impression of sticking to the letter of the law even while flouting its spirit. Civil rights were removed by the Decree for the Protection of People and State of 28 February 1933 and the Reichstag was emasculated by the Enabling Law of 24 March 1933. Through this quasi-legal path the Nazis could tap the powerful springs of respect for and loyalty to established authority that were deeply embedded in German culture. Hitler and his government now represented the *Obrigkeit* to which obedience was traditionally owed by all citizens. Resistance to such legitimately constituted authority was contrary to the deepest instincts not only of German officials but of the vast majority of the German people.

However, although from one perspective the new regime could appear as a normal presidential cabinet, at the same time, equally crucial to its image was the attempt – through torchlight processions, mass demonstrations, radio broadcasts and other forms of propaganda – to convey the impression of the birth of a new order, of a new Germany. The Nazis benefited from the fact that, unlike their political rivals, they clearly bore no responsibility for the discredited Weimar democracy. With the exception of the Communists, who were limited by their narrow working-class appeal, they alone could offer the prospect of a new deal with some degree of credibility. They appealed to a sense of national solidarity which had been generated by the First World War and to populist aspirations, which had long been frustrated by barriers of birth, property and education, and which had been unable to find expression through the traditional parties of the right which were dominated by notables.[17]

The Nazis were able in particular to tap the frustration of a younger generation, which, partly for demographic reasons, was a potent force in the Weimar Republic and which had developed an alternative youth culture. Many were deeply alienated from the liberal democratic political culture of Weimar, which failed to satisfy their romantic notions of politics and their desire for emotional commitment. Young people proved particularly vulnerable to the Nazis' rhetoric and political style. But there was also the more practical consideration that a Nazi regime might improve their dire career prospects. Both of these aspects of the Nazis' appeal ensured that, during 1932–33, university students were one of the Nazi Party's strongest constituencies.[18] This relative youth of the Nazi movement contributed to its remarkable dynamism and its hunger for power.

Thus the new government succeeded in combining the contradictory images of continuity and change, of reassurance – many familiar figures were still in the seats of power – and a promise for the future. One of the main Nazi slogans for the March 1933 election was: 'The old and the young Germany fight together under Hindenburg and Hitler.' And a poster produced for the campaign showing Hitler and Hindenburg side by side reinforced this impression of the link between Germany's past and Germany's future, the field marshal and victor of Tannenberg (1914) and the ordinary front-line soldier, the one representing Germany's traditional military and social elite, the other the ordinary German who had risen through his own gifts and efforts.

The dominant theme emphasised by the Nazis, however, was that of national revival, and the two main terms used to describe this were 'national revolution' and 'national uprising' (*nationale Erhebung*). The latter conveyed the impression of a people rising up and throwing off their 'oppressors', the politicians of the Weimar Republic, the 'November criminals'. It tapped the historical myth of the uprising against Napoleon in the so-called War of Liberation of 1813 – as if the democrats and supporters of the Republic had been a kind of alien force holding down the German people, which now under the new government was regaining its true identity. Indeed, this movement represented a kind of desperate assertion of national unity in the face of the political, religious, economic, social and ethnic divisions which had racked Germany ever since the foundation of the Second Reich in 1871. The only occasion hitherto when Germany had achieved such a sense of unity was on the outbreak of war in August 1914. Since then, the 'spirit of 1914' had been a potent myth for the German right, an occasion when national unity had apparently been achieved without having to go through the painful economic and social reforms necessary to achieve a more just and therefore widely accepted social order.[19] Nazism has in fact been aptly described as 'in part an attempt to reproduce the experiences of 1914 as a permanent condition'.[20] Among many German intellectuals there had long been the hope of a third *German* path between Western capitalism and Eastern Bolshevism.

This was certainly the light in which some Germans saw the new government. Indeed, although the 'national uprising' was in a sense an assertion of national unity, like August 1914, it was a unity forged in war, however this time a war waged not against external enemies but against an internal foe. It was, as the novelist Thomas Mann was quick to see, a kind of 'domestic war of revenge':

> People think they are a great nation again. The war, the defeat did not happen, their consequences wiped out by an *ersatz* war, which calls itself a revolution and, in imitation of the Entente propaganda, is directed against the nation itself.... Concentration camps everywhere with prisoners of war.[21]

In short, the clear intention of the 'national uprising' propaganda was to identify the forces of the right in general and of the Nazis in particular with the nation and to offer an invitation to participate in this movement of national rebirth by supporting the government, with the clear implication that those who did not would be setting themselves outside the nation and identifying themselves as internal enemies. Assisted by more than a decade of extreme nationalist propaganda, which had exploited the experiences of defeat, the humiliation of the Versailles treaty, and the running sore of the reparations question, the Nazis and their Conservative partners succeeded in defining the terms in which patriotism was conceived: the patriotic German was one who supported the new regime. Moreover, this definition was apparently endorsed by the electorate when it gave the new government (though not the Nazi Party – 43 per cent) an absolute majority on 5 March 1933, albeit only a marginal one (51 per cent).

A proclamation issued by the new government under the title 'Appeal to the German People' and broadcast by Hitler on the evening of 1 February 1933 hammered away at these themes.[22] All government activity since the Revolution of November 1918 was subsumed under a blanket term of abuse as 'Marxism' and blamed for the existing state of Germany, while the spectre of communism was invoked as the alternative to the new order: 'Fourteen years of Marxism have undermined Germany. One year of Bolshevism would destroy Germany.' The new 'national' government would 'regard it as its first and supreme task to restore to the German people unity of mind and will' and it would protect 'Christianity as the basis of morality' and 'the family as the nucleus of our nation'. Echoing Kaiser William II's statement to the Reichstag in August 1914 ('I do not recognise parties, only Germans'), which inaugurated the so-called 'peace of the fortress' (*Burgfrieden*), it stated: 'We do not recognise classes but only the German people.' And the proclamation ended by requesting loyalty 'to the command of the Field Marshal [Hindenburg]' and by invoking God's blessing on the new government.

It would be difficult to overestimate the impact of this campaign on the German middle classes, in particular. It played on a wide range of emotions, awakening fears and hopes, deep-rooted loyalties and prejudices. In a society whose bonds of solidarity, fragile at the best of times, had now had imposed upon them the added burden of economic crisis, which sharpened social tensions and added to the existing feeling of national inferiority, a feeling which struck at the core of many people's self-respect and sense of personal identity, a campaign offering the prospect of national unity and revival in a new 'national community' [*Volksgemeinschaft*], and couched in terms that reaffirmed that society's most powerful norms and values inevitably evoked a powerful response.

This was something of which the Nazis were well aware and consciously endeavoured to exploit – among other things by using quasi-religious symbolism. For example, the concept of the Third Reich to describe what the Nazis were in the process of creating had for German ears a millenarian ring to it. Hitler's speeches were littered with pseudo-religious cadences. For example, he concluded his last speech in the 1933 election campaign, which was broadcast throughout Germany, with the prophecy that 'a new German Reich would arise of greatness, of honour, of power and glory, and of justice, Amen'.[23] As he finished his speech, the radio broadcast a recording of a Lutheran hymn followed by the bells of Königsberg cathedral. This quasi-religious aspect of the Nazi appeal during its takeover of power was associated in particular with the role of Hitler as a charismatic leader. Its impact can be judged by a statement from one of the leading German Protestant theologians, Professor Peter Althaus of Göttingen University:

> We as believing Christians thank God our Father that he has given to our *Volk* in its time of need the Führer as a 'pious and faithful sovereign' and that he wants to provide for us in the National Socialist system of government 'good rule', a government with 'discipline and honour'. Accordingly, we know that we are responsible before God to assist the work of the Führer in our calling and in our station in life.[24]

The propaganda campaign of the 'national uprising' reached its height during the fortnight or so between the election and the opening of the new Reichstag on 21 March. On 12 March, it found symbolic expression in a flag decree issued by President von Hindenburg, which laid down that in future the swastika and the traditional black–white–red flag of pre-Weimar Germany, combining 'the glorious past of the German Reich and the vigorous rebirth of the German nation', should replace the black–red–gold flag of Weimar and of the democratic Revolution of 1848.[25] The two should fly side by side as the flags of the new Germany.

This campaign culminated in the ceremony to mark the opening of the new session of the Reichstag on 21 March – officially termed the 'Day of the National Uprising', but which came to be better known as 'Potsdam Day'.[26] The recently created Minister for Propaganda, Joseph Goebbels, had planned the ceremony with great care. It took place in the garrison church in Potsdam, a holy shrine of Prussian royal and military traditions, in whose crypt lay the tombs of its former kings, Frederick the Great and Frederick William I. The atmosphere was a heady mixture of religion, German nationalism and Prussian tradition. An empty chair was left for the Kaiser, now in exile in Holland, behind which sat the Crown Prince – a clever hint at the prospect of an eventual restoration. As a kind of national high priest, Hindenburg descended into the crypt and laid wreaths on the tombs of the dead kings. As the correspondent of *Der Tag* put it: 'The representative of the present day greeted the great men of the past and, ascending out of the crypt as a reverence-inspiring mediator, conveyed the blessings of past centuries to the younger generation.'[27] The high point of the ceremony was a solemn handshake between Hindenburg and Hitler. The photograph that captured the occasion for the world at large and which was turned into a postcard showed Hitler bowing low as he shook hands with Hindenburg – a gesture of homage by the representative of the new Germany to that of the old. Hitler had reinforced this image in his address by referring to 'the marriage between the symbols of old greatness and youthful energy'. The links between past and present were reinforced by a parade involving units of the *Reichswehr*, the Nazi SA and SS, and the Conservative veterans' organisation, the *Stahlhelm*. Finally, the occasion acquired additional symbolic significance from being held on the anniversary of the opening of the first Reichstag of Bismarck's new German Reich in 1871, which also happened to be the first day of spring.

Potsdam Day, or the Day of the National Uprising as it was officially called, marked a kind of sanctification of Hitler's leadership, reinforcing the constitutional legitimacy of the new regime with a quasi-religious one.[28] The occasion was broadcast live on all German radio stations and was marked by ceremonies throughout Germany involving church services, torchlight processions and speeches by local notables and Nazi Party leaders often using pseudo-religious imagery in order to emphasise the significance of the occasion. Potsdam Day marked a crucial stage in the transfer of Hitler's charismatic form of leadership from the Nazi Party to the German people as a whole. In the euphoria which it generated, it must have seemed to many upper- and middle-class Germans as if the prospect which the formation of Hitler's cabinet had held out of a marriage of Prusso-German tradition and Nazi revolutionary dynamism as the basis for a new revived Germany had been fulfilled. The French ambassador commented at the time: 'it appears as if the Third Reich is determined to achieve the fulfillment of the Second'.

What 'Potsdam Day' represented for the German upper and middle classes was signified for the working class by the national celebration of 1 May.[29] Ever since 1889, when the Second International had recommended that there should be an annual demonstration of the international proletariat for the Eight Hour Day, May Day had been the most important date in the calendar of the German socialist movement. The celebrations which took place on that day, which invariably included a procession, represented a public assertion of working-class solidarity and a claim for public recognition and respect. However, the previous history of May Day had been of a struggle against employers and the state for such recognition. Under Weimar only a few states had given it official recognition and so, by passing a law on 19 April making May Day an official national celebration, 'The Day of National Labour', the Nazis were in effect appropriating May Day for the new regime and paying public homage to the dignity of labour. Moreover, by obliging employers to join in the processions, the Nazis were making a public demonstration of their ideal of the classless 'national community'.

May Day 1933 was the first of those gigantic national festivals which were to become such a striking feature of the Nazi regime and its 'aestheticisation of politics' (Benjamin). One and a half million Berliners marched to the Tempelhoferfeld to hear Hitler speak and similar demonstrations were held in every German town and city. In Gelsenkirchen in the Ruhr, for example, a centre of heavy industry, 100 000 people took part in what was described as the biggest demonstration in the city's history.[30] The reporter of the *Nationalzeitung* noted: 'Max Reinhardt can lower his curtain for the last time; the German people put on the greatest drama conceivable.'[31]

The impact of May Day 1933 on German workers was certainly less powerful than that of 'Potsdam Day' on the upper and middle classes, but it undoubtedly made an impression on the less politically committed workers, helping to defuse the deep suspicion with which the new regime was regarded by this section of the community.[32] However, on 2 May, while the workers were recovering from their hangovers after the May Day celebrations, the SA and SS were on their way to close down the Free (Socialist) Trade Unions by force. For, while the elaborate spectacles of 'Potsdam Day' and 'May Day' and the illusions which they encouraged represented one side of the Nazi Revolution, there was another side which was equally significant and representative: terror and intimidation.

The role of terror and intimidation

The Nazis owed much of their success in acquiring total power to the fact that they were a mass movement. This mass support, with its paramilitary cutting edge in the shape of the SA and SS, played a vital role in crushing actual and potential opposition from political rivals, intimidating those in authority at all levels into resignation or co-operation, and providing a basis of democratic legitimacy for the Nazi leadership, which their Conservative rivals conspicuously lacked.

The SA and SS contained large numbers of mainly young men, many of them unemployed, who had joined the Nazi movement partly in the hope that its victory would improve their prospects and partly in order to replace the boredom and aimlessness of unemployment with a spirit of macho camaraderie and a sense of purpose.[33] This sense of purpose they found in propaganda for the movement and in confrontation with their political enemies, the supporters of rival political parties. The main focus of their attacks were the Communists and Social Democrats. This was not so much because of the SA's political views as because they tended to come from a similar social/cultural milieu and because the left had responded to right-wing violence by developing large paramilitary-style organisations of their own in the shape of the *Reichsbanner* (SPD) and the Red Veterans' League (KPD), which were prepared to confront the Nazis with their own violent methods. In terms of the psychological dynamics of the rank and file these clashes seem to have had more in common with those of street gangs or football supporters than with conventional political confrontation.[34] The leadership of the SA and SS, however, many of whom had been involved in the ruthless post-war Free Corps units, had their own political agendas.[35]

In the months prior to Hitler's appointment as Reich Chancellor the SA, in particular, had been becoming increasingly disillusioned with the movement's failure to achieve power and with what they saw as its flirting with a reactionary establishment, a mood which had led to internal conflict and a widespread disinclination to continue propaganda duties. Hitler's appointment, therefore, immediately aroused expectations of a rapid improvement in their personal prospects and of new opportunities to attack their political opponents. In short, they were in the mood for action. Initially, however, this mood had to be restrained to some extent. The first weeks of the revolution were marked by an election campaign in which it was important not to alienate the electorate by too much violence and lawlessness. Nevertheless, even at this stage the SA and SS did acquire a significant role.

During the first phase of the revolution, from the appointment of Hitler to the Reichstag fire on 27 February, the main sphere of action was in Prussia, where Hermann Göring was acting Minister of the Interior in charge of the internal administration, including the police.[36] Here a partial purge of democratic elements had already been carried out following the Papen 'coup' of 20 July 1932, which had overthrown the government of the SPD Prime Minister, Otto Braun. Göring now extended this purge, replacing police chiefs with SA and SS leaders. He also introduced a measure by which, over the following weeks, thousands of SA, SS and *Stahlhelm* members were recruited as 'auxiliary police'. At the same time, on 17 February, he publicly told the police that they 'must in all circumstances avoid giving the impression of persecuting the patriotic associations [i.e. the SA, SS and *Stahlhelm*]' and that they should 'maintain the best relations with these organisations, which comprise the most important constructive forces of the state. Patriotic activities and propaganda are to be supported by every means. On the other hand, 'subversive organisations' were 'to be combated with the most drastic methods':

> Police officers who in the execution of this duty use their fire arms will be supported by me without regard to the effect of their shots; on the other hand, officers who fail through a false sense of consideration may expect disciplinary measures.[37]

In view of this and of the changed climate which followed Hitler's appointment, it was not surprising that, during the election campaign, the level of intimidation by the Nazis of their opponents markedly increased. Reporting after the election campaign had been going on for a fortnight, the *Times* correspondent noted:

> A large class of people welcome the ruthless repression of political enemies. They believe these things are necessary, that there is now a clash of naked forces in Germany, which must be fought out as preparation for the ultimate war of liberation. They think that Nazism will win and that if it fails only Communism can follow, but they think that even this would be a 'national' Communism and would prefer that to a return to Parliamentary democracy. They do not demand a policy from their new rulers: they are told that they are getting a national revival and think this cheap at the price of a few democratic prejudices like impartiality and justice. A man who cries, 'Unser heiss geliebtes Vaterland, Hurra, Hurra, Hurra!' may be forgiven practically all his sins in Germany today.[38]

The election of 5 March initiated a new phase in the Nazi Revolution, in which terror and intimidation by the SA and the SS played a crucial role in the takeover of power.[39] Between 5 and 9 March, the Nazis seized control of those states such as Hamburg and Bavaria in which they did not yet form the government and, during the following days, they seized power in the cities and towns throughout Germany.

The takeover of power at state and local government level typically involved intimidation through mass action on the part of the SA and SS, which was then legitimised by official measures by Nazi ministers at Reich or state level. In the case of the states the takeover began with marches and demonstrations by the SA and SS outside the government offices. The local Nazi *Gauleiter* then informed the Nazi Reich Minister of the Interior, Wilhelm Frick, that the state authorities were incapable of maintaining law and order. He responded by installing the *Gauleiter* as a special police commissioner giving him control of the state police. The state government was then 'persuaded' to resign and was replaced by Nazis.

Having consolidated their hold on the states, the Nazis' attention switched to local government. Here the takeover of power typically involved a march to the town hall and a demand that the swastika flag should be hoisted as a symbolic assertion of Nazi control. Numerous *Bürgermeister* then found themselves suspended on trumped-up charges of mismanagement or corruption, sometimes being arrested under humiliating circumstances. On 13 March, for example, the

Oberbürgermeister of Cologne, Konrad Adenauer, the most important Centre Party figure in the Rhineland, was dismissed and, on the same day, the *Oberbürgermeister* of Wiesbaden, Bonn and Mannheim were all arrested. Opposition city and town councillors were frequently harassed by being taken into protective custody and having their homes searched.

A particularly striking example of the use of terror was the mass arrest on 28 June of the local leaders of the Catholic Bavarian People's Party (BVP), including mayors, local councillors and party officials, some of whom were priests.[40] This group's more or less entrenched hostility to the new regime posed a significant obstacle to Nazi control over the rural areas of Bavaria in particular. Although the BVP leaders were treated gently by comparison with Socialists and Communists and released after only a few days, this kind of cat-and-mouse tactic was clearly calculated to exercise the maximum psychological pressure on respectable middle-class people, for whom imprisonment would have a particularly traumatic effect. The aim was clearly to intimidate them into giving up their offices and to teach them a salutary lesson, without, however, provoking too much local hostility.

Above all, this phase saw the use of mass terror and intimidation particularly against the left and Jews.[41] During the second week of March, local SPD headquarters and trade union offices were raided by gangs of SA and SS, their files, furniture and equipment were destroyed, and their officials taken into 'protective custody'. Whole streets in working-class districts were cordoned off and systematically searched with the aim of terrorising the inhabitants. Individuals, who had been prominent in their opposition to the Nazis prior to Hitler's appointment were also targeted, as were Jews, particularly those in prominent positions, in a campaign which culminated in the official boycott of Jewish businesses and professions on 1 April.

Those arrested during this phase of more or less overt terror, which lasted throughout the spring and summer of 1933, though with varying periods of intensity, were taken into 'protective custody' under the Decree for the Protection of People and State of 28 February. They were arrested by SA and SS units and held in the cellars of the local SA/SS headquarters or, if they were lucky, in police cells. Some were detained only for a day or two, severely beaten with whips and steel rods, and then released. Others, however, were held for longer, with the result that the SA cellars and police cells rapidly became overcrowded. This prompted the Nazis to establish 'concentration camps' in disused factories and warehouses, which were placed under the control of the SA and

SS.[42] The first of these was established by the SS on 20 March in a disused gunpowder plant on the outskirts of Dachau near Munich. It was followed by numerous others all over Germany, in which the prisoners were exposed to the crudest forms of brutality at the hands of the SA and SS thugs who guarded them. It has been estimated that during March and April 1933 at least 25 000 people were arrested in Prussia alone, and this figure does not include those who were arrested temporarily and then released.

The Nazi Revolution was characterised above all by the extent to which the distinction between the Nazi movement and the official forces of the state became blurred. This had been encouraged by the recruitment of SA and SS as 'auxiliary police', but it went much further than this. During this period, various Nazi organisations succeeded in arrogating to themselves powers and responsibilities which had little or no basis in law and yet, such was the atmosphere of intimidation, major changes were largely accepted as *faits accomplis*. It was against this background that the process of 'co-ordination' (*Gleichschaltung*) took place, by which societies, clubs and organisations of all kinds, from chambers of commerce to village gardening societies, were obliged to revise their statutes and adjust the membership of their committees to take account of the new regime and its agenda.[43] In some cases this did not require explicit directives or even overt threats; the organisation simply saw which way the wind was blowing and conformed. Sometimes, the changes were largely nominal, involving the appointment of a Nazi to a leading post, who then acted as in effect a front man, while the organisation continued much as before. In other cases, however, the organisations went further than was necessary, for example by introducing a so-called 'Aryan clause' excluding Jews from membership, although there was no official requirement to do so. In this climate of intimidation the anxiety to show willing, sometimes coupled with racial prejudice, overrode any sense of solidarity with fellow members.

Thus, the Nazi Revolution was marked by, on the one hand, the ruthless dynamic of the Nazi movement determined to seize power and using a judicious combination of legal forms, official action, and informal and unofficial terror and intimidation and, on the other, by a society paralysed by a sense of exhaustion, by feelings of powerlessness and resignation, but also filled with the hope that the Nazis and Hitler in particular might after all have the answers, by the belief that there was, in any case, no feasible alternative on offer, and by the initial impression of a large measure of continuity to calm fears of upheaval.

The revolution in power

Before 1933 the Nazi movement had concentrated above all on acquiring power; there were few concrete plans for what was to be done with that power once it had been gained. The Nazi takeover, therefore, raised the question of what kind of revolution it was going to be. This was of particular importance to the members of the Nazi movement itself, and disagreement over the issue produced the first major crisis of the new regime.[44]

For many members of the Nazi movement the takeover of power had represented above all the prospect of acquiring a job or other material benefits. Priority in the allocation of jobs was given to Nazis, but many were bound to be disappointed, given the excessively high expectations that had been raised. Dissatisfaction at the failure of the takeover to bring more immediate benefits and, in particular, resentment at what were seen as compromises with established institutions were concentrated in the SA, where a substantial proportion were unemployed and which had a strong tradition of populist anti-establishment sentiment. The SA's leader, Ernst Röhm, a *condottiere* figure, had traditional notions of what a revolution should be, which involved something much more radical and violent than was taking place in Germany during 1933.[45] In particular, he resented what he saw as concessions to a decadent Conservative establishment. He poured scorn on the 'bourgeois simpletons' who had 'confused the "national uprising" with the German revolution' and insisted that it was 'high time the national revolution stopped and became the National Socialist one'.[46]

However, while Röhm thought of the revolution in old-fashioned terms of barricades and blood on the streets, Hitler was a modern revolutionary who believed in a more gradual 'cold' form of revolution.[47] For Hitler in 1933 the major priority was the consolidation of power. This involved, in the first place, retaining the support of the German elites and above all the army, which was the only organisation which could seriously endanger the new regime. Secondly, it required the improvement of the economic situation and, above all, the reduction of unemployment, in order to sustain and increase popular support. Both of these priorities necessitated a period of relative stability. On 6 July 1933, therefore, in a speech to the Reich Governors of the states, Hitler formally ended the revolution:

> More revolutions have succeeded in their first assault than, once successful, have been brought to a standstill and held there. Revolution

is not a permanent state, it must not develop into a lasting state. The full spate of revolution must be guided into the secure bed of evolution. In this the most important part is played by the education of the people. The present state of affairs must be improved and the people embodying it must be educated in the National Socialist conception of the state.[48]

This clash between two different views of the nature of the Nazi Revolution was given a sharper edge by Röhm's ambition to transform the SA into a national militia-type army that would integrate the professional army in a subordinate capacity. Anxious to win the support of the army for the impending succession to Reich President von Hindenburg, who was on his deathbed, Hitler was forced to embark on his notorious purge of the SA on 30 June–1 July 1934.

However, this purge was very far from being a 9 Thermidor. For among those murdered were key figures associated with the Conservative Vice Chancellor, Franz von Papen, who indeed lost his own post in the purge. In other words, Hitler and the Nazi leadership were not simply acting against disillusioned radicals but also against disillusioned Conservatives. Hitler emerged from this crisis in a position from which he could continue the revolution in the way he had long envisaged it and which he had already spelled out to 'old fighters' on 19 March 1934:

One does not become a National Socialist in one year, in fact many years are necessary and generations will no doubt pass before we shall have buried the victory sign of our Reich in the hearts of everybody. And only then will the National Socialist revolution have succeeded and the German people have been finally saved.[49]

This revolution in power did not involve a major transformation of the class structure; social change of this kind was restricted to limited opportunities for upward mobility through the new Nazi organisations. The fact that secondary and higher education remained fee-paying constituted a major barrier. In this sense social change was more a matter of perception than reality.[50] The revolution in power took other forms. In the first place, it involved the progressive destruction of the *Rechtsstaat*, the 'rule of law' under which the German state had operated since the mid-nineteenth century. The law increasingly came to be interpreted in terms of the Nazi slogan, 'Justice is what benefits the nation' and political criteria, interpreted by the Gestapo and other agencies, came to take precedence over legal norms.

The undermining and destruction of democratic and legal structures and procedures removed the barriers to the second component of the Nazi Revolution in power, namely eugenic and anti-Semitic legislation and practice designed to turn Germany into a 'racial state'. The Jewish boycott of 1 April 1933 and the sterilisation law of 14 July 1933 were early steps along this path which was to lead to the 'euthanasia' programme, i.e. the mass murder of the mentally handicapped and the extermination of Jews, Gypsies and various 'asocials'.[51] 'The greatest revolution', Hitler told the Nuremberg Party rally on September 1937, had been 'achieved through the systematic implementation of national and therefore racial hygiene. The consequences of this German racial policy', he continued, 'will be more decisive for the future of our people than the effects of all other laws. For they create the new man. They will preserve our nation from the fate of so many previous examples of other races which have ceased to exist because of their ignorance concerning a single issue.'[52]

Hitler's revolutionary racial project was powered, indeed made possible, by the commitment of professional elites to an agenda which involved the perfection of the 'national body' through the promotion of those deemed to possess 'worth' and the segregation and elimination of those deemed 'worthless'.[53] It offered ambitious young men in their twenties and early thirties – the graduates who staffed the SS and the Propaganda Ministry, the doctors and eugenicists involved in the sterilisation, 'euthanasia' and 'criminal biology' programmes, and technocrats like the architect, Albert Speer – unprecedented opportunities for exercising power and influence, for acquiring status, and not least for realising their 'scientific' ambitions in a context where the legal and democratic barriers hitherto protecting individual rights had been removed.

However, it was not only Nazi ideology and the various quasi-scientific agendas associated with it which had revolutionary repercussions. For the impact of Hitler's charismatic style of rule had a corrosive effect on the structures and processes of government leading to a partial disintegration of the state.[54] Moreover, the essence of charismatic leadership is that it is the form of authority appropriate to crisis. The leader derives his authority from his apparent vocation to lead his followers in a crisis. Nazism was rooted in crisis and its whole system was geared, in effect, to the maintenance of crisis as a permanent state. At the same time, Nazism glorified conflict as the core of the natural order and saw war as the apotheosis of politics. Thus, both the nature of the system itself and the ideology of its leadership arguably created mutually reinforcing pressures leading to the supreme crisis of war, a war whose effects would revolutionise Germany in ways that had not been anticipated by Adolf Hitler when he set out on his revolutionary mission in Munich in the early 1920s.

7. Battleground of the Revolutionaries: the Republic and Civil War in Spain, 1931–39

TIM REES

To say that revolution was in everyone's mind in Spain during the 1930s would be an exaggeration, but it would not be a too gross or unpardonable one. Perhaps no other place or time in Europe during the twentieth century – including Russia in 1917 – has witnessed the flourishing of such a number of movements proclaiming such a variety of openly revolutionary ideologies. The most recognised of the revolutionary episodes of the time took place during the Civil War of 1936–39 in the Republican zone, with George Orwell's discovery of Barcelona as a city in the midst of Anarchist revolutionary turmoil the best-known account of it.[1] However, it was not just the war that allowed revolution to flourish nor was anarchism the only example. In fact, the bitterly polemical nature of political conflict during the 1930s as a whole, which was at its most intense during the Civil War, encouraged the expression of political aims in revolutionary terms. Revolutionary movements initially grew in importance with the establishment of the democratic Second Republic in 1931 and encompassed a wide spectrum of ideas – including radical liberalism, socialism, communism and fascism, as well as anarchism. This breadth itself precluded the development of a classical revolutionary situation, conceived in terms of two opposing blocs representing the status quo and a revolutionary alternative. Instead, these multiple notions of a revolutionary future were often at odds with one another during the Republic and openly clashed during the Civil War, with each version seeking to subdue all others. In this way Spain in the 1930s became a battleground of virtually all the European ideologies that could be labelled as 'revolutionary' during the twentieth century.

To accept this view of the 1930s in Spain as, in great part, a struggle between distinctive revolutionary projects necessarily requires a broad view of 'revolution' which transcends timeless or partisan notions. Indeed, Spain in the 1930s is particularly interesting precisely because it does not fit particularly well dominant notions about revolution – certainly when compared to our 'classical' examples like France in 1789 or Russia in 1917. The proposition pursued in this essay is that revolution should be viewed as a contested term, open to multiple ideological definitions and dependent on context. Failure to see it in this light has often obscured the extent to which the political conflicts of the decade can be seen in revolutionary terms. In this sense the Spanish case can be seen as a particularly acute example of the general desire to identify a single experience that defines revolution for once and all time.[2] Because the language of revolution was so ubiquitous, there was a correspondingly strong pressure to deny the competing credentials of other forces that defined themselves in 'revolutionary' terms. Consequently, those involved, as well as many subsequent commentators, were unable or unwilling to look in wider terms at revolution and tended instead to identify one cause as truly 'authentic'. Looking beyond the Civil War, one must also then accept that Europe has seen many more revolutionary movements and revolutions during the century than might be supposed, if we take deep and rapid political change to create a new form of society and government (or in the case of anarchism, no government at all!) as the basic benchmark.

At the same time there must be some limits to our conception of 'revolution'. For instance, not all civil wars produce a revolutionary situation, at least not on the scale that I am suggesting for that in Spain. Likewise, what is 'revolutionary' in one situation may well not be in another. Nevertheless, without being completely relative it is fair to argue that 'revolution' must be located in the minds of its proponents, or at least in the eye of the beholder. Accordingly, my analysis of the Civil War stresses the self-identification of the actors involved as revolutionaries pursuing a variety of revolutionary goals. That these languages of revolution rejected other revolutionary discourses tells us something about not only the nature of political conflict in Spain in the 1930s, but also something about the nature of 'revolution' more generally.

The republican revolution

The primary reason why such an unusual revolutionary situation developed in Spain was that it came out of a regime that was itself the product of a revolution. This was the Second Republic, created in 1931 as

Spain's first liberal democratic system of government and which its main architects also imbued with the mission of radically altering the balance of cultural, economic and social power. This did not indicate, however, that the proponents of the Republic shared exactly the same vision of the new regime, nor that they were politically united in any other respect than wishing to see a change take place. The main intellectual force behind the new order was the collection of small republican political parties, representing mainly the liberal professional middle classes. They provided a moral and political critique of the monarchist form of government that had existed in Spain from 1875. Attacks by republican leaders and intellectuals characterised the system as a politically corrupt *ancien régime*, stressing the oligarchical nature of power, concentrated into the hands of dominant agrarian interests supported by the relatively small industrial bourgeoisie.[3] Regional nationalists, particularly republican Catalans, also condemned the system as dominated by Madrid and Castilian interests at the expense of the rights of the linguistic minorities.[4] As an alternative these groups proposed a democratic Republic based on wide-ranging civil liberties, that would modernise the Spanish polity and society. Meanwhile, the principal material force behind the creation of the Republic was the Socialist Party (PSOE), the largest working-class political organisation in Spain, and its trade union movement (UGT). However, the Socialists had a more divided view of both the monarchy and of a Republican alternative. The reformist right of the party, led by Indalecio Prieto, largely shared the vision of the liberal republicans, seeing a change of regime as a moral political project as well as step towards a more egalitarian social order. In contrast the radical left of the party, dominated by the trade union chief, Largo Caballero, was less concerned with the political complexion of government (even having briefly collaborated with the military dictatorship of General Primo de Rivera that took power in 1923) and more with the economic and social interests of working-class supporters.[5] A long history of dispute between these two wings over strategy and tactics was set aside in the late 1920s, when both agreed that it was desirable to overthrow the dictatorship. In 1930 the PSOE, the republicans and the Catalan nationalists came together in a broad alliance to pursue a change of regime, largely negotiated by Prieto and the leading liberal intellectual, Manuel Azaña, and known as the Pact of San Sebastián.[6]

In many respects the participants in the republican–Socialist alliance were mostly drawn together for negative reasons: they were determined to remove the monarchy from power. Otherwise the variety of their long-term aims precluded the drawing up of a detailed political programme. However, they were agreed that it was not enough to simply replace the monarchy with a Republic. It was necessary not just to embrace a democratic form of government but also to root democracy in new social underpinnings that removed the foundations of the old order. In the context of the time this was a radical proposition, and as a result its supporters self-consciously used revolutionary language to describe themselves. With intellectuals so prominent a part of the coalition, it was also not surprising that a mix of historical and contemporary comparisons figured prominently in their thinking and rhetoric. For the Socialists of all persuasions the Republic represented Spain's delayed 'bourgeois' revolution on the pattern of 1789 and 1848 that would overthrow the 'feudal' old order, in a formulation that cast the republicans as the representatives of a revolutionary bourgeoisie. In some respects the republicans themselves also shared this essentially nineteenth-century vision of the coming Republic – even if they did not share the Marxist terms in which it was formulated. After all, they saw their ideological positions as rooted in the liberal-progressive traditions of the French Revolution and after. However, along with the right of the PSOE, they also saw themselves in more modern guise as the missionaries of the democratic modernism that had spread across Europe after the First World War. In this they saw Spain finally joining a progressive current that had suddenly produced liberal democracy in countries such as Germany, where the Weimar Republic served very much as a model for the kind of reforming revolution that republicans wished for Spain.[7]

With the formation of the San Sebastian Pact and the increasing calls from republican and Socialist ranks for the overthrow of the military dictatorship and the monarchy, it appeared as though a classic revolutionary situation was developing.[8] By 1930 the regime was so discredited among its own erstwhile supporters that Primo de Rivera was forced to step down from power, leaving weakened monarchist politicians and the king, Alfonso XIII, desperately seeking a means to revitalise the regime. Yet despite these favourable circumstances the would-be revolutionaries were unsure and divided over how to proceed. Efforts to organise a rising were farcical, resulting only in an uncoordinated attempt by disaffected army officers on 12 December 1930 at Jaca. The execution of two of the leading figures involved, Captains García Hernández and Galan, compounded the failure and led to the complete abandonment of further attempts to use open force. In the event these deaths discredited the monarchy even further, contributing to an ever-growing sense of paralysis.[9] While the regime could not be overthrown, it was in a state of internal collapse, leaving its opponents to exert pressure through their very existence. The final point came in April 1931 when municipal elections were called as a first step back to the parliamentary system that had existed before 1923. Although the disunited monarchist parties gained a majority of the votes cast, amidst wide accusations of electoral malpractice, it was clear that the king had, in his own words as he slipped away to exile, 'lost the affection of my people'. With the army and police forces unwilling to defend the regime to the last, the republican–Socialist coalition declared the establishment of the Republic in scenes of public celebration by their supporters.[10]

Despite the passive means by which it occurred, the creation of the Republic was hailed as a revolutionary triumph in itself and the beginning of a progressive era for Spain. Parliamentary elections in June merely confirmed this feeling when candidates standing for the republican and Socialist parties swept the board, leaving only a minority rump of monarchists and other right-wingers as deputies.[11] In a jubilant and utopian speech at a celebratory dinner for supporters of his party, Acción Republicana, on 17 July 1931 Manuel Azaña was in no doubt that a peaceful revolution was taking place and that the 'old order' represented by the monarchy had been swept away in the process.

> Let us congratulate ourselves, republicans, that in so short a space of time Spain has achieved the most extraordinary revolution in her history and thrown wide the door to freedom and national prosperity.... We are then the mandatories of revolution twice sanctioned by popular vote in the country. That is the basis of our position. We have no other. Therefore our duty in government is to preserve the spirit which brought us to revolution.... From this revolutionary spirit arose our Republic.... The Republic has already achieved its great work by expelling the dynasty, by restoring political liberty, by allowing Spaniards to live decently as free men...for us the Republic is an instrument, an instrument of war if you like, though I should not dare to call it that for it is a hard saying; an instrument for the building and refashioning of the state, of Spanish society, from top to bottom.[12]

The task of the Parliament and the coalition government produced by it, over which Manuel Azaña presided as Prime Minister, was to create a constitutional framework and to enact an ambitious series of fundamental reforms. Long-standing conflicts in Spanish society were to be addressed through measures such as the separation of Church and state, the creation of a secular education system, the redistribution of the land, modernisation of the Officer Corps, the granting of rights for women, regional self-government for the linguistic minorities, and improvements to wages and conditions of work. The vision was of wide-ranging changes to the institutions of state and government, the distribution of economic power on the land and in industry, to the position of the Catholic Church, in the rights and position of women, in culture and education. Once these had been accomplished Republican Spain would then be an unchangeable reality, deeply rooted into the fabric of society.[13]

Although this point would mark the end of the process of liberal-democratic revolution in the eyes of its protagonists, it would also mark the beginning of the full functioning of that democracy. It was assumed that once the constituent phase was over new elections would be held to the first proper Parliament. The coalition of parties that had toppled the monarchy and collaborated in the agreed programme of reforms would naturally break apart. Individual movements could then pursue their particular aims, in competition with each other but within the boundaries of the Republican system. That the compromises that had underpinned the revolution would be at an end was of particular importance to the forces that represented the political limits of what was assumed would become the new status quo. For the republican right, represented by the Radical Republican Party and the Liberal Republican Right (formed by ex-monarchists), and the Socialists, this would be an opportunity to define in greater detail what the Republic would mean in the longer term: maintaining it as a conservative democracy or moving it towards an egalitarian socialist society.

This understanding of the future of the Republic, shared in broad terms by all the partners in the coalition that had brought the regime into existence in April 1931, was never to be realised in practice. An important reason for this was that in reality the republican–Socialist coalition lacked sufficient cohesion. Divisions and rivalries appeared almost immediately over the practical details of the Constitution, the reform programme and of day-to-day policy. In December 1931 the Radicals split from the government, partly because of objections to the scope of the reforms but also in a bid to consolidate themselves as the party of republican conservatism.[14] The difficulties of achieving meaningful reforms also created frustration within the ranks of the Socialist Party, leading it to break with its republican allies in order to pursue a path more directly to a socialist society.[15] By the end of 1933 the government was exhausted and new elections were called in November.

Such tensions might have been lessened, or at least their significance could have been mitigated, if another unanticipated development had not changed the whole political trajectory of the Republic as assumed by its creators. This was the rise of the powerful Catholic–conservative movement, the Confederación Española de Derechas Autonómas, Spanish Confederation of Autonomous Rights (CEDA) to become the first real mass organisation of the political right in Spain. It rallied exactly those interests – most notably the landed and business elites, conservative peasants and the Catholic Church – that had underpinned the monarchist system and which republicans and Socialists had believed to have been permanently removed from influence. Although working within the institutions of the Republic, the CEDA was ambiguous, at best, about the regime and it certainly actively opposed nearly all of the reforming measures initiated by the Azaña governments.[16] Its existence and actions contributed hugely to ever-growing social and political conflict. Polarisation continued under a two-year period of Radical-led government that followed the 1933 elections, which were won by an alliance of the Radicals and CEDA. Many of the reforms of the previous two years were reversed or amended. An important turning point came with the abortive rising of October 1934 called by republicans, Catalan nationalists and Socialists who were convinced that the Republic had been delivered into the hands of its enemies following the entry of CEDA into government. Further elections in February 1936, which were won by a Popular Front alliance, led to the complete abandonment of the Republic by the right and a turn towards military conspiracy to destroy it.[17]

Revolution out of revolution

Clearly, while the Republic did form a new status quo that supplanted the monarchy, it was not a stable or uncontested one. The result of the mixed success of the liberal-democratic revolutionaries of 1931 in consolidating the regime fully was that the spread of alternative revolutionary ideas and movements was encouraged. This proliferation was made possible by the political freedom introduced by the Republic. Although this was never perfect, in the sense that there were periods of political suppression under the liberal regime, a complete spectrum of ideas could be openly expressed for the first time in Spain. Furthermore, the architects of the new regime established the use of revolutionary political language themselves. Accordingly, the arrival of the Republic both heightened expectations on the far left that further change beyond the bounds of liberal democracy was possible and spurred on the radical right which despised the democratic state, in a manner remarkably similar to the situation in Weimar Germany or Russia after February 1917. All these revolutionary forces certainly played upon, and exacerbated, the tensions of the time. However, there was no clear-cut struggle between a Republican status quo and a revolutionary bloc that amounted to a classic revolutionary situation. The wide range of competing revolutionary opponents of the Republic were inconsistent in their positions. There was often no clear distinction between the status quo and its alternatives, as the blurred line between them shifted according to different contexts. As a result, patterns of revolutionary activity and their significance were both complex and changing during the life of the Republic.

The greatest range of revolutionary options was on the political left.[18] At the time of the Republic, in fact, every variation of the ideological left was to be found in Spain. In particular, the country was the home of the largest Anarchist movement to be found in the world, based around the anarchosyndicalist trade union federation, the Confederación Nacional del Trabajo (CNT), and the semi-secret Federación Anarquista Iberica (FAI) created to preserve Anarchist ideals. The Anarchists rejected all forms of the state, including liberal democracies, calling instead for their revolutionary overthrow and replacement by a decentralised collectivist society and face-to-face democracy.[19] In contrast, Marxist communism was a minority movement in Spain during the Republic, though one which grew in significance. Its orthodox face was the Spanish Communist Party, Partido Comunista de España (PCE), which was linked to the Communist International. Like all the member parties of Comintern, the aim of the PCE was the establishment of a Soviet-style regime in Spain.[20] Meanwhile dissenting Communists, outside Comintern control, who organised themselves in opposition to the PCE, rejected this view. Two bodies were established at the outset of the Republic: the Bloc Obrer i Camperol (BOC), the Workers' and Peasants' Bloc, led by Joaquín Maurín, and the Izquierda Comunista Española (ICE), the Spanish Communist Left, under the leadership of Andreu Nin. In September 1935 they merged to form the Partido Obrero de Unificación Marxista (POUM), the Workers' Party of Marxist Unification.[21] Although they refused the label 'Trotskyist' with which the PCE attempted to label them, these organisations did draw their example from the Bolshevik Revolution while denouncing the Soviet Union under Stalin as a betrayal of its promise.

These Anarchist and Communist movements provided a range of competing revolutionary alternatives to the liberal-democratic Republic, though in practice their attitudes to the new regime were more ambiguous. For instance, many of the supporters of the CNT–FAI and PCE tacitly supported the foundation of the Republic as an improvement over the Primo de Rivera dictatorship, which had vigorously suppressed both movements. Although not followed by the Anarchists, the leadership of the Communist Party initially went as far as publicly welcoming the transition to a democracy. However, they very quickly moved to distance themselves from the 'bourgeois state' under pressure from the Comintern's 'class against class' line which forbade collaboration. In any event, disillusionment at the slow pace of reform and official discrimination in favour of the socialist unions and against other workers' organisations by the Azaña governments set in early on among rank and file supporters of both the PCE and Anarchists. Both organisations, followed by the POUM and its forerunners, began actively to oppose the Republic and to call for its replacement by their alternatives – in effect creating an undeclared revolutionary alliance. In the case of the Communists of all varieties, the effects of this did not amount to much given the small number of adherents they commanded. But attempted revolutionary strikes and Anarchist-led 'uprisings', particularly during the first two years of the Republic, though ineffective, did place considerable pressure on the regime.[22]

Discontent at the course taken by the Republic also affected the Socialist Party, where internal divisions over the role that the party should play under the regime gradually surfaced. In effect this became a dispute between two different revolutionary discourses based on the two long-standing strands of thought within socialism: on the one hand that of the liberal democratic revolution, which the party had espoused in 1931, and on the other that of revolutionary Marxism. Increasingly there was a swing within socialist ranks back towards support for the second option, particularly among trade unionists who were the bedrock of support for Caballero. In the elections of 1933 the PSOE broke with the republicans and fought an exclusive campaign. Defeat and a turn towards more conservative government only accelerated the trend towards a more revolutionary stance, involving an immediate move beyond liberal democracy towards a socialist society. Even further fuel was provided by the perception, common to all Socialists, republicans and regionalists, that the Republic was in danger of falling into the hands of its enemies. For the left of the party this suggested that a socialist Republic was the only choice remaining. As Luis Araquistáin, an advisor to Caballero, wrote in the opening editorial of a new socialist theoretical magazine:

> The dilemma in Spain, finally, is not between Monarchy or Republic.... The basis of the dilemma is whether the Republic has to be of a fascist type, which is the dream that the right has started to make a reality, or whether it has to be a social Republic, as the working class wants. One has to choose between them.[23]

A sharp increase in revolutionary rhetoric accompanied this shift within the PSOE, dividing the party still further, but with little in the way of practical revolutionary activity to show for it.[24]

Hopes of revolution on the political left proved to be entirely that: wishful thinking. In part this was due to the fact that the Radical–CEDA governments were immune to any such threat while they controlled the apparatus of the state, particularly the military and police forces, and were prepared to use them as they did in October 1934. This attempted rising also showed the other reasons for the failure of revolution: lack of unity and will. Although a range of leftist groups opposed the Republic by 1934, joined in theory by left-wing Socialists, no real revolutionary bloc existed in practice. All seemingly favoured co-operation to overthrow the regime, or at least the current government, but all attempts to achieve unity broke down at the national level. Long-standing rivalries were simply too strong for such a possibility. This was compounded in the case of the Socialists by the suspicion, largely correct, on the part of other parties that they had no real intention to launch a revolution and that Socialist leaders, particularly Caballero, used revolutionary language to cover a vacuum of ideas.[25] In the event, the October rising was more of an attempt to preserve the Republic in the form in which it had been conceived in 1931. Only in Asturias, where a local alliance of working-class parties had been forged, were there anything approaching serious revolutionary events.[26]

Although a failure, Asturias entered revolutionary mythology. In particular, the PCE credited itself with a leading part, even though the actual role of the party had been negligible, using this propaganda to boost its profile within Spain and to impress a sceptical Comintern leadership that the party was making some progress with 'the Spanish Revolution'. However, in other respects there was a pragmatic swing back towards a defence of the Republic of 1931 in reaction to the failure of the rising and its aftermath. This led to the creation of a Popular Front alliance to fight the elections called for February 1936 following the fall of the Radical–CEDA administration. Although this coincided with, and used the language of, the Comintern's new moderate policy downplaying without eliminating the importance of revolution announced at the

Seventh World Congress of 1935, at the heart of this was the restoration of the alliance between the Socialist Party and the republicans. A whole range of centre-left parties including the PCE and POUM joined them, though there was no formal participation by the Anarchists.[27]

After victory, however, the limits of this co-operation were also revealed as none of the working-class parties joined a republican-led government. This was of crucial importance in the case of the Socialists where Caballero's supporters prevented the inclusion of the PSOE, as Prieto had wished, effectively ending any hopes of recreating the alliance that had created the Republic. A bizarre compromise resulted whereby the Socialists supported a republican government that was dependent on their parliamentary votes but at the same time campaigned for a programme of socialist change. At a time when pent-up social tensions erupted in a wave of strikes and land occupations that lasted during the spring and summer of 1936, Caballero feared that the party would lose its own supporters if it did not take this stance – a position that was borne out to some extent when the Socialist Youth defected to the PCE.[28] In practice, the other parties of the left shared this position as well, even though there was still no formal unity between them. Although they had showed their preference for the Republic in the elections, when push came to shove, they could not commit themselves to abandoning revolutionary language and aims that went beyond the reforms that the republican government began to implement once more.

The notion that the revolutionary left posed a serious threat was common currency on the political right. Many saw the Republic itself as an illegitimate revolutionary regime, making anything further to the left even more of an anathema. Yet this did not mean that only conservative and reactionary thinking existed on the right. It could even be argued that the aims and ideologies of many groups on the right had, despite all appearances to the contrary, a revolutionary element to them. For instance, the two different brands of monarchism, Alfonsine and Carlist, openly called for the overthrow of the Republic, and the CEDA was ambiguous on its attitude to the regime until it too abandoned legality in 1936.[29] Willingness to see forceful change was also accompanied by a preference for alternative regimes that had a utopian tinge to them. This was not so surprising, given that straightforward reaction failed to address the problem of why the hated Republic had come into being in the first place. A simple return to a pre-1931 status quo, was not, therefore, entirely plausible. Accordingly, all sections of the right that looked to the past for political inspiration tended towards an idealised version of it. They found this in the integrist version of Catholic social and political doctrines that was the common currency of the right. Dominant Catholic ideas stressed a 'golden age' of harmony and greatness undermined by liberalising tendencies from the nineteenth century onwards. They provided a powerful underpinning to the political ideologies of all sections of the non-republican right.[30]

Though this was an imagined past, projected as an ideal future, it is nevertheless not really plausible to see these ideas, and the movements that espoused them, as truly revolutionary in nature. This was because their own supporters did not see them as such; nor did they project themselves as revolutionaries. The only movement on the right to do this wholeheartedly was Spain's fascist movement, the Falange. This had emerged from the amalgamation of two parties, the Falange Española and the JONS (Juntas de la Ofensive Nacional Sindicalista) in 1934, under the leadership of José Antonio Primo de Rivera, the son of the dictator.[31] Like fascist movements elsewhere, it shared some of the assumptions of the authoritarian right. This included the acceptance of much of Catholic social doctrine. As one of the party's leading figures, Ernesto Giménez Caballero, said: 'The fascism for Spain is not fascism, but Catholicism.'[32] However, the core beliefs of the movement were much more self-consciously revolutionary in nature.

Though Falangists condemned the threat of leftist revolution, instead of seeking a reactionary alternative they proposed to substitute their own revolution, arguing that what was needed was not a better version of the past but a radical future. The ideological basis for this was dubbed National Syndicalism, a set of ideas largely adopted from the JONS. In articles in the party newspaper, the leading theoretician of the JONS, Ramiro Ledesma Ramos, made clear the direction that he saw the movement taking: 'We are and could not be anything else but revolutionaries. What the JONS seeks is exactly a national revolution'[33] and 'We only accept the battle against Marxism on the terrain of revolutionary reality.'[34] This sense of battling for supremacy on revolutionary ground was reinforced in the symbolism of the party which, like similar movements elsewhere, involved party uniforms, the straight-armed salute and the language of revolutionary change. Even more self-consciously the party flag placed the Falangist emblem, the Yoke and the Arrows, on a background of red and black borrowed directly from the Anarchists. The National Syndicalist revolution that was enshrined in the Falangist programme, the so-called 26 points, shared many of the notions of radical Italian fascism. The party projected itself as a 'third way' between communism and capitalism, distancing itself from the reactionary right, proposing instead an ultra-nationalist alternative based on corporate lines. The individual would be submerged within the nation, with each person contributing to the whole according to his or her talents and position in life. Political parties and trade unions would be banned as divisive. At the same time the programme endorsed measures such as redistribution of the land and the need for social rights, considered by the conventional right as a dangerous threat to property and the status quo.[35]

For most of the Republic the Falange was a rather isolated force on the political right. Conservatives and reactionaries were wary of its revolutionary agenda.[36] Even so, there was some seepage of Falangist ideas into the mainstream. After all fascism was at that time *the* fashionable new movement in Europe and many non-Falangists admired what they perceived as its achievements. This was most striking in the case of the CEDA, where its leader, Gil Robles, took on much of the trappings of fascism and Nazism in the form of party rallies and in his oratory in an attempt to give the party a modern image despite its decidedly conservative character in other respects. On balance, however, this was more a matter of style than substance. The exception was the youth organisation of the party, the JAP, whose programme was much closer to that of the Falange.[37]

The Falange otherwise remained a small movement with little real importance while the conservative and reactionary right dominated during most of the life of the Republic. Though the left tended to label the right as a whole as 'fascist', the threat of a revolutionary alternative from that quarter was negligible while conventional right-wing politics seemed to be working in its supporters' interests. While maintaining a commitment to revolution, the Falange's only route to some influence was in grudging co-operation with other parties in opposition to the liberal left. This involved engaging in conventional politics, much as sections of the revolutionary left such as the PCE and POUM did at times, in the form of electoral pacts. It was only when the right as a whole abandoned such activities in the wake of the electoral defeat of February 1936 that the Falange was able to break from this pattern and to begin to come into its own as a radical alternative to the Republic. At that moment the CEDA, in particular, lost all sense of purpose as an organisation dedicated to defending conservative interests within the regime and it began to disintegrate to the benefit of the Falange. The first signs of this came in the spring of 1936 when the JAP defected to the party – curiously mirroring the situation of the Socialist Youth at the same time. Meanwhile, Falangists became active in paramilitary activities, physically attacking political opponents, and contributing to the sense that the

Republic was now facing a revolutionary crisis from both the left and right.[38]

Ultimately, of course, the Republic was not overwhelmed by revolution, although the government was certainly weakened by the loss of a significant body of support for the regime. While the stance of the Anarchists, Communists, POUM and left-Socialists gave all the appearance of a revolutionary menace from the left, arguably there was little real substance behind it. At the same time, the republican government dealt with the Falangists by banning the party and arresting its leaders. By the summer of 1936 the social and political situation seemed to be stabilising. The direct threat to the regime then emerged, not from the revolutionary extremes, but from within in the form of a military conspiracy by disaffected army officers.

Revolution versus revolution

The irony of the military rising of 17/18 July 1936 that began the Civil War was that the small group of military plotters that led it unwittingly achieved almost exactly the opposite of what they had intended. Their aim was for a swift *coup d'état* that would decapitate the Republic and remove the threat of revolution from the political left which they identified with it.[39] Mostly reactionary conservatives, they had only the vaguest of intentions as to what would follow, envisaging a military directorate that would temporarily rule in conjunction with the main parties of the right. But instead of a surgical pre-emptive counter-revolution the rising only succeeded in some areas of the country, mostly where the balance of local political forces favoured the right. Elsewhere, where the army stayed loyal or in areas where forces of the centre and left resisted, it failed. Spain was divided into two zones, Republican and Nationalist, and was plunged into three years of brutal war.[40] The initial result of this attempted coup was that rather than restoring order – as the generals proclaimed was their mission – the insurgents actually created chaos.

Only in one respect could it be said that the rising succeeded in crushing a revolution. For all practical purposes the Republican project of 1931 was effectively destroyed as soon as the army revolt began. This was because the elected government offered no real resistance to the insurgents, and they were defeated in large parts of Spain by local actions. Central control was lost as the state disintegrated and power flowed to those within the Republican zone that were able to pick it up.

The chief architects and supporters of the liberal democratic revolution of 1931, the republican parties and the Socialist right, quickly realised that the outbreak of war meant that they, and their vision of Spain, were finished. This did not mean, of course, that they ceased all attempts to preserve the Republic in its original form. But the future of the Republic, if it had one, was not now entirely in their own hands and even though the regime might continue in name it could never be exactly as it had been. Symbolically, both Azaña and Prieto, though they continued to serve in office, were thrown into irrecoverable despair by the disaster of war.[41] Through their actions the army effectively eliminated any prospects of returning to the previous status quo and the war became, among many other things, a struggle to define what would replace it. The revolutionary currents that had developed with the Republic now had the ideal conditions to become the main focus of that contest.

It was within the Republican zone that the best-known and most divisive revolutionary experience took place.[42] In the aftermath of the military rising the existing government was paralysed, unsure and unable to act decisively. Central authority and state institutions simply broke down, obviously so in those areas in which the insurgents seized control immediately but also where the rising had failed. Across the Republican zone local people, and above all the political party organisations and trade unions that remained, were forced to take responsibility for running their own affairs in the absence of the state. With amazing rapidity, committees were formed to take control – usually dominated by the working-class parties and unions which had played the most important role in defeating the rising and which now held the balance of power. They took responsibility for securing and running their own areas; organising militias and police forces for defence and to secure social and political order, and directing economic and social affairs. Gradually a measure of local order emerged out of confusion.

What did differ from region to region, however, were the forces imposing that order and the nature and significance of it. In areas such as Aragón and Catalonia that were strongholds of the Anarchists and POUM, the opportunity was seized to create a revolutionary new order. For the Anarchists, in particular, having struggled vainly to destroy the state for so long they suddenly found that it had conveniently disappeared in front of their eyes. For them the kind of decentralised control that became necessary was actually the fulfilment of their revolutionary dreams. The POUM also revelled in the revolutionary possibilities presented by this situation, though the party differed greatly from the Anarchists in how the future was understood. While the Anarchists saw the destruction of the state as an end in itself, the POUM saw it as a chance to create a new state that would guarantee a revolutionary new order. In the meantime, however, both groups were at the forefront of pushing local change to its limits. Privately owned land and industries were seized from their owners and farms and enterprises were collectivised, to be run by committees composed of peasants and workers. Networks of Anti-Fascist Militia Committees and regional councils took practical control of the war effort and the running of everyday life. Great changes were introduced at a local level, abolishing money, dissolving formal marriage, and attacking class divisions and signs of privilege. It was into this maelstrom of revolutionary change that Orwell arrived as a volunteer in the POUM militia.[43] There was also a dark side to this new order. Everywhere suspected Nationalist sympathisers were arrested. But the Anarchists, in particular, were most associated with the outright persecution of political opponents. In the areas under their control, but elsewhere as well, an uncontrolled 'red terror' of revolutionary violence and destruction operated against rightists, the Church and its clergy, fuelled both by the desire for revenge but also as a means to suppress counter-revolution.[44] For Anarchists and members of the POUM this was a supreme moment of euphoria, celebrated at the time and ever since as *the* revolution by its supporters, who were determined that the war against the Nationalists should be fought to defend and advance the gains that they had already made in the aftermath of the rising.

However, the victory of this revolution was far from complete or secure within the Republican zone, let alone in the face of the Nationalists. Though largely powerless, central and regional government still continued to exist. There was still a cabinet and Parliament in Madrid, and the Catalan regional government (the Generalitat) still survived in Barcelona. A new regional government was even formed in the Basque country, where the Basque Nationalists had opted for the Republican side despite their previously strong associations with the political right. The POUM urged that these bodies should be taken over as well, effectively seizing control of state power. But for many Anarchists this signified both a betrayal of their principles and was not necessary, as these bodies had simply become irrelevant anyway as far as they were concerned. In other respects as well the Anarchists and POUM were not in complete control in the Republican zone. Even in the areas where the Anarchist revolution had triumphed, other groups that had opposed the army continued to operate, and elsewhere they were the ones that dominated. Socialists, republicans, Communists and regional nationalists all remained as opponents of the Nationalists and allies in the war effort against them. They too were involved in resisting the army rising and in creating some semblance of order in the areas that remained out of military hands. The pattern of local committees and councils was repeated in areas where these groups were strong; power was often shared, including with Anarchists in regions such as the south of Spain with a great mix of organisations. Socialists, Communists and even republicans were also involved in seizing the property of opponents and in the creation of collective enterprises.[45]

However, this did not mean that they took the same view of developments as the Anarchists and POUM. Not surprisingly, the republicans, regional nationalists and right-wing Socialists – representing the Republican status quo – were aghast at developments. They rejected the revolution proclaimed by the Anarchists and POUM that was being built upon the ruins of the regime they had created. In their view the revolution was a disaster that was objectionable in itself and which threatened to divide support for the Republic by alienating the liberal middle classes. Above all they saw the revolutionary approach to the war, fighting it with militias, as doomed to fail in the face of an organised, centrally led Nationalist army. Local control was for them a temporary necessity; restoring state institutions, re-establishing law and order, preserving liberal democracy and creating a conventional army to pursue the war against the Nationalists were their aims from the start. But real power had slipped away from their hands at the outbreak of the war, they lacked the force of numbers to reimpose order and the restoration of a now discredited republican government was an impossibility.[46]

The desire to re-establish the state and to pursue a conventional war effort was also shared by the Socialist left and the Communists. Both were ideologically predisposed to the notion of a strong state, but in other respects differed from the Socialist right and the republicans in that they had revolutionary credentials themselves. Faced with the possibility of revolutionary advance that the war brought about, and with the proclamation of a revolution by the Anarchists and the POUM, they were placed in a dilemma over how to proceed. Nevertheless they reacted rather differently to it. Supporters of the Socialist left were often deeply involved in collectivisation and the local committees, and Caballero was sympathetic to a revolutionary advance, though not to the kind of decentralised society that the Anarchists proposed. Instead he wanted a revolution that was government-led and which could win the war by producing a strong conventional army that would defeat the Nationalists in the field. This compromise position, and the fact that the Socialists were the largest most important political party in the

Republican camp at the start of the war, made Caballero the natural choice to succeed as Prime Minister in September 1936. He then formed a Popular Front government that was an uneasy coalition of all the political groups opposed to the Nationalists. This even included, after much soul-searching and internal dissent, representatives of the CNT.[47]

The position of the Communists was and remains more controversial. Critics of their position, particularly Anarchist and POUM supporters, have portrayed them as the betrayers of revolution and the agents of Stalinist foreign policy as directed by the Comintern.[48] As the only serious international backers of the Republic, it was certainly true that the USSR wielded great influence in Spain. It was equally certain that Stalinist policy favoured a downplaying of revolution in order to try to secure a broad international alliance against the fascist powers. However, the role of the PCE was far more ambiguous than might be supposed from this interpretation. Initially, the party leaders failed to appreciate the extent of the collapse that followed the army rising. They did not see the committees and spontaneous collectivisations as anything more than *ad hoc* measures that would disappear when normality reasserted itself. Even when it became clear that something more serious was happening, and that Communist supporters were also involved, the party leadership did not recognise that a revolution was under way.

This was not just because of the dictates of Stalin and the Comintern, but reflected the ideological view of revolution that was held by the Spanish Communists. True revolutions in their view, and that of all Communists linked to Comintern, could only be led by Bolshevik-style parties following the example of Russia in 1917. Any other claims to revolutionary status were fraudulent by definition. In this sense the PCE did not reject revolution because it had become counter-revolutionary, but rather it simply could not recognise as revolutionary anything that it did not lead. Moreover, the active hostility of the party, particularly to the POUM, which was regarded as a renegade organisation, was guaranteed as any other claims to revolution were to be seen as an attempt to divert the Spanish working class away from their true path. Accordingly, the activities of the Anarchists and POUM were characterised by the Communists as the actions of 'uncontrollables', and not without some justification given the chaotic and spontaneous nature of their version of revolution.[49]

This logic also allowed the PCE to continue to see itself without hypocrisy as a revolutionary party and to continue to see themselves as in pursuit of a 'Spanish revolution'.[50] There was an acceptance that the Republic of 1931 was a thing of the past and that a revolutionary situation, if not a real revolution, now existed. However, there was no real consensus among Communist leaders on the aims of the war or how best to conduct the war effort. They were predisposed to the re-establishment of the state, favoured a centralised war effort and a conventional army, but without any overall master plan beyond this. Nor did the Comintern offer much of a useful lead. The Popular Front policy, stressing the need to build anti-fascist alliances and to downplay immediate revolution, certainly propelled the PCE towards collaboration and this led to the party joining the Caballero government, after it had initially rejected the idea in August 1936. Otherwise there was not much in the way of specific guidelines. Meanwhile, the nature of the PCE was transformed in terms of its size and importance. The party benefited greatly from the fact that it was uncompromised by the failures of the pre-war Republic, was seen as a disciplined and united force, was closely identified with the support of the USSR, and embodied the Popular Front ideal more than any other group. Increasing heterogeneity made it all the more difficult to act decisively. So for rather different reasons, therefore, the party initially opted to follow the compromise position of the Socialist left; maintaining the self-image and language of revolution, albeit one quite distinct from and opposed to that of the Anarchists and POUM, but also working to rebuild a Republican state.[51]

A clash within the Republican camp between those who wished to recreate the state and those dedicated to its destruction was virtually inevitable.[52] In many senses though this was not a conflict between a status quo and a revolutionary bloc – though this was how supporters of the Anarchists tended to conceive it. Rather it was a difference between versions of 'revolution' in a situation where the republican norm had already broken down. Even so the conceptions of the war and its aims were very different and completely mutually exclusive.[53] As soon as the Caballero government began the process of forming new organisations of state power, the path to some kind of conflict began. Government ministries, provincial authorities, courts and police forces were reformed and they gradually sought to exercise practical control. Even more importantly, steps were taken to create a conventional army. All these bodies were supported and manned, not surprisingly, by those groups like the republicans, Socialists and Communists who wanted a conventional war effort – even if they had different ideas about its aims. Effectively a system of dual power was gradually created in the Republican zone.[54] Failures in the military struggle against the Nationalists increased the frustration of those who saw central direction of all aspects of the war effort as the only way to secure victory.

Meanwhile, the leaders of the POUM and many Anarchists increasingly warned that their revolution was in danger, not just from the Nationalists at the front but also within the Republican zone. Tensions mounted with a series of minor disputes and more serious clashes, particularly in Barcelona. Even so, in early 1937 the visitor to Spain, Franz Borkenau, could comment in a comparative article on the progress of 'revolution' in Spain that: 'Surprisingly enough, until now the Spanish Revolution has been spared the most typical bitterness of all previous revolutions: fraternal strife in the revolutionary camp.'[55] Almost immediately he was proved wrong.

The open struggle for power that erupted suddenly in May 1937 in Barcelona, sparked off when the police attempted to take over the Anarchist-controlled telephone exchange, was relatively short-lived but decisive. It was resolved in favour of the forces of centralisation and marked the dissolution of the Anarchist revolution by force. Divided over how to respond to this resurgence of the state, the Anarchists collapsed. The POUM was left isolated and was singled out for harsh treatment: the party was banned and its leaders were arrested or fled, and Andreu Nin died under interrogation and torture. A further casualty of this conflict was Largo Caballero who was ousted from power by a coalition of the right Socialist faction, the republicans and the Communists within the cabinet. Perceived as too vacillating and indecisive, his value as a compromise Prime Minister came to a final end with the rupture in the Republican camp. A new Popular Front government under the Socialist, Juan Negrín, then oversaw the full centralisation of the war effort.[56]

From the perspective of the Anarchists and the POUM, counter-revolution had triumphed within the Republican camp. However, while their revolution was defeated, there could still not be a straightforward reversal to the pre-war Republic. As a result revolutionary language and ideals as a whole did not die in 1937. In particular, the Negrín government still had to articulate a purpose for the war that could unite and motivate a population eager for change. Yet the right Socialists and the republicans were not well placed ideologically to provide a political rationale on these lines. Instead it was the Communists who took the leading role in reformulating Republican war aims. Though they had abandoned Caballero and the compromise position of the left Socialists, this did not mean that they had openly embraced the status quo. As before, Communist leaders proclaimed the continuation of the 'Spanish Revolution' while denouncing the POUM as traitors and the events of May as an attempted *putsch*. Nor was this mere cynicism, or a blind obedience to the dictates of Stalinist policy, even though it was true that the Communists' self-image lent itself to the convenient rationalisation that, as the only true revolutionaries, by definition any actions or political position that they advocated were bound to be revolutionary in nature. For them no revolution had been dissolved because none had really existed.

Accordingly, the Communists did not see themselves as the agents of counter-revolution and pressed instead for a 'progressive' version of the Republic while maintaining the broad Popular Front approach to the war: a position that delicately combined the pragmatic need for unity with the maintenance of revolutionary aspirations, albeit ones short of a Bolshevik-style regime in Spain. The rhetoric of a 'Republic of a new type' that the Communists provided was adopted wholesale by the coalition government, and defined its approach to the war until final defeat in 1939.[57] In practical terms this meant that many of the developments that had occurred after the start of the war were maintained, but under government control. So, for instance, both rural and urban collectives often continued to exist but under a central economic authority. A whole host of informal organisations were also brought under the umbrella of the Republican state. This was particularly the case with the remaining militias, but also covered a wide variety of political bodies from local committees to women's groups and the trade unions. In many of these the Communist Party was prominent, leading to conflict with other forces in the Republican coalition who feared a takeover. Accordingly no permanent settlement of internal tensions within the Republican camp proved possible and open unrest broke out again in March 1939 when an attempted anti-Communist coup was launched against the Negrín government. Though it failed, the Republic was in its death throes and all hopes of revolution on the left, or of a new form of status quo, were finally swept away by the collapse of resistance to the Nationalist forces.

The defeat of the Republic and with it any possibility of revolution from the left was an aim shared by all of the political coalition that rallied to the Nationalist cause. This did not mean, however, that they were united in a straightforward campaign of counter-revolution. In many respects the Civil War created conditions in which revolutionary ideas could flourish in the Nationalist zone as much as in the Republican. Military officers and members of right-wing political parties exercised loose authority at a local level in the absence of central authority. At the same time the outbreak of war discredited groups like the CEDA, which were seen as compromising with the Republic, effectively collapsed, encouraging a trend towards the extreme right. Though effectively in competition with each other in the uncontrolled atmosphere of the early months of the Civil War in the Nationalist zone, these groups shared a dictatorial vision of the future. In the case of the conservative Catholics, monarchists and Carlists the war was conceived as primarily a means to impose a pre-1931 status quo. But for the Falangists of the radical right the suppression of the Republic only fulfilled the first part of their political plans. To replace illegitimate 'red' revolution with their 'national-syndicalist' revolution was their ultimate intention. As a result the Nationalist camp also experienced internal tensions over revolution, though in quite different ways from the Republicans.[58]

The importance of this revolutionary current within Nationalist ranks would have been muted if the Falange had remained a minority force. However, in a process that also paralleled developments in Republican ranks, the party grew enormously in size after the war began. Recruits came from a variety of sources, including the previously politically uncommitted eager to show their support for the Nationalists and former members of the CEDA. Many existing Falangists, already disturbed by the party's compromise with the reactionary right in supporting the military rising, viewed the newcomers (the 'new shirts' in contemporary parlance) with suspicion. Certainly many of them had little close knowledge of the party programme or aims, but this did not necessarily mean that the revolutionary fervour of the movement was diluted, as has been claimed. The newcomers were opting to join a movement that was unmistakably radical in its broad aims and political style, and which stressed its ideological distance from more conventional political alternatives that could have benefited equally from this new support. Moreover, though José Antonio, the party leader, was captured and executed, the replacement leadership remained committed to the original programme. The promise of a new order that rejected all past political failures was something that had a strong appeal once the war began, and the image of youth and vigour that the Falange projected also suited the times well. That the Nationalists also received their greatest international support from Italy and Germany also undoubtedly boosted the appeal of a radical fascist message. Not surprisingly, therefore, the claims of the Falange to political influence grew enormously once the war was well under way.[59]

The Falange never translated the growing strength of the party into a revolutionary seizure of power within the Nationalist zone. At the local level, particularly in areas that the party dominated, Falangists attempted to apply the doctrines of national syndicalism leading to some conflict with more reactionary groups and the Catholic Church. At the broader level, however, there were no serious moves to act decisively to fulfil the party programme by creating a Falangist state. Partly this was due to the indecisiveness of the new leadership of the Falange, under the ineffectual Manuel Hedilla, which continued to talk of the need for revolution but resisted the urgings of some leading Falangists for action. But the most important reason that no bid for power was made was that the desire to destroy the Republic was so overwhelming that no organisation of the political right was prepared to break ranks in what was always to be a repressive war of coalition.[60] Nor would the more conventionally reactionary groups in the Nationalist camp and, most importantly, the army have stood by while such a unilateral development occurred. It was the military which had initiated the war and they made it clear that they intended to lead the struggle against the Republic, a position confirmed in September 1936 when General Franco was appointed to supreme military and political command by leading figures from the officer corps. This move signalled that central authority was to be imposed in the Nationalist zone, though Franco had no blueprint at this stage for the form that any future state might take. Like the other political forces, the Falange reluctantly accepted the situation as a necessary compromise for the war effort while effectively remaining loyal to the principles that the party leadership hoped would prevail in the longer term.[61]

The methods chosen by Franco and his advisors to impose political control in the Nationalist zone were a mixed blessing for the ambitions of more radical Falangists. While the different political groups were allowed to operate unfettered, Franco was leader in name only. This situation was allowed to persist until April 1937 when a decree was published announcing the forcible unification of all political movements into a single party, the clumsily titled Falange Española Tradicionalista y de las JONS. Having previously rejected the idea of starting his own party, Franco opted instead for an amalgam of existing options. Protests from the Falangist leadership at this loss of political autonomy were met forcefully with the arrest of dissidents, most notably Hedilla who was sentenced to death. The loss of independence was not complete in practice, however, as each of the different political currents within the Nationalist camp effectively continued on under the umbrella of the new party. Nor did this bring to an end competition over the future political direction of Spain in the event of victory over the Republic. Instead this became focused within the new party as the different forces vied for power over it. Falangists could continue to hope, therefore, that their ideas would prevail by indirect means.[62]

As the single party developed during the war it seemed that in many respects it was indeed becoming a vehicle for radical Falangist ambitions. While Franco was its titular head, his close advisor and brother-in-law, Ramón Serrano Suñer, who was a member of the Falange having defected from the CEDA, directed it. Serrano Suñer was not just guided by party loyalty and the need to placate a powerful political current but also by the sense that Spain needed a new regime that represented modernity and was distanced from the immediate past. The Falange offered just such a vision. Consequently when he drew up the party structure and programme, it was from the Falange that most of the principles and practice were drawn. The pre-war Falangist programme was incorporated wholesale, committing the new party to national syndicalism, and many of the ancillary bodies of the Falange such as the Women's Section and Youth Movement became official organisations. At the level of political imagery and symbolism as well, Falangist models predominated: the use of 'comrade' as a form of address; the adoption of the straight-armed fascist salute; the singing of the anthem, 'Face to the Sun' and the ubiquitous display of the Yoke and Arrows emblem. Also 1936 was described as Year 1 of the new era in Spain, rhetorically emphasising a break from the past, and public political discourse stressed the radical nature of the promised New State. Not surprisingly, conventional conservatives protested that the Falange seemed to be winning power, not so much as through the back door but by being invited in from the front.[63]

In the event conservative fears proved largely unjustified. The emerging Franco dictatorship was never to institutionalise the 'national syndicalist revolution' of radical Falangist dreams. Despite his political allegiances, Serrano Suñer was careful to limit the real influence of the Falange both within the single party and in the wider state apparatus of francoism. The outwardly fascist appearance of the FET y de las JONS was deceptive, disguising the extent to which it retained a careful balance of all the political forces on the Nationalist side. Leading posts within the organisation were shared out between the different tendencies, none of which really ever lost their own identities. This ensured that the Falange was never able to gain monopoly control over the movement. Nor was the power of the party allowed to dominate the state in the way that national syndicalist doctrine demanded. As a government apparatus was gradually constructed by Franco during the war all the different, competing, forces within the Nationalist camp were given a share of institutional power. Only some areas of administration (media, youth, women, and syndical apparatus) were handed over to the control of the party. Otherwise the army and the Church were allocated important areas of responsibility, along with a conventional bureaucracy of government ministries.[64] At the highest level of the regime, as well, the same policy of balancing different institutional and political forces operated. When Franco appointed his first cabinet in 1938 the party gained the largest number of posts, but radical Falangists of the pre-war school only received a minority of them. Though the early governments often spoke in the language of national syndicalism, describing their intentions as 'totalitarian' for instance, only in a few areas were Falangist ideas put into practice and then often in a muted form.[65]

While containing radical Falangism made political sense for the new regime, ensuring it a wider basis of support and reassuring more conventional conservatives, it also introduced a revolutionary tension within early francoism. Radical party members were bitterly disappointed at the failure of the party to achieve its aims, sometimes even speaking of betrayal by the dictatorship which used the Falange as a 'fig leaf' to cover up a reactionary reality. In the immediate post-war period such feelings were to become even more acute during the battles for influence and control that opened up among the victors. These were the final struggles to secure a fully revolutionary future for Spain. But by this time the task was virtually impossible and eventually the Falange was to emerge as the biggest loser. Having played an important part in the defeat of revolution from the left, the Falangist vision of revolution was itself shorn of most of its real significance by the forces of the reactionary right. In this sense Falangism shared a similar fate to the more radical wings of Italian fascism and German Nazism, both of which were curbed in the rise to power by leaders seeking to placate more conservative interests.[66]

Conclusion: the end of revolution?

The end of the Civil War brought to a close this remarkable cycle of unconventional revolutionary episodes. In a decade of almost continuous conflict, in which revolution had been pitted against revolution, there was no truly revolutionary outcome or a resurrection of the status quo ante. For the defeated Republicans the counter-revolutionary and reactionary nature of the Franco regime seemed clear. And indeed, the justification of the war as a crusade against the threat from the revolutionary left was a central plank of francoism. But neither was there complete reaction; the tumultuous turns of events precluded any such simple return to the past. The ground for such a return had been cut away by the arrival of the Republic in 1931 and the military rising of 1936. In the process a great many Spaniards came to see revolution as the only common-sense future. The Franco regime, therefore, inhabited a political territory somewhere between revolution and reaction, even after the radical vision of the Falange suffered its final collapse. Much of what the dictatorship stood for did indeed hark back to an imagined perfect past, but it was also forced to embrace 'modernity' in order to distance itself from some of the failures of the immediate past. It was, for instance, a monarchy in name, but no monarch was restored in the fear that this would lead to a resurgence of the Republic. This also meant that the revolutionary element within the dictatorship was never to completely die. Radical Falangism continued to have its adherents, who acted at times as virtually an internal opposition to the regime. For intellectuals, students and some workers, in particular, national syndicalism provided a language which could be used to criticise without necessarily provoking the outright repression that was directed against all outside opponents.[67]

Nor was revolutionary discourse eliminated from the political vocabulary of the Spanish left; if anything it became even more central to it. In exile the remnants of the Republicans engaged in unrestrained polemical battles over who was responsible for their defeat. For decades these coloured not only the views of the direct participants and sympathisers of the Republican cause, but also those of academic commentators on the war. Again and again the issues that had divided the Republicans were rehearsed, as though somehow the right formula for victory would emerge in defeat when it had failed to do so during the war itself. At the forefront of these rhetorical battles remained the question of revolution, and in particular the 'might-have-been' revolutionary path of the Anarchists and POUM, whose adherents continued (and continue) to claim theirs as the true revolution and, because it was never fully followed, the real route to victory. In turn the role of the Communists was denounced by all other parties as sectarian, including their former Republican and Socialist allies eager to distance themselves from failure and by dissidents from their own ranks. In the shadow of the Cold War after 1945, Spain became a prime example of Communist perfidy for anti-Communists of all political persuasions. At the same time, the PCE and USSR glorified the role of the party in the Civil War and maintained the description of their policy as a step on the road to a 'Spanish revolution'.[68] In fact, then, conflict about 'revolution' did not come to an end in Spain. What occurred was the fate suffered by many periods of revolution this century: they live on not as reality but as rhetoric.

8. Yet Another Failed German Revolution? The German Democratic Republic 1989–90

JONATHAN OSMOND

Prediction and hindsight

In early 1989 Germany comprised two republics and a battered, divided former capital, part of which was a western enclave deep in the heart of the German Democratic Republic. Large contingents of American, British, French and Soviet troops were quartered in Berlin and also throughout the territories of the two states. The GDR was headed by the 76-year-old General Secretary Erich Honecker of the Socialist Unity Party of Germany (SED), who had been at the top for nearly 18 years. His counterpart in the Federal Republic of Germany was Chancellor Helmut Kohl of the Christian Democratic Union (CDU), a man of 58 who had then been in office for over six years but had, dare one say it, bigger aspirations.

If at that same point in 1989 there had been those blessed with the gift of being able to see ten years into the future, they would have beheld a Social Democratic Chancellor of the whole of Germany, Gerhard Schröder, in charge of a Red–Green coalition government about to move into a renovated and remodelled Reichstag in the centre of the capital of Berlin, now a sea of cranes and new high-rise buildings. Without knowledge of the intervening decade they would have wondered what kind of revolutionary change had taken place. What blend of nationalism and liberation had come to pass, and how had the international divisions of the Cold War been superseded? Had the Germans managed to combine national unification with democratic left-leaning politics in a way which had eluded them in 1848 and in 1918, and for that matter in 1815, 1832, 1871, 1933 and 1945? The economists among these putative visionaries would have noted that not only had the Mark of the GDR disappeared with the state itself, but that the Deutsche Mark, pillar of post-war West

German economic stability, was on its way out as well. They would have also noted levels of German unemployment unknown since the dark days of the early 1930s. Looking further afield on the European map our imaginary prophets would have sought Czechoslovakia and the Soviet Union in vain. They would have found a rump Yugoslavia, the Serb capital of which was being bombed daily by NATO forces, of which Germans formed a contingent. NATO itself now included Hungary, Poland and a separate Czech Republic. The reverberations of the events of the revolutionary autumn of 1989 are indeed still being felt in Germany, Europe and world-wide.

Some of the upheavals elsewhere have involved extreme violence and criminality, but in Germany itself the changes have – with a few notorious exceptions of terrorist assassinations, racist murders, state security brutality, and an assault on Dresden railway station – been remarkably peaceful. However, the surprising scale of Schröder's victory and the entry into the Bundestag of the reformed Communist Party of Democratic Socialism (PDS) on the basis of 5 per cent of the national vote and 25 per cent of the east German vote testify pacifically to the prolonged agony of adjustment in the east and the consequent uncertainties in the west. The German revolution of 1989 leaves much unfinished business even now in its own territory.

Yet there can be doubts as to whether Germany has experienced a revolution at all. Perhaps the external withdrawal of Soviet support for the Honecker regime – rather than any domestic initiative – was the principal cause of the changes, and the swift absorption of the former GDR into an enlarged Federal Republic evidence of the lack of political will in the population of the GDR. As soon as nationalism – or perhaps the desire for the Deutsche Mark – took hold before Christmas 1989, the emancipatory, truly revolutionary features of the demonstrations of the late GDR dissipated. The CDU, one of the old subservient bloc parties of the GDR, won the first democratic elections in March 1990. The treaties of union between the two German states – though heavy in paragraphs – transposed practices of the Federal Republic to the territory of the GDR in almost all respects, first monetarily in July then politically and socially in October. The economic infrastructure of the old GDR was dismantled, sold off or closed down, with consequent dramatic levels of unemployment. The population became a mostly willing target for an invasion of western products from butter and beer to motor cars, bank accounts, insurance and foreign holidays. The public slogans of communism were replaced in turn by the electoral hoardings of the western parties and then by the mass advertising of the consumer society.

In the light of all this, should one even speak of a revolution? Was 1989 – like 1848 and 1918 – to end up as a half-hearted German attempt to forge a new type of democracy, foiled by popular apathy and the resilience of existing power structures? It will be argued here that despite the undoubted presence of both these features, there *was* a revolution in the German Democratic Republic which taken all in all succeeded in most of the demands for liberation which lay behind it. A substantial proportion of the population – not a majority, but revolutions never have a majority – at then unknown personal risk rebelled against those in authority over them by leaving the Republic *en masse* or by taking to the streets, both serious offences under GDR law. The ruling party and governmental system were first changed under popular pressure, then removed by democratic election. The subsequent political accommodation in an enlarged Federal Republic had and still has serious flaws, but it was the outcome of an expression of democratic will, only possible because of the popular revolution, if later supplemented by the machinations of the political parties of Bonn and Munich. The outcomes of revolution – which always disappoint many, and sometimes most, of those involved and affected – cannot be the only yardstick by which the term is defined. It is the process too which must be judged as 'revolutionary' or not. It is argued here that this process did represent a revolution and that the domestic and international outcomes were also revolutionary in their long-term impact.

The analysis of revolutions can suffer, of course, from the ease with which hindsight is applied in order to explain a sudden outburst of demonstrations, political activity and/or violence which become what we call revolution. A characteristic account involves a list of critical 'factors' or 'dysfunctions' – in the economy, in society and in the political system – to which are added the resistance of the regime to change and a contingent event which 'sparks' the situation into revolution.[1] This summary may be expanded by consideration of either the inability or the unwillingness of the regime to defend itself, which seems to have been the characteristic of the GDR case. The cynical view of such accounts is that they operate teleologically from the outset, simply marshalling the evidence of crisis and not the counter-indicators and uncertainties. They give more credence to processes of change than to those of stability. After November 1989 there were implications of this latter stance, as much play was made in the western media of the failure of commentators to predict the breaching of the Berlin Wall and the end of the apparently stable, orthodox and economically relatively successful GDR.

Everyone, it appeared, had been taken by surprise. Similar comments have appeared in later academic treatments of the subject.[2]

In a sense, of course, the events of November 1989 were a complete surprise, partly because the opening of the Berlin Wall in the way that it actually happened appears to have been the result of a momentary misunderstanding between SED leader Egon Krenz and Politburo member and press spokesman Günter Schabowski.[3] It has to be said, though, that by November a revolutionary process was already in train and that even a more orderly opening of the border would surely have led to the pressures which were condensed spectacularly into the night of 9–10 November 1989 by the crowds at the crossing points and the eventual good sense of the border guards. And, while it is true that the *particular* circumstances of the turbulent autumn and their rapidity were not predicted, there was ample expert appreciation that the GDR was in danger not just of serious crisis but of complete collapse. In order to spare anyone else the indignity of scrutiny with hindsight, these are extracts from 'outlook' commentaries produced by the present author in October 1988 and in January 1989. Apart from headings, the passages are quoted in full:

> While the leadership question is unresolved, there will be a paralysis in the system. If that means, as it probably will, that the economic situation deteriorates, then the pressure for political change – including pressure from Mr Gorbachev – will increase. We may see more actual public disturbances in East Germany, reflecting a wide range of discontent in the population.[4]

> As it embarks upon its 40th anniversary, the German Democratic Republic is far more unstable than its official image would suggest. The country is internationally recognised, has flourishing contacts with West Germany, has one of the strongest economies of the CMEA area, and has for a long time been politically quiescent. And yet East Germany is the state which can least afford to accept change from Mr Gorbachev. *Perestroika* and *glasnost* threaten the ruling elites and social systems of all the states of Eastern Europe, but only in East Germany (and in Yugoslavia, for different reasons) is the very existence of the state in question. Political liberalisation in East Germany would make the Berlin Wall a nonsense, and a demolition of the wall would presage the dismantling of the GDR. It is for this reason that the East German leaders are and will continue to be adamantly opposed to political reform. It would not only mean an end to their

careers, but also an end to the state which they have constructed. [...] Before the advent of Mr Gorbachev, it would have seemed idle musing to discuss the reunification of Germany in the foreseeable future. It is still not a proximate event, but it is not beyond the realms of the possible. What it would require to become possible is either a complete breakdown of the economic and political structures of East Germany, which is not likely under the firm hand of the present regime, or the arrival of a reforming East German party leader with the imagination to be able to deal with West Germany on a constructive basis. There is no sign of such a person as yet, and though the next party congress has been brought forward to the spring of 1990, exciting rumours of Mr Honecker's departure, the old guard will be making all the speeches. [...] The current situation is far from calm. While most of the East German population is apathetic and resigned, and not immune to propaganda about the achievements of the German Democratic Republic, there is a core of Church based dissent which is continually being renewed, there are signs of disillusionment and aimless violence among young people, and there are applications lodged by between 3 and 7 per cent of the population to leave the country entirely. The authorities respond with violence and harassment against demonstrators, schoolchildren, and those who have made known their desire to depart. Meanwhile, for all their rhetoric, the economy is clogged by inefficiency, failure to supply demand, and lumbering bureaucracy. Some of the leading politicians know this, but to open the gates to reform and restructuring could lead to a flood of changes.

The political future of East Germany is at present impossible to predict, but the longer Mr Gorbachev stays in power and continues his reforms, the greater the probability that East Germany will be the focus of major internal and international crisis. Mr Honecker is hanging on now, but when he does go, be it in two years or five years time, the situation will require a personality to replace him of a kind not yet evident in the higher ranks of the party.[5]

If the hedging of bets were an audible process, there would be cacophony here. Furthermore, there is a gross underestimation of the timescale of the crisis and an overestimation of the preparedness of the regime to use force against its own population. On the latter point, however, one may cite the knife-edge situation in Leipzig on 9 October 1989 – with demonstrators and armed security forces massed against each other – as evidence that the potential for major bloodshed and for alternative political outcomes was great indeed. Overall, however, this and many other western observers were noting well before November 1989: leadership crisis and inaction, severe economic deterioration, popular unrest, nascent right-wing extremism, a potential flood of emigration; and the possibility of the demolition of the Berlin Wall, the end of the GDR and German reunification. The details were, of course, beyond human prescience.

We now know too that the awareness of impending crisis was even greater in the minds of many participants. Post-1989 memoirs have to be read carefully to avoid *ex post facto* self-justifications, but even so the more sensitive ones indicate knowledge of the depth of the disaster for the GDR.[6] This is supported by contemporary documentation from the Ministry for State Security, charting the extent of popular discontent with living conditions and hostility towards the regime.[7] The scale of the economic calamity – masked by bogus statistics and the withholding of crucial information – had been presented to Erich Honecker and Economics Secretary Günter Mittag by Chair of the State Planning Commission Gerhard Schürer on and off since the early 1970s.[8] They chose to ignore it.

What should have been clear to all – whether upholders of the system or its critics – but was perhaps shunned as an uncomfortable problem, was the logic that there was no justification for the existence of the GDR apart from its political and economic system. This is not to suggest that there is some ideal form of authentic, legitimate state which the GDR did not match; it was after all a relatively durable polity which had developed out of specific international and domestic power relations. The same could be said of many states in history.[9] Nonetheless, when it came to debate in the GDR in the period between the ousting of Honecker on 17 October 1989 and the elections of 18 March 1990 both sides – Krenz, Schabowski and then Prime Minister Hans Modrow on the one hand and the citizens' movements on the other – were arguing about reform within a German Democratic Republic, possibly in some loose association with the Federal Republic, rather than looking squarely at unification. It is easy now to see this as a blind spot, but at the time, of course, no one – including Helmut Kohl – could be certain that Mikhail Gorbachev would agree to the creation of a unified Germany, certainly not a Germany within NATO. In this context too the voice of the people – revolutionary in impact if not in behaviour – proved decisive. The election of Kohl's ally, Lothar de Maizière of the CDU, in the spring of 1990 – coupled with the growing economic catastrophe – set an agenda for a particular kind of unification which even Gorbachev did not resist.

Theories of revolution

There are now many narrative histories of 1989–90 in German and in English, the best of which place the events against a much longer-term background.[10] It is not the intention here to rehearse those details once more, but to investigate the broad origins of the crisis and the salient features of the revolution. The emphasis is on the crisis, rather than upon the details of the subsequent unification process and its aftermath, which are subjects in themselves. They derive from the revolution but were not strictly part of it.

Alongside the narrative histories, some more interpretative than others, there have been many individual and collective attempts to provide theorisation of the revolution in the GDR.[11] The approaches vary enormously, including mass psychology, economic determinism reminiscent of Marxism itself, sociology, demography, political science and religion.[12] There is not the scope here to reproduce all of these, but comments on some of them may be illuminating.

There is a potential link between some of the analyses of the nature of SED rule and the psychological disturbance of the population highlighted by others. Charles Maier writes of 'paternalistic control' and Gert-Joachim Glaessner of 'party patrimonialism', while Mary Fulbrook has recently suggested 'modern party absolutism' as a description of the system.[13] All three, deliberately rejecting a revival of totalitarianism as a descriptor, emphasise the control and policing features of SED practice, which have been explored from the recipients' perspective in searing fashion by Hans-Joachim Maaz.[14] His psychoanalytical approach finds echoes too in the comments from the man in charge of the Stasi archives, Joachim Gauck: 'Many people in the old GDR were pure bundles of nerves, because they had to endure all this and continually faced an invisible enemy.'[15] The importance of these interpretations is that they highlight the *Entmündigung* of the population, that is the treating of people as less than capable of dealing with their own affairs. The revolution was a statement writ large that the people of the GDR were asserting their own capacity and individuality.

Following on from this is the more collective emphasis in Maier on the reassertion of civil society and communitarianism.[16] He perceives this as a common feature of the revolutions in Communist Europe in 1989. Certainly the adoption of such terms as 'citizens' movement', 'New Forum', 'Civic Forum' in the Czech lands, 'Hungarian Democratic Forum' and even – with its deliberate appropriation of Communist terminology – 'Solidarity' in Poland suggests a discourse of seizing back from the state that which it had taken inappropriately from the people.

Theoretical approaches incur the temptation of seeking one underlying explanation of 1989–90. A purely economic approach, for example, while it can chart the failures and distortions of the planned economy without difficulty, cannot of itself explain why the crisis came when it did. The same applies to geopolitical interpretations, which view the long-term development and decline of states.[17] Socio-political modelling has produced some of the strangest ways of approaching the problem by trying, for example, to correlate 'necessary' and 'sufficient' variables of the collapse of the SED and German unification or, in another instance a table of 'Average Correlations Within and Between Two Subdimensions Of Unconventional Political Participation in 1991 in East and West Germany'.[18] One may question whether this kind of approach helps us to understand German politics, or anything else for that matter.

Some cases hinge upon the definition of events. The very choice of terminology at the time and in subsequent literature gives clues as to how interpreters view the situation. German words used as alternatives to *Revolution* include *Wende, Zusammenbruch, Umbruch* and *Untergang*, some of which are more easily translatable than others.[19] Of these *Wende*, though including the 'turning' element present in *Revolution*, suggests a gentler process than does the common conception of 'revolution' and was at the outset associated more with change under Krenz *within* the SED system rather than with the overthrow of that system. The other terms emphasise the collapse of the state rather than the assault upon it, reducing the agency of those who left or protested. The choice of these words relates to the question of the long-term inherent flaws in the GDR, especially where – as with Armin Mitter and Stefan Wolle – the decline is perceived through the entire history of the GDR.[20]

An alternative or an addition to a full-blown theorisation of the revolution is to view it as a series of coincidences befalling a system already so weakened socially, politically and economically that it no longer had at its disposal the economic or political means to defend itself, a view taken by Claus Offe. It is possible to list a series of contingent events which each increased the pace of change, a 'chain reaction', as he describes it.[21] This approach bears similarity to conventional accounts of revolutions in France, where significant *journées* like the execution of the king in 1793 or the June Days of 1848 stand out as marking turning points in the revolutionary calendar. Karl Marx himself charted the 1848 Revolution in France in this way, with a very specific chronology from day to day and week to week.[22] In the case of the GDR, such a list would include: the Hungarian dismantling of the barbed-wire frontier with Austria and the protests against local election fraud in May 1989; the Honecker regime's support of the Tiananmen Square massacre in June; Honecker's illness at the Bucharest summit in July; the opening of the Hungarian border and Hans-Dietrich Genscher's speech at the Prague embassy in September; the 40th anniversary celebrations of the GDR, the Dresden station violence, the Leipzig demonstration stand-off, and the removal of Honecker in October; and in November the opening of the inter-German border. Each of these events unleashed further fear, anger or expectation which fuelled the mounting emigration and domestic protest. To take the example of Honecker's fall, for instance: while the change in leadership did not of itself lead to or need to lead to more general upheaval, it was already coupled with popular and Politburo reactions to the pomposity of the 40th anniversary ten days before and to Gorbachev's critical presence on that occasion. It would be hard to imitate Marx in ascribing specific changes in class relations to these one-off events (though of course the regime did perceive class conflict as the underlying cause of the process), but this does not mean that the events were just 'coincidence'. Honecker's illness was not determined by the inherent structure of the GDR, but on the one hand it exposed the incapacity of the remaining leadership to take charge of a growing crisis and on the other it emphasised the complaints from within and without the SED that the leadership was old, ill and out of touch.

Offe uses his 'chain reaction' approach to suggest that the revolution was therefore not based upon the agency of those on the streets. When he says that the collapse of the state was not due to a '*will* for national unity' nor to the '*intentions* of the short-lived democratic-revolutionary people's movement'[23], though, he is in danger of underestimating the purposeful actions of those marching in Leipzig and of those voting in March 1990 for parties set on monetary and political union. It is true that the emigrants were not by their individual actions setting out to bring down the SED or the GDR, but their retraction of any confidence in the system was also a positive act, taken at considerable personal cost to themselves. Heinz Bude goes so far as to ascribe to them the pivotal role:

> The '*Wende*' was brought about rather by the young families who left the country via Hungary. They demonstrated to the political class in the GDR the failure of socialism. For things were not obviously going badly for them and they were also not persecuted by the '*Stasi*', but nevertheless they simply turned away.[24]

The emphasis on the 'young families' here is also significant; for all its efforts since 1946 the SED had not managed to reproduce itself sufficiently across the generations.

Stalemate in the system

Theoretical models can be helpful in unlocking parts of the revolutionary process but cannot explain it in total, and here a more empirical historical approach is of more use. In order to explain the combined fragility of the state and the outbreak of unrest, we need to link the morass of economic problems and the constraints upon the political actors.

The ruling ideology of the GDR, Marxism-Leninism, assumed economic determinism of the superstructure, class struggle and – in 'real existing socialism', as it was known – the rational planning of production in the interests of the working population. One need not espouse Marxism-Leninism to see the relevance of economic determinism to a discussion of the final crisis of the GDR. By the end of the 1980s the GDR economy was characterised by industrial and agricultural inefficiency in international terms, poor-quality goods, widespread visible and breathable pollution, dilapidated building stock and massive hard-currency debt. The last of these was in a sense the crucial one. Borrowing from the West and from Japan had increased dramatically during the 1980s, and it had been used primarily to underwrite the championed social benefits of living under socialism: full employment and subsidised housing, childcare, transport and basic foodstuffs. The debt burden was by now, though, a block in the way of any realistic economic reform. The regime which under Erich Honecker's 'unity of economic and social policy' had as its priority the provision of the population with social amenities and products, could not deliver the goods without the kind of price rises and job cuts which were contrary to the entire ethos of the GDR and would themselves spark unrest. A class analysis also played a part, despite over 40 years of Communist rule. The regime could live with high-profile but minority intellectual hostility, fed by allegedly bourgeois and Christian assumptions, because this opposition was well infiltrated by the Ministry of State Security (Stasi) and because the SED thought it could rely upon the support or at least the quiescence of the working class in whose name it ruled. The compact with the working class meant, however, that no dramatic reappraisal of the economy was possible.[25] It was probably too late anyway. The GDR had fallen so far behind the quality production of Western

Europe, North America and the Far East that its products could not compete. It was dependent instead on the re-export of relatively cheap Soviet oil and – with Honecker in the van – placed its hopes in the ridiculously expensive reinvention of the microchip. Furthermore, the pain of adjustment in the capitalist economies which had taken place in the 1970s and particularly in the 1980s had ostensibly been spared the planned economies, but in practice they had to catch up on that trauma too.[26] Unfortunately, a rigidity of thinking in the SED prevented even a limited attempt to deal with real issues. As Hans Modrow puts it, thinking back to the late 1970s, 'More and more we lost the power to discuss really complex questions – until we could no longer think in complex terms and now scarcely noticed that we had lost that capability.'[27]

The economic crisis underlay the frustration and anger which was vented in 1989, but there was no one moment where the economic situation sparked unrest, as it had way back in June 1953. During the summer 36 years later it was the opportunity of escape spotted initially by holidaymakers in Hungary that shifted the gear of change. Of course, the motives were many and various of those who chose to risk leaving everything behind in order to cross the border from Hungary into Austria and thence to the Federal Republic or to take refuge in West German embassies in Prague or Warsaw, but frustration about the economic incapacity of the GDR was part of the impulse. A deeper sense of never being treated as free mature adults was present too, as it was in the minds of the demonstrators in Leipzig. The economic dimension really came to fore, though, once the Berlin Wall and the inter-German border were opened on 9 November 1989. Thereafter the East Berlin regime had no real control over its workforce, its currency, its inter-German trade or its prices. It could also no longer depend upon the CMEA barter arrangements and the hard-currency transactions which had been the bedrock of its position in international trade. From the Bonn perspective too, the opening of first the Hungarian and then the inter-German border threatened major social crisis and expenditure, as the GDR threatened to lose a large proportion of its population to the West. From early 1990 it was in the interests of both governments to stabilise a situation veering out of control, but Bonn had the whip hand – and used it.

The political situation in the GDR in the late 1980s could be described as a many-sided stalemate, long in the making. All the players in the game were in one way or another pinned into positions from which they could not escape without crisis. The top leadership around Erich Honecker was bound by long-held ideological positions, by wilful ignorance of the severity of the economic crisis at the base, and by the appreciation that the GDR could survive as a political project only if it was defended by the state authorities and if necessary the Red Army. The senior figures outside Honecker's closest circle shared many of its preconceptions and habits, but some – Schürer, Stoph, Schabowski and others – did see that the GDR was running into deep economic and political crisis. They were hampered, though, by the circumstances and mechanisms which – deliberately – discouraged the coalescing of faction and opposition.[28] They had seen in the past too how speaking out about problems could be not just ineffective but actually detrimental to one's own career prospects and the cause of reform. Rivalries and mutual suspicion played their part; in fact many of the leading figures loathed each other. None of them envisaged radical economic change in the direction of the free market, but neither could they see the resources necessary to overhaul the economic infrastructure within socialist parameters.

More broadly in the structures of the SED there were those wedded to their positions by long years of power and sometimes corruption, and others – primarily Hans Modrow in Dresden – whose association with a critique of central policy had left them excluded from crucial decision-making. In Modrow and others there remained too such a fundamental loyalty to the party and to the state that their options for imaginative manoeuvre were very limited. Similarly, local party secretaries and ordinary members, even those dismayed by the sclerotic rule of Honecker, were bound by a long-established doctrine of party discipline, and were in any case unable to influence matters further up the hierarchy. Only when the challenge came from the demonstrators on the streets did some in the SED feel able to think constructively and independently. As Hans Modrow puts it, 'The rebels could reach and move many functionaries, because they suddenly acted as their bad consciences.'[29] The democratic, libertarian and socialist rhetoric of the GDR – flouted in practice throughout its history – was now being used by the internal opposition. As the now famous chant had it, '*We* are the people!' The SED, by implication, was not.

Those who were explicit in their criticism of the regime, whether from a religious, civil-rights, environmentalist or pacifist perspective (usually a mixture of several of these), did not for the most part propose an overthrow of 'socialism' as such. Many of them too were bound by loyalty to the idea of the GDR, albeit one transformed into an open democratic state. They were also shackled by the limitations on their freedom of discussion and organisation. They knew that they were under the surveillance of the Stasi, from time to time they had to account to the authorities for their actions, but even they did not know how widespread was the net of Stasi activity in their own circles, be it in the churches, in 'alternative' cultural groups or among lawyers who acted on their behalf. Furthermore, opposition circles had over the decades been depleted by voluntary or compulsory loss of GDR citizenship. It is also a mistake to see the 'opposition' or the citizens' movements as homogeneous, even with the emergence of New Forum on a mass base in late 1989. Rivalries and suspicions were as alive in the citizens' movements as they were in the Politburo.[30] Once the power of the SED was broken, many in the citizens' movements were understandably unable to be sure that this moment had come and were still fearful of Modrow's intentions and of a revival of the Stasi. They were unable or unwilling to take charge of affairs of state even when incorporated into Modrow's Government of National Responsibility in February 1990 and New Forum decided not to constitute itself as a political party. This left it at a serious disadvantage in comparison with those groupings which tied themselves to West German political parties. Its formless nature and its continued espousal of socialism then failed to impress the electorate.

The churches, primarily the Protestant churches, had long played a role as an alternative forum within the GDR. They were indeed the only organisation not incorporated in one way or another into the state, and in the years and months leading up to the revolution they provided a focus for dissent which was not necessarily Christian in origin. It is not surprising, therefore, that many of the local and national spokesmen of the revolution were pastors, Rainer Eppelmann, Markus Meckel and Joachim Gauck being the most notable. One should not overestimate, though, the freedom of the churches before 1989; they too were part of the stalemate. The SED had attempted with some success to bind the churches into the system through the Church–state agreement of 1978, religious and related activities were thoroughly infiltrated by the Stasi, and prominent Church figures, lay and clerical, had to or chose to have dealings with the SED and the security forces. Bishops were not always pleased by the agitatorial role adopted by some of their junior brethren, and in the events of 1989 the churches as institutions generally took a conciliatory rather than a radical role.[31]

The population at large was hemmed in by the border fortifications, although most people had never seen their full extent, since – except in Berlin – they were not allowed anywhere near them. People were bought off by full employment and by the subsidies of housing, transport and basic goods, but never satisfied by them, especially in the face of the thriving capitalist economy in the neighbour German republic. The possibility of breaking out from their situation arose quite specifically when the Hungarians – encouraged by Bonn – created an escape route via Austria. The ensuing reaction of the authorities, harsh under Honecker but then directionless during his illness in the summer of 1989, provoked the popular demonstrations in Leipzig, Dresden and elsewhere. And finally the GDR was itself in a stalemate position, trapped between its loyalty to the USSR and its financial dependence on the Federal Republic. A move in one direction caused difficulties in the other. Honecker was confounded by the changes under Gorbachev which he saw – rightly as it happened – as threatening socialism and the basis of the Soviet Union itself. This led the SED to restrict access to material emanating from the Soviet Union, including the whole or parts of Gorbachev's speeches, at the same time as maintaining the propaganda of the GDR's permanent alliance with the USSR. The Federal Republic was denounced for bribing the treacherous Hungarians, an accusation which was largely true if by now irrelevant. By the time in early 1990 that Modrow was explicit in seeking large financial assistance from Bonn, he was already sidelined in terms of Kohl's policy and was promised nothing.

Revolution throughout the GDR

For all the symbolism of the Wall and the Brandenburg Gate, the revolution of 1989 was not just a Berlin event. It is only to be understood as an outcome of crisis throughout the GDR, with the city of Leipzig a particular focus of developments. In this respect, 1989 bears comparison with previous upheavals in German history, and – for all its centralism as a state – the GDR displayed the same regionalised dimension as Germany on those other occasions. In 1848–9 Berlin had been only one revolutionary locality among many, alongside Munich, Vienna, Leipzig, Dresden, Frankfurt am Main and – latterly – the urban and rural districts of the south-west. The 1918–19 Revolution originated in north-west German mutinies and in Munich, with major political unrest in industrial centres in western Germany, in Hamburg and Bremen, and in Saxony. The National Socialist 'revolution' witnessed Hitler being offered power in the Reich capital, but it could scarcely be understood without the previous nationwide radicalisation, not least in the so-called *Hauptstadt der Bewegung*, Munich, where Ludendorff and Hitler had launched their first abortive lunge for power ten years earlier. The transformation following defeat in 1945 was of necessity a decentred process, dominated by the policies of the occupying powers in their respective zones, although Berlin soon became the focus for domestic and international tension. Even the uprising of June 1953, though most closely associated with the workers of the Stalinallee and demonstrations at the Brandenburg Gate, was in fact a popular protest affecting numerous towns and cities and even – on a smaller scale – some rural areas.

This regional dimension needs to be addressed, particularly but not only the role of Leipzig. There is no one simple explanation of why this city should have been marked by protest, but there are several significant indicators. In the first place, of course, pressures upon the population existed throughout the GDR and there is no reason to assume that a revolutionary process must take place only or primarily in a capital city. More than this, however, although the GDR was a small state, it was subject to the same kind of popular provincial suspicion of the capital as may be found in other countries. Indeed, the constant insistence in GDR propaganda that (East) Berlin was not just 'Berlin' but 'Berlin – Capital of the GDR', exacerbated the feeling elsewhere in the state that resources and initiatives prioritised the capital at the expense of other districts.[32] This was not necessarily true in all respects, but it certainly was the case that investment in other towns and cities was very uneven and subject to political patronage and the dictates of central economic policy and official propaganda. Regional rivalries themselves played a part, but the success of local initiatives was always dependent upon approval from the centre. Hans Modrow gives numerous examples of the quashing of developments in his district of Dresden because of suspicion in Berlin or the favouring of some other city. Rather than the kind of comradely co-operation which he claims to have worked for, 'False ambition, local egoism and the denunciation of disagreement as faction-building prevented all real co-operation.'[33]

Of the major cities of the GDR outside the capital, Leipzig was in fact the one which benefited most from development, because of its status as the twice-yearly international *Messestadt*, but this also exposed residents to greater western contacts than those of other cities. The centre of Leipzig looked more like a comparable West German city than most in the GDR, despite the evident signs of shoddy construction and the large areas of dilapidated older buildings in and beyond the centre. The combination of resentment at Berlin with a high degree of civic and – below the surface at first – Saxon pride lent strength to the protests once they began. These were also fuelled by a series of previous antagonisms about high-handed official policy towards the city's fabric and its public events.[34]

As important, though, was the long-term development in Leipzig of Church-based protest which was allowed to take hold on a small scale at the Monday evening Nikolaikirche meetings and demonstrations, before burgeoning by the autumn of 1989 into the symbolic circling of the city centre by the protesters. By the time of the potential bloodbath of 9 October, it was local initiative on the part of Gewandhaus conductor Kurt Masur and local party officials, as much as instructions from Berlin and the Soviet military, which defused the situation.

The phenomenon of district party officials breaking from the dogmatism of the Berlin leadership was also to be seen in Dresden, where Mayor Wolfgang Berghofer and SED District Secretary Hans Modrow opened up the possibility of dialogue with the opposition. This was in the aftermath of the chaotic and violent scenes outside the city's main railway station at the beginning of October when trains passed through from Prague carrying those allowed by Honecker to emigrate, but only via GDR territory. In the same way that the GDR's 40th anniversary celebrations in Berlin on 7 October 1989 – in Gorbachev's presence – raised the tension and stimulated the anti-Honecker demonstrations, so in Dresden emotions were heightened and aptly symbolised on the same evening by the performance at the Semper Opera of Beethoven's *Fidelio*. The barbed-wire set for the Prisoners' Chorus drew attention to the words of the libretto: 'O Freedom! O Freedom, do you return?' The Stasi itself could have been evoked by the prisoners' words: 'Speak softly, restrain yourselves! We are observed by ears and eyes.'[35]

Leipzig and Dresden built up their own momentum, which then encouraged protest in Berlin itself, culminating in the massive demonstration of 4 November. It should not be forgotten, though, that in many parts of the GDR, groups were coalescing to hold discussion of possible reform, anticipating the later 'round tables' of late 1989 and early 1990.[36] Once the full potential of change was unleashed by the opening of the inter-German frontier and by the collapse in SED power, local initiatives abounded, not only 'round table' discussions but also occupations of district Stasi headquarters.[37] And finally, even in Berlin itself the local dimension played an important part. As the television pictures of the dancers on the Berlin Wall sped around the world, the most important feature of that night and the following days in Berlin itself was the reuniting of a city and of its inhabitants.

If the revolution had important local dimensions, it was also, of course, a global event of the television age. The dissatisfaction of the

GDR population had for many years been fed by their reception of the West German media, but in 1989 television coverage of China and of Hungary and Poland hastened the pace of change. The fall of the Wall in its turn encouraged the democratic revolution in Prague and the much nastier occurrences in Bulgaria, Romania and eventually Albania. Yugoslavia was already descending on its own awful path into chaos.

A failed revolution?

Debates about whether or not there was a revolution in the GDR – and if there was whether it failed or not – centre implicitly or explicitly on the disappointment of those who sought an alternative to dogmatic SED dictatorship within the borders of the GDR. This disappointment embraces, however, many very different strands. In retrospect, such prominent SED figures as Schabowski, Krenz and Modrow suggest that they too favoured reform within a socialist context, a claim more convincing in some cases than in others. They clearly played a major part in the revolution of 1989, but their complicity in the old system restricted it to that of gravediggers. Even Modrow, whose contribution over several months to the genesis of new forms of debate and representation should not be downplayed, was so wedded to the ideals of the GDR from its creation that he misconstrued the new situation and failed to appreciate his own lack of any democratic legitimacy. A genuinely humane and modest man, he was nevertheless restricted by his continuing contempt for the Federal Republic, fed by the way in which he was treated by Helmut Kohl.[38]

The bitter disappointment of the spokesmen and -women of the citizens' movements was that 'their' democratic revolution was stolen from them in early 1990 by the West German government parties playing upon the economic worries of the population and pushing a nationalist agenda not present initially in 1989, and by the removal of the main power debate to the international arena in the Two-Plus-Four talks. Without questioning the reality of these phenomena, the interpretation is flawed. The citizens' movements were certainly crucial in providing a temporary organisational framework and a democratic vocabulary. However, they were following popular protest rather than initiating it, at the same time as showing a rather patronising arrogance towards the people whose concerns were more immediate and tangible.[39] Furthermore, their conduct at the round table talks simply did not match up to the scale of the crisis.[40] Debates about a new form of basic democracy in a continuing socialist GDR, perhaps noble in themselves, were by now beside the point. As Hans Modrow, not an impartial observer certainly, put it:

> I believe that increasingly New Forum blocked its own path. Moral rigour stood in the way of political pragmatism. Political incapacity, at first a virtue against functioning in the GDR system, became now a surly and provocative ambition not to help to carry out socialist renewal in co-operation with the remnants of the government. I believe that this stance of refusal contributed to the collapse of the citizens' movement.[41]

The citizens' movements' failure to produce a strong alternative political coalition to both the PDS and to the Federal Republic set the scene for their resounding defeat in March 1990. The one political party which had been expected by many to benefit from the crisis – the SPD – was weak and fractious in the GDR and undermined by the inept handling of the situation in the west by Oskar Lafontaine. He chose to pander to real West German fears about the impact of unification, thereby reducing his appeal in the east and eventually falling foul of the nationalist discourse in the west as well. As far as the population was concerned, democracy and efficiency did not have to be sought in the GDR; they were already available in the western parties, and those parties most able to deliver were those already in government, the CDU and their partners.

Some participants' disappointment at the particular outcome of political upheaval cannot be used as a measure of revolution. Otherwise there will be found to have been few or no revolutions in history. It is contended here that a popular uprising against a state in deep crisis did in the GDR constitute a revolution. Masses on the streets, political demands articulated by new if transient citizens' movements, and compromises by some representatives of the old order combined to alter fundamentally the nature of economy, state and society in the GDR. One peculiarity of the German case in 1989–90 was perhaps that the new system was so to speak bought off the peg rather than tailor-made, but even here one should not draw too sharp a distinction between the GDR and, say, Poland and Hungary. In those countries too capitalist forms were adopted at breakneck speed with both positive and negative social consequences. It is surely the national dimension which remains unique to the GDR, though even here there was a mixture of popular demand and West German imposition.

Theories of revolution will no doubt continue to abound and to be applied to the GDR in 1989–90, but in essence the explanation is straightforward. The SED had created a system which bound together all facets of economy, politics and society in such a rigid way that when external circumstances changed and internal problems mounted it could not defend itself against the forces of popular discontent its own policies had fostered. The nature of the revolution was not inevitable and the timing was not predictable. Or was it? We may conclude with a percipient commentary from 50 years ago:

Even if communism were temporarily victorious it doesn't carry with it such a hopeless teleology of tyranny – even if tyrannical in its present phase – as did Nazism. In short anything [that] is a revolution must keep moving or it doesn't revolute: by its very nature it contains within it the seeds of its own destruction, so by 1989, say, everything ought to be hunky dory, all of which certainly doesn't make it any easier to live in 1950.[42]

Malcolm Lowry, extraordinary novelist and phenomenal alcoholic, was more chronologically precise in his prediction than any political scientist, historian or sociologist of more recent days. 'Hunky dory' is a phrase, however, which few would use today to describe post-Communist Germany, let alone the wider world since 1989.

9. The Age of Paradox: the Anti-revolutionary Revolutions of 1989–91

RICHARD SAKWA

Belinsky was as much an idealist as a negationist. He negated in the name of his ideal. That ideal had quite a definite and homogeneous quality, though it was called and still is called by different names: science, progress, humanity, civilisation – the West, in short. Well-meaning but ill-disposed people even use the word *revolution*.[1]

The end of the revolution has been proposed many times before, and such announcements have invariably proved premature. As Fred Halliday notes, the year 1989 gave the idea of revolution a 'special contradictory confirmation': it marked the 200th anniversary 'of the emergence of the modern, and modernist, concept of revolution during the French revolution'; but it was a year that began 'with sage warnings on how revolution was no longer a relevant concept, [but] it ended with the collapse of the communist regimes in a process that should, by all but the most dogmatically teleological of criteria, be termed "revolutionary" '.[2] These were indeed revolutions, but revolutions of a special type.

My argument will be that the revolutions of 1989–91 have put an end not only to a particular revolutionary cycle (namely, that focusing on the Russian Revolution of 1917), but mark the conclusion of the whole era of what we shall call Enlightenment revolutionism, and indeed, to a whole epoch of how we understand politics and processes of social change.[3] By the end of the eighteenth century the American Revolution was no longer the exception but the exemplary case – joined later by the French Revolution itself – of Enlightenment revolutionism. Koselleck described how Enlightenment utopianism became transformed into a philosophy of history in which, in his view, the necessarily separate sphere of politics was subverted by the social, cultural and moral demands made on it. The growing gulf between state and society, politics and ethics, gave rise to the challenge in the form of what he calls *critique* (one type of which was revolutionism), and this in turn provoked a *crisis* in which the autonomy of politics and statecraft was undermined.[4] As we shall note below, *crisis* can itself contribute to political regeneration, but when allied with revolutionism its impact can be devastating. It assumes that complex problems of human organisation can be resolved by radical intervention if those intervening have made the correct critique and bear the correct philosophy of history.[5]

The exhaustion of Enlightenment revolutionism does not mean that there will no longer be uprisings, upheavals, overturns and *bunty*, but that the philosophical significance of these events has changed. The uprisings of the slaves in the ancient world might once have been seen as revolutions from the Marxist perspective, but today even that dwindling band would tend to categorise them as desperate acts of the exploited and humiliated rather than prefigurations of a better order. Today, too, there is no shortage of conditions to provoke revolt, but now once again, as in antiquity and up to the modern era, there is no secular universal belief system to sustain hopes that a political overturn can inaugurate the rule of the just heralding the onset of a better world. This is not the same as the end of utopianism (although that, too, appears to have run its course) but focuses more on the exhaustion of the millenarianism associated with the revolutionary act of Enlightenment modernisation itself.

What is the anti-revolution?

A revolution is an event or series of events that fundamentally challenges the political order of things, relations between people and between objects, and which alters perceptions of reality. The taxonomic and structural studies of Crane Brinton, Samuel Huntington, Ted Gurr, Charles Tilly, Theda Skocpol, Jack Goldstone, Michael Kimmel and others[6] are primarily concerned with modernising and agrarian revolutions, together with the impact of inter-state conflict, whereas the anti-revolutions affected urbanised, modern industrial societies in a time of peace. In his latest work Tilly, indeed, appears to reject the very notion of revolution as a 'singular' event, considering it part of a spectrum of collective political mobilisation encompassing rebellions, riots and social violence.[7] According to Tilly and others, war has precipitated most European revolutions, and once again this distinguishes the revolutions of 1989–91, although of course the Cold War was a species of war which imposed intolerable strains and distortions on East European, and in particular Soviet, society.

The Communist revolutions were part of the triumph of modernist discourses associated with the Enlightenment project, of rational organisation and progress, and thus by implication denied culture and tradition.[8] The East European anti-revolutions reflected the end of belief in the liberating potential of revolutionary socialism, and associated with that the end of belief in the radical emancipatory potential of the revolutionary act itself. Revolutions of the oppressed and the downcast will of course continue, whether as 'singular' events or not, but the special late eighteenth-century view of revolution as a distinctly emancipatory act casting aside the burden of superstition, obscurantism and tradition to allow access to the sunlit uplands of modernity is irrevocably dead. The view that a particular class by rising up will achieve some universal goals in the development of humanity has gone.

Revolutionary socialist ideology drew liberally from the Enlightenment perspective of progress, deculturation and denationalisation. Condorcet's project called for 'the destruction of all historical civilisations and the standardisation of mankind according to the pattern of the Paris intellectual'.[9] For Marx 'the revolution is necessary not only because the *ruling* class cannot be overthrown in any other way, but also because only through a revolution can the *overthrowing* class reach the point where it gets rid of the old filth (*Dreck*) and becomes capable of a new foundation of society'.[10] In other words, a change of institutions was not enough but the revolutionary act itself was assumed to lead to a change of heart that would inaugurate a qualitatively new epoch. The destructive storm launched by Lenin after October 1917 failed even to reach the level of 'the Paris intellectual' but was patterned after the standards of a deracinated 'Russian' intellectual with a severe behaviourial disorder. Walicki has recently demonstrated how close the Bolshevik Revolution remained to the basic Marxist vision, above all the destruction of commodity production and all that this entailed.[11] While the trajectory of the Bolshevik Revolution included numerous personal choices and surprises, the words of Frederick Engels when he wrote to his Russian friend in 1885 are only partially applicable in this case: 'People who boasted that they had *made* a revolution have always seen the next day that they had no idea what they were doing, that the revolution *made* did not in the least resemble the one they would have liked to have made.'[12]

The Russian Revolution was the first large-scale attempt to implement Marxist revolutionary theory, the first attempt to build a society based on the rejection of Western modernity while trying to fulfil it. This utopian project, as it is now called, displaced political discourse from pragmatic reason towards a political practice that generated closure and exclusivity. In his recent work *The End of the Communist Revolution*, R. V. Daniels details this process in a chapter entitled 'The Long Agony of the Russian Revolution'.[13] Neil Harding, also, talks in terms of 'the Marxist-Leninist Detour'.[14]

The revolutions of 1989–91 in Eastern Europe challenge not only a redefinition of revolutionary theory, something argued for by Robert Dix,[15] but also suggest that the concept of revolution itself is anachronistic. The revolutionary epoch, begun in the early modern period with the dissolution of the feudal order and monolithic religious system, reached its apogee in the eighteenth century and ended with the decline of modernity itself. The age of Enlightenment revolutionism ends with a revolution. The paradox is deliberate: the revolutions of 1989–91 were anti-revolutionary revolutions. As Andrew Arato puts it, we are confronted by 'the historical novelty of "revolutions" that reject *the tradition* of modern revolutions'.[16]

The events of 1989–91 were not counter-revolutionary but anti-revolutionary in two senses: they tried to overcome the actual revolutions that had taken place in these countries in 1917 and 1945–48; and they repudiated the whole logic of revolutionary thinking that had haunted the European imagination for some two centuries. Our argument is that the end of the revolution in Russia and Eastern Europe signifies the end of Enlightenment revolutionism as a form of political action in its entirety.[17]

Features of the anti-revolution

The anti-revolutionary syndrome is characterised by a number of features, one of which is that the distinction between concepts of reform and revolution loses its traditional political resonance. The struggle between revolutionary and evolutionary socialism dominated the early years of the twentieth century, between Lenin's militant brand of vangardist revolutionism and Bernstein's insistence that 'Everywhere in the more advanced countries we see the class struggle assuming more moderate forms.'[18] Today the notion of revolutionary socialism both as a method and an aim commands few followers, and the East European anti-Communist movements undermined the whole notion of revolution. Gorbachev himself could never quite decide whether *perestroika* was a reform or a 'revolution without shots', finally settling on the notion of a 'revolution from above'.[19] The hybrid nature of these events provoked Timothy Garton Ash to coin the ugly term 'refolution';[20] a fundamentally new phenomenon had emerged that was both reform and revolution, but at the same time neither. The erasure of the distinction reflected not a convergence but the emasculation both of the revolutionary ideology and the ideology of revolution.

A paradoxical feature of the anti-revolution is that while denying revolution as a method, its consequences were on the whole more revolutionary than many *soi-disant* revolutions themselves. The last revolutionary act of East European societies was to choose, as Ralf Dahrendorf puts it, between an *open* or a *closed* society at a time of *constitutional*, as opposed to *normal*, politics.[21] The distinction is one drawn from Abbé Sieyès, who distinguished between *pouvoir constituant* and *pouvoir constitué*, with a revolutionary dynamic to the politics of the former,[22] a theme present also, Arato notes, in *The Federalist*.[23] Constituted power, or *normal* politics, however, as we shall note below in the context of the politics of 'crisis', does not entail surrender to the given but can have a radical edge that modifies the original constitutional settlement. As the Japanese demonstrated following the so-called Meiji Restoration of 1868, under the carapace of restoration a radical transformatory mission may be pursued.[24] The transformation, moreover, was directed solely towards the renewal of Japan and made no pretensions to universality.[25]

Communist revolutions represented a revolt against the trappings of modernity associated with Western societies while trying to fulfil the modernist Enlightenment project in other ways. Marx had argued that the Communist revolution would be the last revolution, since the revolt of the last exploited class would put an end to exploitation as a whole. In the event, it was the anti-Communist revolution that proved to be the last genuinely universal revolution. The anti-revolution, however, was both universalising, in the attempt to rejoin global processes, but also particularising, to restore native traditions. The anti-revolution thus fulfils the Enlightenment project but at the same time transcends it – preparing the way for the rejection of some central features of Enlightenment politics.

The contortions induced by the attempt to force the events of 1989–91 into conventional revolutionary theory are nowhere more evident than in a recent view that they 'make sense as a species of "bourgeois revolution" '.[26] This is true as far as it goes, in so far as the notion of a bourgeois revolution makes any sense at all, but misses much of importance in analysing the direction of change. Earlier revolutions were stamped with the whole gamut of modernist (Whig) assumptions about progress and the perfectibility of society. For the Eastern European revolutions, and with them certain events in the rest of the world (e.g. the Philippines), the model of the better world was no longer located in the future but could be found somewhere else: expectations shifted from the temporal to the spatial axis. These were revolutions of manoeuvre, moving laterally rather than forwards. The systems against which the revolutions of 1989–91 were directed were already modernised, in the sense of urbanised, literate and technologically sophisticated, but this was a peculiar sort of parallel modernity that might be labelled mis-modernisation. The anti-revolutions were designed to set them back on the track of mainstream modernising processes. They were indeed 'rectifying revolutions', as Jürgen Habermas put it, in which 'the fall of communism is a revolution that does not and cannot go far enough',[27] but their purpose was not to rectify the revolution but to put an end to it.

The 'anti-revolutionary' elements in 1989 derive in part from the fact that these events took place in circumstances where Marx had expected revolutions to occur, in societies that were already substantially modernised, but were intended not to supersede capitalism but to restore it. Thus they were in stark contrast to the two main types of revolution in the early modern and modern world: 'bourgeois' revolutions (England, America, France); and 'elite–peasant' revolutions in Russia and China.[28] The absence of many of the classical sociological features considered essential for democracy, however, exaggerated the role of political actors. The centrality of strategic processes has led to much emphasis on 'pacting' in the literature, describing the various round tables and 'negotiated revolutions', and has even tempted some to apply game theory to these transitions.[29]

The subject of the anti-revolution was no longer an elite band of intellectual revolutionaries, nor the desperate mass of exploited peasants or immiserated workers of classical revolutionary discourse, but society itself – reflecting not the amorphous classlessness of earlier debates about the 'end of ideology' but positive goals of the universal class of modernity. Adam Michnik detailed the strategy whereby the insurgency against the Communist regime made redundant not only the classical antinomy between revolution and reform but also rejected classical revolutionary strategies. In his seminal article 'A New Evolutionism' of 1976, Michnik concluded that the systems were unreformable and thus proposed a third strategy in which civil society itself, rather than the state, became both the subject and the object of the changes.[30] The notion of anti-politics undermined the deadly serious pretensions of revolution as a style of politics. The concept is most closely associated with George Konrád, but his work is at best confused.[31] The notion of anti-politics that can be constructed from the works, *inter alios*, of Havel, Michnik and Konrád, focuses on a notion of power and politics that moves beyond the Weberian idea of the state as the 'monopoly of legitimate violence'. State power is delegitimated and societal resistance elevated to the status of the classic heroic resistance movements against oppression. Havel stressed the element of moral recuperation in the revolutions of 1989, declaring on 10 December 1989 to a crowd in Prague that they had achieved a revolution 'against violence, dirt, intrigue, lawlessness, mafia, privilege and persecution'.[32] Konrád noted that 'I know of no way for Eastern Europe to free itself from Russian military occupation except for us to occupy them with our ideas.'[33] And the idea, of course, was the notion of 'living in truth', the politics of parrhesia.

For Havel, the attempt to seek power in the state was a diversion from more important tasks, while Michnik sought to ground resistance politics precisely on society. Konrád insisted that 'Centralised political authority is one pole; decentralised spiritual authority is the other.'[34] Konrád, however, was mistaken when he argued that 'Autonomy's slow evolution does not culminate in new people sitting down in the panelled offices of authority',[35] and when power, as it were, fell into the laps of the 'autonomists' in 1989 they lacked a language of institutional politics to cope with it. They did, however, have a strong moral grounding. Anti-politics was concerned with what can be called the 'remoralisation' of politics, a view that considers the division between left and right at worst an anachronism and at best an irrelevance, and in which the old struggle between capitalism and socialism is a mark of a bygone age. In other words, the notion of anti-politics heralded the anti-revolution.

The 'anti-political' style of the struggle of civil society against the Communist state marginalised the role of institutionalised political leadership. Revolutionary movements of the Leninist sort played absolutely no part in the overthrow of the Communist systems – and, it might be recalled, they had contributed little to the overthrow of Tsarism in February 1917. While the absence of organised leadership in the popular revolutions of the late 1980s is not a new phenomenon, the explicit nature of the politics of the self-organisation of civil society can be explained less by theories of spontaneity (against, in particular, Lenin's idea of revolutionary consciousness) but reflected the inherently normative character of these anti-revolutions. The 'self-limiting' nature of these revolutions reflected obvious tactical considerations, but their 'gentleness' was more than incidental but intrinsic to the very model of transformation to which they aspired.[36]

The shift in the subject of the revolution was accompanied by a renewed emphasis on Tocquevillian themes, the primacy of culture over socially determined modalities of political action – and indeed, the relativisation of directed political action. Contrary to Marx (in Ash's words), 'consciousness ultimately determines being...the key to the future lies not in the external, objective condition of states – political, military, economic, technological – but in the internal subjective condition of individuals'.[37] Ethics and morality, 'living by truth' and rejecting the lie, act as potent weapons against the party-state. The new culturalism, however, has not gone unchallenged, and Skocpol insists that 'anthropological ideas about cultural systems' are full of pitfalls in complex stratified societies.[38]

Post-communism is post-modern in the sense that it returns to traditions truncated by the triumph of modernity from the late eighteenth century. The link forged in the furnace of the industrial revolution between social conditions and social classes and mass political action has been broken, and now once again 'postmaterialist' (or more accurately, 'pre-materialist') values come to the fore. The cultural logic of political action in new social movements from the West complements the anti-revolutionary revolutions from the East. The new humanism appeals to universal values, most evident in the writings of Havel, rather than to class-based or partial values. The anti-revolutionaries of the new social movements and anti-communism appeal to the autonomy of civil society, the autonomy of the subject and to the role of morality in politics.

These were anti-revolutions in yet another sense. In the past those who opposed revolutions were called 'counter-revolutionaries', a term coined by Condorcet[39] and applied by the Bolsheviks to define their opponents in their own terms. The revolution was everything and everything was conducted within its frame of reference. The concept of revolution itself, in other words, in the French and Russian revolutions became one of the main forms in which the tyranny sustained itself. The events of 1989–91, however, moved beyond the discourse of revolutionary thinking that kept them in thrall, and precisely in this sought freedom. To borrow Joseph de Maistre's distinction, the rejection of revolutionary socialism was not 'a *contrary revolution*' (a counter-revolution, narrowly defined), but 'the *contrary of revolution*' (opposed to the revolutionary process in its entirety).[40] The former found few takers while the latter triumphed.

Those who opposed the events of 1989–91 were not labelled counter-revolutionaries because that would have legitimated their opposition and conceded precisely the intellectual terrain that the anti-revolutionists sought to free (liberate). It would have meant adopting the language of the system that they sought to transcend (destroy). The avoidance of the traditional militarised lexicon of revolutions (liberate, destroy) also made obvious tactical sense, since, if it came to shooting, the regimes were clearly at an advantage. The exhaustion of revolutionary discourse, moreover, was apparent in the fact that very few defenders of the old regime themselves had the courage to talk in terms of defending the gains of the revolution. The order on which revolutionary socialism was based, as Horvath and Szakolczai point out, had already undergone a long process of internal dissolution even before the events of 1989–91 shouldered it aside.[41]

The revolutions of 1989–91 generated a miserably weak counter-revolutionary movement for the obvious reason that the historical conjuncture that the original socialist revolutions reflected had long since disappeared. The concept of socialist revolution had itself become an irrelevance, and in the absence of a new universal transformatory ideology, the whole concept of revolution fell into decrepitude. The Japanese option of transformation without revolution appears to have triumphed. It is now clear that the absence of revolutionary change in India represented the way of the future rather than China's dramatic (and disastrous) 'leaps' into modernisation.

The anti-revolution, finally, was marked by a distinctive style of politics. This had been prefigured in the rise of Solidarity, symbolised by Lech Walesa's pen. In Gdansk in August 1980 Walesa signed the famous accords, legalising the Solidarity trade union movement and thus breaching the Communist power monopoly, with a monstrously outsize pen. It seemed as if not only was the Communist system for the first time allowing systemic pluralism, but that the very style of politics would forever change, the grey seriousness of the revolutionary project would give way to a more self-mocking 'post-modernist' approach. The 'lightness' of post-Communist politics was reiterated during the August coup in the USSR. Following days of tension, at the meeting of the Russian Parliament on 23 August 1991, after Gorbachev's humiliation, Yeltsin turned to the deputies with an ironic smile and said: 'For some light relief, comrades. Allow me to sign a decree suspending the activities of the Russian Communist Party. (Tumultuous applause growing to an ovation).'[42] And thus 74 years of party rule came to an end, not on the barricades but in the convention hall, not with a gun but with a pen.

The exhaustion of revolutionism

Revolutionary socialism had exhausted itself intellectually even before it expired as a political movement. From Edmund Burke, Joseph de Maistre to Max Weber, Bernstein, Karl Popper and many others, the Enlightenment notion of revolution (and in particular its rebellious offspring, revolutionary socialism) has been accompanied by a sophisticated and explicitly anti-revolutionary ideology. In his *The Protestant Ethic and the 'Spirit' of Capitalism*, for example, Weber criticised the limitations of the 'intellectual tools' of Marxism, and above all condemned the political strategy for modernisation it advanced. In methodological terms, Weber rejected the Marxist hierarchy of determinations in history, and his analysis of the development of bureaucratic paternalism, 'a social order in which maximum regulation, instrumental reason and impersonality had triumphed at the expense of individual responsibility' led him to believe that socialism 'was poised to intensify this system rather than to abolish it'.[43] Rather than representing the cutting edge of modernity, revolutionism as a mode of action and political discourse, in Weber's view, itself became archaic and represented the greatest obstacle to social self-regeneration.

In Russia itself the idea of revolution had taken hold in the nineteenth century, but had provoked an equally strong reaction, and it is in Russia that the myth of revolutionism, the idea that a better society can be built through violence and human will, was most profoundly developed and most profoundly challenged, a combination that allowed opposites to be made equals. Dostoevsky's subtle exposure of the revolutionary Stavrogin in *The Devils* was given an anti-Russian twist by Joseph Conrad in his *Under Western Eyes*. Similarly, Solzhenitsyn's view of Communism as a disease afflicting Russia was countered by Milan Kundera's view that *the disease is Russia*.[44] The end of revolutionism in Russia was prefigured even before the revolution had taken place. The epochal significance of the *Vekhi* (*Landmarks*) collection of essays of 1909 was that for the first time in such a formal manner a group of the Russian intelligentsia, many of whom had been sympathetic to social-

ist aspirations, repudiated both the concept and the content of revolution.[45] A century of Russian political thinking was dramatically
reversed. The critique of revolutionary philosophy and the philosophy
of revolution was developed in the later book with some of the same
authors, *Iz Glubiny* (*De Profondis – From the Depths*) of 1918, where
they reflected on the terrible consequences of the intelligentsia's thirst
for revolution.[46] In that tradition *Iz pod Glyb* (*From under the Rubble*),
published at the height of Brezhnev's stagnation, called for the reassertion of moral values against the incompetent cynicism of a decayed revolutionism.[47]

All modern revolutionary regimes have sooner or later fallen (or been
forced to adapt to the world system that they had originally rejected),
even though most have left a permanent mark on their societies. Why
have all revolutions failed? One reason is that their predominant ideas
have tended to come from abroad, and sooner or later the societies have
rejected them. This is not the case in France, and it is precisely here that
the legacy of the revolution is strongest. Another explanation is that they
have been constrained and ultimately undermined by the international
system. The presence of an alternative, and apparently more successful,
form of social organisation in the West undermined the legitimacy of the
Soviet 'alternative modernity'. These are important factors, but there are
deeper reasons for the universal failure of revolutionary regimes.

The revolutions were not followed by the anticipated *metanoia*, that
change of heart on which a new society could be built, but rather than
the regimes after the delay of the anticipated millennium adapting to the
environment and native traditions,[48] it was precisely the *impossibility* of
adaptation that endowed them with a fundamentally tenuous quality.
The revolutionism at the heart of the post-revolutionary settlement has
meant that they have been unable to create a viable political order
(*Ordnungspolitik*). The absolutism of revolutions gives rise to political
absolutism: not only is politics as a form of social mediation necessarily foreclosed but the lack of reciprocity between state and society condemned these regimes to the endless manoeuvres of 'stability politics'.[49]
The revolutionary regime could not escape from its own contradictions,
and the ideology and organisation that had once served as its sharpest
swords now fused to form an iron cage locking it for ever, not quite as
Gertrude Schroeder put it, on 'the treadmill of reform',[50] but in the air-
less antechamber of pseudo-reforms.

Oleg Rumyantsev noted that 'revolutionism is a tragic legacy for
twentieth-century Russia'; derived from Lenin and developed by Stalin,
Bolshevik revolutionism foreclosed the possibility of reforms, and

indeed 'reformism', a theory of moral limitations, became a dirty word.[51] Colburn notes that revolutions, like nationalism, have a weakly developed ethical–philosophical dimension.[52] Whereas wars are regulated by certain rules of engagement and conduct, these are lacking in civil wars, of which revolutions are the sharpest expression. The moral absolutism of revolutions – like the primordial rights often associated with a particular nation – is reinforced by analyses that focus on deterministic or structural theories that underrate the moral constraints of the human agency that makes the revolution. The appeal to historical necessity and the ultimate benefit of the revolutionary process to the mass of the people negate the value of the individual human being. Traditional class-based analyses of revolutionary action have neglected the political–ethical context of the human agency at the heart of the revolutionary process. In the anti-revolution Enlightenment revolutionism gave way to a new humanism marked by the return of neo-Kantian principles.

The revolutions of 1989–91 put an end to the age inaugurated by Marx's *Economic and Philosophical Manuscripts* of 1844, which tied the idea of revolution to the notion of the liberation of a class. The Marxist revolution was thus inalienably associated with 'civil war', not necessarily taking a violent form but dominated by the logic of a society riven by conflict and characterised by a shifting war of position between two great forces in which politics was no more than instrumental. The domestic roots of the 'cold war' should thus be stressed, a cold war in which the domestic protagonists were allegedly locked into a battle until the end of history. All this was swept away in 1989, together with the ideology of civil war and its concomitant Cold War played out on the larger stage. Revolutionary socialism had exhausted itself and with it, almost as an afterthought, the Leninist party. In a peculiar inversion of Marx, the end of the socialist revolution put an end to all talk of revolution.[53]

In an interview in 1994 Alexander Yakovlev, the driving force behind the theoretical innovations of *perestroika*, examined the ideological basis of the insurgent movement in 1990–1 and noted that 'The stage announced by the revolution of 1991 has not produced a single new idea.'[54] François Furet,[55] Habermas and others have elaborated the argument that the 1989 revolutions offered no future-oriented or theoretical innovations beyond the attempt to implement the agenda of the French Revolution and to impose the given order of the West. A whole raft of literature puts forward variations on the theme of the unoriginal and negative nature of the 1989–91 revolutions. Leslie Holmes calls them the *double rejective revolution*, rejecting both the Communist power system and what was seen as external domination.[56] Neil Ascherson describes 1989 in Eastern Europe in terms of 'constitutional representative democracy as a "return to normality" ',[57] and Misha Glenny talked in terms of the 'return of history'.[58] But these revolutions were not only restorative, rejective or returning, but mimetic, fighting again the battles that were long ago won elsewhere, and at the same time emulating revolution to defeat revolution. The anti-revolutions share one component with the classical 'great revolutions', the breakdown of regimes, but they lack the other, a universal utopian vision borne by special groups.

Lenin argued that without a revolutionary theory there cannot be a revolution and the events of 1989–91 proved him right, with the paradoxical twist that their main originality lay precisely in the anti-revolutionary philosophy designed to subvert the notion of revolution itself. These revolutions might not have had utopias of their own, but this itself marked a break with the age inaugurated by millenarian peasant revolts and Enlightenment revolutionism. These were not simply restorative revolutions, since other than in a purely symbolic sense there was little of the pre-Communist order left to restore, but normative remoralising movements. These had a strong agenda of their own focused (not always compatibly) on the themes of liberalism, democracy, nationality *and* anti-revolution. While the anti-revolutions might not have generated much that was original, they demonstrated that precisely those elements that were original in revolutionary socialism were unviable. Whereas the bourgeois revolution dealt with the real, the revolutionary socialist revolution dealt with the ideal.[59] The Bolshevik Revolution offered little, if anything, that was new *and* sustainable. Thus it fell to the anti-revolutions to fulfil the salutary if unexciting job of returning the social philosophies of these countries to something approaching normality. This was hardly likely to move the masses, but it was hardly likely to kill them either.

The anti-Communist revolution might not have had ideals of its own to realise but it relegitimated the ideals of others, above all the moral critique of politics. Ferenc Fehér noted the important new features of the 'gentle revolutions' (otherwise called 'velvet revolutions'), including 'limitations on violence, the concern for civil society, and, especially, a new leisurely rather than accelerated consciousness of time', and Arato stresses 'the rejection of utopian narratives and the hubris of making history after an absolute break from a unified, self-conscious point of view'.[60] The revolutions of 1989–91 represented the end of the whole revolutionary epoch since the eighteenth century, the end of revolution as a way of achieving social and political change, and in particular the end of the Jacobin tradition of subordinating the individual to overriding social purposes. The typical dramatics associated with the 'great' revolutions were absent, with the cast of 'friend' and 'enemy' replaced by an inclusive concept of everyone as victor, *sans* political trials, revolutionary tribunals, expropriations and civil war.

Possibly the closest analogy would be the February (bourgeois) Revolution of 1917 in Russia.[61] Here, too, popular mobilisation took the form of unified and good-natured crowds, and the role of political parties, retribution and organised force was minimal. An enormous constitutional break took place within the framework of attempts to maintain constitutional continuity and the sanctity of human life. In certain respects February was far more revolutionary than October, inverting pyramids of authority and subverting traditional values. Like the anti-revolutions of 1989–91, political reconstitution would no doubt have been followed by profound social changes and economic reorganisation, but the social revolution as such lacked political form in early 1917 as in 1989–91. The problem, of course, with February was that this was a bifurcated revolution, in which the nineteenth-century revolutionary tradition became a material force in its own right, and whose only achievement was to delay the implementation of February's programme by 74 years.[62] The crisis of the Russian state that provoked the February Revolution, however, is not yet over, but the search for solutions has returned to the themes of February rather than October, the revolution of democratic secularisation against the quasi-religious nostrums of Marxism-Leninism.

The fall of the old regime in August 1991 was marked by a genuine national consensus which relegitimated the Russian government and the democratic project as a whole. This was far more than the 'euphoria' of victory, a term used by sceptics to trivialise and denigrate the genuinely popular and revolutionary nature of the events of August 1991.[63] The divisions of Russia's revolutionary epoch began to be healed. Above all, the bridging of the gulf between the intelligentsia and the government meant that in August 1991 for the first time in over a century the intelligentsia felt that it was defending *their* government in the White House. The division between the intelligentsia and the workers was also undermined as sectarian class politics gave way for a time to a new definition of the national interest. The coup opened the door to political modernity, which in contemporary political science is usually associated with liberal democracy and pluralistic politics. There may well be other forms of political modernity, perhaps taking the more authoritarian forms of some of the Asian societies, but Francis Fukuyama, for example, would argue that these are only transitional societies not yet having reached the end point of history, namely liberal democracy.[64]

The anti-revolution represented numerous repudiations. The anti-revolution took up the tradition of the Right Hegelians, with their respect for the state as the supreme integrative and universalising moment in a society fractured by civil society and the family. The Marxist view that the state is no more than an instrument of class rule was rejected and class politics itself was to a degree delegitimated. Class theory, indeed, in Eastern Europe returned to where Vico and others had left it before Marx and the Left Hegelians took it up. The emphasis now is on the separation of powers, and the whole liberal view of the necessity of maintaining and restraining the state within the framework of law. The anti-revolution is marked by the politics of retreat, including the decolonisation of the state by invasive Leninist power structures. The triumph of the Scottish Enlightenment view of the state as a civil association against the (Marxist) view of the state as the provider of substantive political goods returns us to the problems of an earlier age.[65] Much of this, indeed, is reminiscent of early modern Europe and the rise of liberalism, and the similarity is deliberate. These were mimetic revolutions, mimicking the struggles of liberalism in an earlier age. The anti-revolutions rebutted the view that there is meaning and logic to history, and thus while history might have returned it did so with a small 'h'.

Problems of anti-revolutionary order

The central paradox of the anti-revolutions of 1989–91 is that at the very time that they were repudiating the very notion of Enlightenment revolutionism, they were themselves perhaps involved in one of the most profound revolutionary experiences of the twentieth century. Leonid Gordon has argued persuasively that Russia was indeed engaged in a revolutionary process;[66] and many others have noted that the very logic of Yeltsin's insurgency against the old regime was itself a type of anti-Bolshevik neo-Bolshevism.[67] The logic of this revolution, however, was societal self-organisation, the reconstitution of civil society, or, to put it in more traditional terms, a liberal if not quite yet a democratic transformation. All the great modern revolutions, in France, Russia and China, led to the ultimate demobilisation of the masses (or their instrumental and subaltern mobilisation at the behest of the revolutionary leadership, albeit with elements of autonomous participation), whereas the anti-revolution precisely sought to achieve the creation of an autonomous civil society.

An independent civil society, however, is not necessarily synonymous with democracy, as post-Communist societies are today discovering to their cost, and indeed civil society can in certain circumstances (and not only from a Marxist perspective) be counterposed to democracy. Modernist themes like justice, equality and sovereignty are in danger of being thrown out with the bathwater of revolution. The anti-politics of civil society, moreover, has clear dangers, above all in the lack of responsibility of the new elites in power over the mass movement. In Poland, the country that had taken the revolution of civil society to the extreme, the Solidarity leadership in the years of persecution in the 1980s lost contact with its trade union membership, and once in power after 1989 pursued policies that were diametrically opposed to those it had espoused as part of the insurgent movement in 1980–1, the goals of a self-managing society. Thus the very logic of the anti-revolution, based on the autonomy of society, undermined the bases on which a post-revolutionary political community could be built and was profoundly subversive not only of the Communist state, but of governance in its entirety.

The triumph of the anti-revolution over Enlightenment revolutionism gives way to new challenges focused on the revolt against modernity and modernisation. In developed societies the environmental critique of modernity is allied with a variety of new social movements campaigning for the radical revival of civil society. In countries on the threshold of full-scale modernity (a position in which Russia now finds itself) there have been revolts in defence of culture and traditions. The archetypal case is the Iranian Revolution. As Foucault put it: 'I felt then that I understood that recent events did not represent a withdrawal of the most outmoded groups before a modernisation that is too brutal. It was, rather, the rejection by an entire culture, an entire people, of a modernisation that is an archaism in itself.'[68]

Russia might at last achieve the modernisation (i.e. Westernisation) that it has sought since Peter the Great's time but, paradox of paradoxes, that very model of civilisation exhibits symptoms of advanced exhaustion. The debate over the civilisational choices facing the country found the opposition advocating Eurasianism and condemning *mondialism*, and in general seeking a way of avoiding the 'necessary' repetition of the Western experience, with all of its dead ends. Much of this is couched in terms of the conservative rejection of the Enlightenment tradition, one of whose fruits was the concept of revolution itself. Thus the rejection of that most typical feature of the Enlightenment, revolution-ism and the belief in the perfectibility of human society, is accompanied by an assault on other features of the Enlightenment tradition. While 1991 saw the end of one revolution in Russia, the completion (philo-sophically) of the revolution of modernisation, it might signal the begin-ning of another, the revolution of archaisation, designed no longer to destroy tradition but to restore it.

Russia sought to join the mainstream of modernity at time when that mainstream itself entered a period of profound crisis, partially as a result of the triumph of the anti-revolutions themselves. The end of utopia, paradoxically, did not lead to the complementary decline in dystopias but in fact our *fin de siècle* is accompanied by a peculiar proliferation of the genre. The collapse of revolutionary theory and the theory of revo-lution provoked a profound debate over the nature of contemporary modernity, and indeed, the denial of revolutionism as a form of political change and action is central to the whole notion of post-modernism. The Enlightenment gave birth to 'the concept of revolution as conscious human action',[69] but the heightened awareness of the limits to the per-fectibility of human society and the dangers of grandiose social engi-neering gave rise to a widespread political timidity.

The death of the universally rational and the triumph of unfettered individualism give rise, according to our latter dystopians, not to politi-cal equality between citizens but to the *equality of opinion*. Fukuyama's reworking of Nietzsche's 'browsing cattle' theme in the prologue to *Also Sprach Zarathustra*[70] is termed *doxophilia* by Eric Voegelin, the empire of 'opinion', contrasted to *episteme*, true belief or knowledge. As Tamás puts it, 'if mind is not capable of being a vehicle for universal rational-ity, and if nature is nothing but a rag-bag of "cultural constructs", who can have the presumption to refute, neglect, or marginalise any opinion which is always, after all, a genuine expression of someone?'[71] Thus the anti-revolution and its associated anti-politics are redefined as some-thing detrimental to the very basis of political community.

Today we no longer have revolution but we still have crisis; but now a crisis no longer born out of a belief in progress but by its absence. The very language we use to describe politics, the language of political analysis and the terms used to describe political concepts, are buckling under the enormous pressures generated by the anti-revolution. Many have noted the theatricality of post-Communist Russian politics, and use the writings of Yurii Lottman and Bakhtin to describe the Bacchanalian and Dionysian features. Russian politics appears a badly scripted play with enormously tragic figures striding across the stage, marked by rhetorical devices (e.g. for democracy) and characters moving into the limelight and then back into the shade. Elsewhere, too, the price to be paid for the end of communism has been noted by the philosopher Bernard-Henri Lévy: 'In France, politics has always been defined by the Revolution. If the Revolution ceases to be desirable, then so does politics. Perhaps what we are witnessing now is the death of politics.'[72] The revolution might have ended, but a 'disenchanted' order takes its place in which the unpredictable and multiple consequences of political intervention paralyse conscious political mobilisation. As Peter Wagner puts it, 'the space from which such an intervention could be undertaken, previously held by the state, is seen as non-existent and empty'.[73]

We need to go back to Greek thinking and the origins of politics in tragedy and the theatre to understand this. We can perhaps better understand the political processes in the modern world by using the concept of revolution less and rethinking the notion of *krisis*.[74] For the Greeks *krisis* meant a decisive state of reappraisal, a moment of reflection, doubt and retrospective assessment which takes place periodically in the life of the city. While revolution represents the imposition of new certainties, *krisis* is the application of individual and collective consciences to challenge the malaise and enfeeblement of moral and communal life. Rather than the utopian or millenarian search for the source of renewal from outside the society or in the invocation of a new set of nostrums from new prophets, *krisis* is the alternative to revolution, a questioning of fundamental meanings and a form of social mobilisation in support of the renewal of the political bases of community. In other words, once the anti-revolution has completed its work permanent revolution gives way to state of permanent *krisis*, constant renewal takes the place of revolution. This is the meaning of the anti-revolution, and why the anti-revolution philosophically puts an end to a whole epoch of morally blind revolutionary absolutism that was so destructive of the rudiments of political association. Of course, the failure to adapt to the constant political reformism implicit in a theory of *krisis* may well provoke a new age of revolutions.

10.   The Revolutionary Idea in the Twentieth-Century World

KRISHAN KUMAR

1789 and 1989/1991

In July 1989, as tourists poured into Paris for the celebration of the bicentenary of the fall of the Bastille, Parisians were to be observed setting off in droves for their country retreats. As had become increasingly clear in the preceding months, the French were disenchanted with 1789, bored with the very idea of revolution.[1] In this they reflected the scholarly consensus that had built up steadily over the post-1968 years in the West. It was shown in the triumph of the 'revisionist' historiography of the French Revolution, illustrated in the characteristically engaging – and *engagé* – remark of Richard Cobb that 'the French Revolution should never have happened, possibly never did happen, and in any case had no effect one way or the other on most people's lives'.[2] It was shown in the general disparagement of revolution as a mode of transformation, the view that if revolutions had indeed once been, as Marx put it, the locomotives of history, 'in our industrial (or "post-industrial") age, the locomotive has become an outdated means of historical transport'.[3]

Elsewhere things suddenly looked very different. In the very months that Western disillusionment with revolution was expressing itself in this sour attitude towards the bicentenary of the French Revolution, the idea of revolution was reborn in Eastern Europe. Between June and August 1989, the Polish workers' movement Solidarity emerged after years of repression to take over the reins of power. It was the signal for revolution throughout Central and Eastern Europe, eventually reaching the Soviet Union itself and bringing about its collapse in the last days of

1991. Revolution, apparently buried in Western Europe, had achieved a remarkable resuscitation in the East.[4]

But was what occurred in Eastern Europe in 1989 'revolution'? And if so, how does it connect up with the Western revolutionary idea? Does it, as some have claimed, renew it, give it a new lease of life at a time when it appeared to have become moribund, at least in Europe? Or does it in some sense mark the end of revolution? Does it confirm a widely expressed view that the revolutionary tradition, as that has been understood in Europe, is played out?

We shall return to these questions at the end of this discussion. What we must examine first is the fate of the revolutionary idea, in Europe and the world at large, as it left behind the experiences of the eighteenth and nineteenth centuries that had given it its characteristic form and meaning.

From Theory to Technique

'1789 and 1917 are still historic dates, but they are no longer historic examples.' Albert Camus, contemplating the idea of revolution amidst the ruins of Europe in 1946, concluded that the classic concepts would no longer do. National revolutions, on the French or Russian model, were now out. The rise of the superpowers, the USA and the Soviet Union, had so transformed the conditions of revolution that the only kind of revolution worth serious discussion was world revolution. But that world revolution would bear little resemblance to the old Trotskyite dream of an international revolution brought about 'by the conjunction or the synchronisation of a number of national revolutions; a kind of totting up of miracles'. Stalin was the greater realist. World revolution, if it ever were to occur, must now mean a revolution carried on the bayonets of foreign armies across the world. It would begin with a military occupation, or the threat of one, and would become significant 'only when the occupying power has conquered the rest of the world'.[5]

It has indeed been said that 'all revolutions start in principle as world revolution', that they all aspire to universalise their aims and symbols.[6] No one can doubt this of the two classic examples cited by Camus, the French Revolution of 1789 and the Russian Revolution of 1917. No less do they exhibit the characteristics of the 'international civil war' that Sigmund Neumann, writing about the same time as Camus, noted as the hallmark of the wars and revolutions of the twentieth century.[7] The appeal to general principles of humanity and society, the summons to the oppressed groups of every nation, foreign intervention and international war: all of these can be seen as much in the French and Russian cases as in any later instances of revolution, such as the Chinese and Vietnamese revolutions.

So there are continuities as well as discontinuities between the past and present of revolution. The Russian Revolution probably illustrates this best. In its theory it looked back to the reflections of Marxists and others on the European revolutions of the seventeenth to the nineteenth centuries. In its practice – in the conditions of society that made it, in the nature of the forces that contended for mastery, in the organisational forms that emerged from it – it looked forward to the 'Third World' revolutions of the twentieth century (though, it must be said, Mexico in 1910 and China in 1911 had already partly inaugurated the pattern of Third World revolutions).[8]

But Camus was surely right to feel that as the century progressed the divide between the old and the new style of revolution had grown. The international dimension, always present to some degree in past revolutions, had swollen to unprecedented proportions.[9] It had proved to be so as much in the Spanish Civil War as in Central and Eastern Europe after the Second World War. It was clear in China, where Mao led the Communist forces to victory largely through conducting a nationalist struggle against the Japanese, and where his main opponent, the Kuomintang, subsisted on American arms. It was clearer still in Vietnam, Algeria and Cuba, where the attitudes and actions – or inaction – of the major international powers were critical to the outcomes of the internal conflicts in those countries. And in case anyone had forgotten the lesson of the Spanish Civil War, and thought external intervention a purely non-European phenomenon, the international factor showed its continuing force in largely determining the course of the Portuguese Revolution of 1974, and in conditioning both the outbreak and the outcome of the revolutions of 1989 in East-Central Europe.[10]

If the balance of forces on the international plane entered as a decisive element in revolutionary fortunes, the change in the relative strengths of the contending parties within the state was scarcely less significant. This was possibly of greater relevance in the advanced industrial societies, though by no means negligible in the less developed ones. Already in his 1895 Preface to Marx's *Class Struggles in France*, Engels had drawn attention to the great growth in the military power of the modern state. Revolutionaries were increasingly disadvantaged in the struggle for state power. Rebellion in the old style, Engels concluded, with street fighting and barricades, had progressively become obsolete since 1848.[11] The fate of urban insurrections in this century has proved him right. 'The city', as Fidel Castro correctly observed from Latin American experience, 'is a cemetery of revolutionaries and resources.' Without peasant support, without the prior weakening or destruction of state power in international war, all purely urban insurrections have failed. And since Engels wrote, practically every new development in weapons technology and in systems of communication has benefited the government at the expense of insurgents.[12]

One consequence of this situation has been the retreat from theory to technique. The classics of nineteenth-century revolutionary theory – de Tocqueville's study of 1789, Marx's writings on 1848 and 1871 – concerned themselves with the long-term causes of revolution, and with the prospects for revolution in changing social circumstances. Their framework was the evolution of whole societies in historical time. They were genuine sociologies of revolution. The twentieth-century classics of revolution have reflected an obsession with the techniques for making revolution. 'How to Make a Revolution' might adequately sum up their burden. The existence of revolutionary forces, and of revolutionary situations, has been taken for granted, disastrously in many cases. All states, it was assumed, could be overthrown, given the necessary will and preparation. The revolutionary, said André Malraux, 'doesn't have to define the revolution, but to make it'. Or as Régis Debray put it: 'A political line which, in terms of its consequences, is not susceptible to expression as a precise and consistent military line, cannot be considered revolutionary.'[13] The outstanding successes of post-1917 revolutionism, China and Cuba, stood, it was felt, as witnesses to this.

Revolutionary thinkers consequently devoted themselves to the strategy and techniques for seizing state power. The formidable power of the modern state apparatus was acknowledged; all the more important then to analyse it, to find its possible weaknesses for exploitation by revolutionaries. Starting with some of the Comintern publications of the 1920s, the texts produced by twentieth-century theorists of revolution increasingly came to mirror the professional military manuals of their opponents. Revolution took from counter-revolution the view that military success was the overriding consideration; revolutionary thinking was converted into thinking about war. In the writings of Mao, Clap, Guevara and Debray the modern techniques of counter-insurgency were coolly scrutinised and answered point by point. In producing counter-strategies for revolution, a military understanding seemed more important than an understanding of the society in which revolution was plotted. Worked out largely in relation to the conditions of Third World societies, and having some relevance there, such thinking took on overtones of fantasy when transplanted to the cities of the industrial world.[14]

New contexts imply – though they do not always necessarily get – new concepts. Several students have complained of the excessive dominance of the French and Russian cases in our approach to twentieth-century revolutions.[15] The changing conditions of revolutionary action, in the West and the wider world, have forced modifications in the traditional conceptions of revolution. It is not clear that anything new has taken their place, or even that it could or should. Post-modernists would wish to consign revolution to the dustbin of modernist ideas, along with truth and progress. Others, for different reasons, may also feel that revolution has had its time, that it no longer connotes any species of meaningful action. Before assessing that radical conclusion, we need to consider some of the attempts that have been made to redeem the concept of revolution.

Utopia and revolution

If, as many have held, ours is 'the century of revolution', this can have little to do with the West. Revolution, as a concept and a practice, is a Western invention. The concept, as so often, has taken on a career of its own. Like cricket or the English language, it is no longer under the control of its creators. The practice, though, has to date largely been absent from twentieth-century Western industrial societies. Not only has there not occurred the proletarian revolution hoped for and expected by Marx; there have been remarkably few revolutionary attempts of any kind.[16] The 1989 and 1991 revolutions in East-Central Europe and the USSR may constitute an exception but, as we shall see, it is by no means clear that they mark a departure from this general picture.

The dearth of revolutionary experience in the recent history of the West has, in a familiar pattern, accompanied and perhaps caused a conceptual inflation. As Western society, for the bulk of its population, forgets its revolutionary origins, its intellectuals have increasingly distilled some of their deepest longings into revolution. No longer merely a change in the political system, or even the social system, revolution comes to mean the transformation of humanity at its core.

This utopian conception of revolution was also present in the early Marx, of course, and in certain other nineteenth-century thinkers, such as Fourier.[17] But it did not predominate in societies which lived with the fact of revolution as a regular occurrence and an ever-present possibility. Revolution, a concept taken from astronomy and applied to society in the seventeenth century, had until the mid-nineteenth century a preeminently political meaning. This was, for all the secondary undercurrents, the main legacy of the English, American and French revolutions. The slogan of the French Revolution, 'Liberty, Equality, Fraternity', more or less adequately summed up the political goals. Variously interpreted these could take on utopian dimensions; but for most revolutionaries the historic examples of England, America and France suggested achievable ends and something of the institutional means towards them.

In 1848, as both Marx and de Tocqueville observed, the 'social question' raised its urgent voice. To the 'national' or political revolution of the earlier tradition was now added the demand for a social revolution. After the further experience of the Paris Commune of 1871, and the official adoption by the Third Republic of the 1789 Revolution as its founding event, the call intensified. The 'Internationale', the anthem of the workers' revolution, challenged the 'Marseillaise', the battle-cry of the bourgeoisie. Marxists and anarchists warred over the precise form of the future socialist society; nihilists and populists added a new fervour to the debate. All agreed with Marx on the insufficiency of the 'partial, *merely* political revolution' that left 'the pillars of the building standing'.[18]

But up to and including the Russian Revolution of 1917, revolution remained primarily within the mould of the French Revolution of 1789, the 'model' revolution for the nineteenth century. When the Second International was founded in Paris in the centennial year 1889, the founders were fully conscious of the homage they paid both to the date and the place. The new revolution would obviously have to go beyond the aims and accomplishments of that quintessentially 'bourgeois' revolution, but it was accepted that the French Revolution still remained the cardinal point of reference. All revolutions aspired to imitate it, even as they hoped to go beyond it. 'A Frenchman', said Lenin in 1920, 'has nothing to renounce in the Russian Revolution, which in its method and procedures recommences the French Revolution.'[19]

It is the primacy of the French Revolution, as the model revolution, that has come under attack in the twentieth century. The Russian Revolution did not so much displace the French – at least in the West – as add to the doubts surrounding it. It did so not by deviating from the model but by what appeared to be its almost slavish imitation of it. In doing so – and doing so, moreover, with a success and a thoroughness that had evaded its great predecessor – it brought out with disconcerting clarity the elements of the model that had alarmed not just counter-revolutionaries but, increasingly, the friends of revolution.

The outcome of the Russian Revolution – the suppression of the soviets, one-party rule, state socialism – threw into question all the principal features of the classic French model of revolution. No longer could one take for granted, as the necessary and desirable elements of all revolution, the revolutionary party, the seizure of power, 'revolutionary terror', and the use of centralised state power to transform society. Trotsky's reflections on 'the Soviet Thermidor' crystallised for many Western Marxists their reservations about the Russian Revolution as the new model form.[20] Henceforth revolution must mean, over and above the question of gaining power, a concern with matters of democracy, ethics, education and culture. The Bolsheviks and their allies had debated these things; in the event their revolution denied them.[21]

Gramsci's and Luxemburg's prison writings, and those of Trotsky in exile, became the source of a comprehensive rethinking of the concept of revolution among Western Marxists. The relationship of intellectuals to the revolutionary party, and of the party to its mass following, were re-examined with an eye to avoiding the Russian precedent. The 'incorporation' of the working class into bourgeois society, and the possible means of extricating it, were the subject of intense debate: here it was the Frankfurt School of 'critical theory' that set the terms.[22] Hungary in 1956, Czechoslovakia in 1968 and Poland in 1980 added fresh material for reflection. For the New Left of the post-1945 era, revolution emerged as a category in which the political and economic dimensions of past revolutions were overlaid, redefined almost, by cultural aspirations. If an example was sought as a model for this conception, it was not Russia but China and Mao's 'Cultural Revolution'.[23]

But education and culture, the hallmarks of the new concept of revolution, were not enough for some. Or rather, as generally understood, they did not go far enough. This in the end was what in Western eyes disqualified the Chinese and Cuban revolutions, for all their elements of novelty, as true exemplars. There persisted in the minds of many Western radicals the conviction that revolution still concerned itself mainly with external forms. The repeated failure of revolutions to realise their promise was attributed to their indifference to the human material that carried through the revolution. Regarded alternately as cannon fodder for the revolution and as the readily re-educated citizens of the new society, the human masses went through the revolution carrying most of the baggage of their unreconstructed past with them. The political and economic forms changed; 'human nature' remained the same.

Oppression and submission persisted, perhaps literally, in the minds and bodies of men. Hence the common fate of all revolutions hitherto. Conceived in freedom, they ended by restoring despotism. The revolutionary cycle from freedom to despotism seemed a mocking echo of the original astronomical meaning of the term. Like the revolutions of the heavens, human revolutions seemed destined to go through unvarying cycles that would always bring them back to their starting point. So they would, as long as human needs and desires remained mired in their pre-revolutionary past.

Reflection on this phenomenon drove many intellectuals away from revolution altogether. Revolution, along with the communism with which it has been associated for much of this century, was the god that had failed. Others, however, were inspired by the early Marx and 'utopian socialists' such as Fourier to rethink the concept of revolution along the lines of what Aldous Huxley called 'the really revolutionary revolution: the revolution in the souls and bodies of human beings'.[24] The ultimately revolutionary programme of the Marquis de Sade, to reconstruct bodily desire, was here recalled; so too the aesthetic and sensuous utopia of William Morris. The Surrealists' exploration of the unconscious, and their emphasis on spontaneity, supplied another building block. Above all there was Freud, as purged of his conservative philosophy by 'Freudo-Marxists' such as Wilhelm Reich and Herbert Marcuse.

Freud's importance lay in pointing to the 'instincts' as the crucial stumbling block to revolutionary designs. He threw down the ultimate challenge: selfishness, aggression and war were inherent in the biological nature of humans. Revolution could no more change that than it could change the colour of their skins. In seeking to show that that was not so, that acquisitiveness and aggression were the products of historically formed social systems, the Freudo-Marxists aimed to strengthen the concept of revolution at its most vulnerable point. They accepted the importance of the 'instincts'; no revolution could succeed that ignored their power. The limited achievements of past revolutions were a testimony to this. But the energy of the instincts was not, as Freud had thought, for ever frozen in anti-social drives. It could be harnessed and redirected to serve revolutionary ends. Pleasure, the principle of sex, could (and should) become the principle of work and politics as well. Eros could conquer Thanatos.[25]

The common theme in the new Western concept of revolution was the insistence that revolution, if it were to be successful, must ultimately work at the level of everyday life. Revolution must come down from the high thrones of politics and economics and enter the humble abode of the family, the home, and the sexual and emotional lives of individuals. It must transform not just the political and economic realms but the 'biological' and 'instinctual' need structures of individuals. It must acknowledge the importance of the beautiful. Work and leisure must be given the character of artistic creativity and enjoyment; society itself must be regarded as a work of art.

Many of these themes came together riotously in the French 'May Events' of 1968, especially as expressed in the thinking and practice of the group of radicals known as the Situationist International. The Situationist graffiti and manifestos proclaimed a conception of revolution that made it synonymous with a total change in the human and social order. 'Be realists – demand the impossible.' 'All power to the imagination.' 'It is forbidden to forbid.' 'Those who speak of revolution and class struggle', wrote one of the leading Situationists, Raoul Vaneigem, 'without referring explicitly to daily life, without understanding the subversive element in sex and the positive element in the rejection of constraints, have a corpse in their mouths.'[26] The variety of influences in this concept of revolution is sufficiently indicated by the titles of some of the action committees that sprang up in Paris in these weeks: 'the Freud-Che Guevara Action Committee', 'the Committee of Permanent Creation', the 'Comité Révolutionnaire d'Agitation Sursexuelle'.[27]

The boundary between revolution and utopia, precariously enough maintained even in the nineteenth century, here fairly obviously dissolves. This does not mean that utopian conceptions of revolution, any more than utopianism in general, are worthless. But it does raise acutely the question of how such a revolution will or can occur. The students in Paris appeared to act at times as if they felt the state could simply be ignored, its power bypassed as being of no moment. They learned that while they might ignore the state, it had no wish to ignore them. It is not even clear how seriously revolution was contemplated or hoped for in these months. More important seemed to be to raise the standard of a different kind of revolution from the past – to put down a marker, as it were, for future revolutions.[28] But this does little to clarify the question of future forms of revolutionary action. As Leszek Kolakowski said shortly after the events, we know reasonably well what people mean to do when they say 'we want land' or shout 'down with the tyrant'. 'But supposing they were to shout, "Down with alienation?"' Where does one find the palace of Alienation and how does one destroy it?'[29]

There is another problem with what we might call the 'totalistic' concept of revolution, revolution as total transformation of the individual and society.[30] Past revolutions provided, both for themselves and future imitators, a distinctive imagery and iconography of revolution. Delacroix's *Liberty Guiding the People*, with its symbolism of the barricade, supplied a powerful myth of revolution for the national and bourgeois revolutions of the nineteenth century.[31] The storming of the Winter Palace in Eisenstein's film *October*, and posters such as El Lissitsky's *Beat the Whites with the Red Wedge*, played a similar role in the iconography of the proletarian revolution.[32] What are the icons of the totalistic concept of revolution, the revolution against alienation? Since there are no actual revolutions of this kind to give rise to them, not surprisingly they are hard to find. The elements that lie to hand – Situationist posters from 1968, some of Jean-Luc Godard's 'Maoist' films of the 1960s, such as *La Chinoise*, the sexual politics of Dusan Makavejev's *WR: Mysteries of the Organism* – are mostly couched in a mocking or ironic vein, lacking the full-blooded commitment necessary to the achievement of iconic status. The lack of any convincing image of the future revolution is not the least of the problems surrounding the concept of revolution in the West.

Salvation by the Third World?

If the advanced industrial West failed to provide any clear instance of revolution in the twentieth century, a failure that was reflected in an increasingly desperate search for a new and more inclusive concept, this manifestly does not apply to the societies of the undeveloped 'Third World'. The theoretical works dealing with twentieth-century revolutions give us a rich variety of cases to contemplate; almost all of them are from the Third World. Among them we might list Mexico in 1910, China in 1911 and again in 1949, Vietnam in 1945, Algeria in 1954, Cuba in 1959, Iran and Nicaragua in 1979. This is a woefully incomplete list. Fred Halliday has said that 'if we look at the 120 or so countries of the Third World, up to two dozen of them can be said to have had social revolutions...since the end of the Second World War'.[33] Moreover there are disputes about the dates, about the classification 'Third World' and about the very designation of 'revolution' as applied to all of these. Nevertheless, putting this aside, there can be no doubt that if ours is indeed the century of revolution, this can have little to do with Europe or the West and almost everything to do with non-Western or Third World societies.

This might make a discussion of these revolutions in a volume of this sort seem out of place. Nothing could be more mistaken. In the twentieth century, to a greater degree than ever before, all revolutions are world revolutions. This applies as much to the rare instances of revolution in Europe – such as the Portuguese Revolution of 1974, stimulated by the anti-colonial struggles in Angola and Mozambique – as to revolutions outside it, where the participation of European or North American powers is only too clear (as in Algeria or Nicaragua). Revolution in the twentieth-century world is a matter of global politics. Influences flow reciprocally from the centre to the periphery and back again.

But it seems unnecessary to labour the point. The link between revolutions in the Third World and the European or Western revolutionary tradition is plain for all to see. The West supplied the revolutionary conditions, in the form of colonialism and world war. It also supplied the revolutionary theory. What after all is Marxism, the legitimating ideology of so many Third World revolutions, but a Western invention? What too of imperialism, democracy, revolution itself – are these not also Western exports that, as concepts and practices, fuelled the revolutionary struggles in the Third World? Most Third World revolutions were led by Western-educated intellectuals – Mao, Ho Chi Minh, Castro. The European revolutionary tradition provided them with the categories through which to see their revolutions, even when they had to engage in some fairly unorthodox interpretations (a lesson already taught by Lenin). When Kwame Nkrumah cried 'seek ye the political kingdom and all the rest shall be added unto you', or when Achmed Sukarno confessed to being 'obsessed by the romanticism of revolution', they were both reflecting the legacy of European revolutionism.[34]

For many Third World revolutionaries the models of revolution inspired by the classic European revolutions remained – unlike the case in Europe itself – highly relevant. In his trial speech after the failure of the assault on the Moncada barracks in 1953, Fidel Castro ransacked the entire European revolutionary tradition in justification of his actions.[35] The French and the Russian revolutions, both in their theory and their practice, remained guiding models for countries which still had to achieve national independence and to establish modern political and economic institutions.

Nevertheless, as with twentieth-century Europe, there has also partly been a revulsion from these models, and what they may connote by way of theory and action. The reasons are also much the same: the models, it is felt, do not go deep enough into the structures of exploitation and oppression. If this is true for groups within European societies, how much more likely is it to be true for groups subjected to entirely alien rule, as have the societies of the Third World.

But in reacting against these European models of revolution, Third World revolutionaries have not for the main part reacted against European thought. Rather they have engaged in the same act of retrieval and reinterpretation attempted by their Western counterparts. They have turned to the very thinkers – Hegel, Nietzsche, Freud, and Marx as seen through the eyes of these – who have been influential in the reformulation of the revolutionary project in the West. This is especially the case with Frantz Fanon, the most important of the theorists of Third World revolution in the recent period.

Fanon, French-trained psychiatrist and supporter of the Algerian Revolution, rejected most of the terms of classic European revolutionism – the class struggle, the leadership of the proletariat, the revolutionary party led by the intelligentsia. However relevant these might still be in Europe, the situation in the Third World was different, and in need of a new kind of understanding. The colonies and ex-colonies had to fight against themselves as much as against their European masters. Their subjugation was by now at least partly self-imposed. The effect of colonial rule was to infect the native populations with a colonialist and racist mentality. Unless they rid themselves of this, national revolution would mean simply a continuation of dependence. The traumas and neuroses engendered by colonialism, the self-hatred and self-estrangement, could be purged only through violence. 'Violence', said Fanon, 'is a cleansing force.' Through collective violence the colonised populations would find themselves; through violence they would liquidate the legacy of colonialism not just in its political and economic but, more importantly, its psychological manifestations. In his Preface to Fanon's *The Wretched of the Earth* (1961), Jean-Paul Sartre wrote:

> The native cures himself of colonial neurosis by thrusting out the settler through force of arms. When his rage boils over, he rediscovers his lost innocence and he comes to know himself in that he himself creates his self....To shoot down a European is to kill two birds with one stone, to destroy an oppressor and the man he oppresses at the same time: there remain a dead man, and a free man....[36]

In Fanon, said Sartre, himself a key influence on Fanon, 'the Third World finds itself and speaks to itself'. But there was a paradox here. Fanon wrote in French, in the passionate rhetorical style of the committed French intellectual. His works draw upon much the same set of thinkers – Lukacs and Sartre as well as Marx and Freud – as were currently informing the thinking of Western radicals. Moreover though he developed an influential theory of Third World revolution he was always better known in Europe and North America than in the Third World itself. This impact was not restricted to Western intellectuals. 'Every brother on a rooftop can quote Fanon', it was said in the Chicago riots of 1967; and *The Wretched of the Earth* was a revered text in the Black Panther movement in America.[37] As with other Third World revolutionaries such as Mao and Guevara, Fanon found himself incorporated into the very revolutionary tradition from which he had sought to free himself.

There is a further problem. Despite Fanon's undoubted prestige among Third World intellectuals, the kind of revolution he envisaged nowhere fits the actual pattern of Third World revolutions – not even in Algeria, where he threw himself into the struggle. Fanon put his trust in the poorest and most marginalised of the peasants, as the groups least contaminated by the colonialist mentality. Certainly he seems to have been right in rejecting the revolutionary potential of the urban proletariat. But nor have Third World revolutions been in any real sense peasant-led. Westernised middle-class intellectuals have in all cases provided the leadership, and their organisation of a nationalist struggle has in most cases also been indispensable to success (not to mention the effect of world war in weakening or destroying the power of colonial elites). Moreover it is not the most wretched of the peasantry who have been the mainstay of revolutionary struggle but the 'middling' peasants – as we would expect from the well-attested theory of relative deprivation and social action.[38] Fanon provided a powerful myth for Third World revolutions; but as with current concepts of revolution in Western industrial societies its relationship to actual practice remains problematic.

In arriving at his concept of Third World revolution, Fanon refused to have any truck with theories of negritude, the 'African cultural heritage', and similar ideas current among his fellow radicals from Africa and the West Indies. These smacked to him of racism, and black racism was as unacceptable as white. The Third World would be regenerated not by such backward-looking 'primitivist' conceptions but by looking to an entirely new future. It would be a future that rejected not just Europe but its own pre-colonial past, now in any case irretrievably lost. 'It is a question of the Third World starting a new history of Man....'[39] Fanon was vague about the 'new man', but he never wavered in his conviction that he would be in some sense socialist. For all his antipathy to Europe,

Fanon remained indebted to European social thought and the European revolutionary tradition.[40]

Others, however, have been at pains to deny the universalism of European categories of thought and practice, and to stress instead native particularisms. In several varieties of Third World theory, revolution has been seen as an affair as much of recovery as of new creation. The nineteenth-century Russian *narodniks* were perhaps the first to speculate along these lines. Lenin sternly stamped on such 'reactionary' thinking, but in other versions of socialism, such as Maoism, it became an increasingly pronounced feature. It gained a particular prominence in the 'African socialism' of such national leaders as Senghor, Touré, Nkrumah and Nyerere. Here an allegedly classless traditional African society was seen as the fortunate legacy that permitted the creation of a 'communal' socialism representing, Rousseau-like, the will of the whole people rather than of a particular class. Latterly, the departure from Western models has been even more profound in the Islamic fundamentalism of the Iranian Revolution of 1979. Iran's example has been infectious. Currently there are probably more revolutionary movements in the world agitating under the banner of Islamic fundamentalism than of any other ideology.[41]

Attempts have been made to deny the validity of some of these non-Western cases as authentic instances of revolution. Revolution, it is said, as a theory and a practice is historically linked to the effort to establish a new order of freedom and equality. What Condorcet said of the French Revolution is held to apply, with suitable modifications, to revolution as such: 'The word "revolutionary" can only be applied to revolutions which have liberty as their object.'[42] On this view not only are 'revolutions of the Right', such as the Nazi Revolution, but also religious revolutions, such as the Iranian Revolution, misnomers. They are the abuse of a concept too important to be abandoned to the vagaries of demagogic rhetoric.

There may be good grounds for trying to hold to such a normative definition of revolution. Certainly within the revolutionary tradition of the West there is a continuity of ideas and aspirations that supports the view of a common project. Liberal and Marxist varieties of revolution share a common inheritance. They are both heirs of the European Enlightenment, and their concepts of revolution are in various ways directed to the realisation of Enlightenment ideals. Movements which consciously turn their backs on such ideals – the ideals of reason, freedom, equality – cannot therefore be called revolutionary. So, at any rate, it can be maintained.

But no part of the globe can permanently lay claim to a political or moral vocabulary. Christianity discovered this very early; more recently, and equally painfully, Marxism and democracy have had to come to terms with it. Revolutionism is clearly a Western principle, born of Western practice. But along with industrialism and other Western ideas and institutions, it has been freely exported to the non-Western world, which has interpreted it as it saw fit. We can no more legislate against that than we can against the Grand Canyon.

Had there been a greater experience of revolution in the West in this century, it might have been possible to insist on a stricter use of terms, to point to a dominating and defining tradition of revolution in the Western mould. The revolutions of this century have, however, not been here but mostly in the Third World. The absence of a relevant experience to reflect on in twentieth-century industrial societies has meant that we are compelled to acknowledge that revolution in our time may depart sharply from the norm established by nineteenth-century revolutionism, up to and including the Russian Revolution. It can take other, sometimes strange and exotic, forms. The Nazi Revolution may be one such; the Iranian Revolution another. Some have argued that recent Latin American revolutions, such as the Cuban and the Nicaraguan, with their absence of a mass peasant base and their reliance on guerrilla cadres – a new type of 'social banditry' – represent a new species of revolution, different from all those of the past. There is also the category, familiar since the Meiji Restoration of 1868, of 'revolutions from above': the largely military-led revolutions of Turkey in 1922, Egypt in 1952, North Yemen in 1962, Peru in 1968, Portugal in 1974. The risings in the Communist world – East Germany in 1953, Hungary in 1956, Poland in 1980 – again seem to be phenomena requiring their own form of analysis. And one still does not quite know what to do with May 1968.[43]

In the face of such conceptual luxuriance, sensible scholars may feel driven to reject the concept of revolution altogether, at least as applied to contemporary forms. And there are certainly signs of such a reaction. But though we must accept the variety of revolutions in the contemporary world we need not feel that there must be, or has been, a lapse into total arbitrariness. There are at least 'family resemblances' between European revolutions and the revolutions of the Third World, even those seeking to appeal primarily to non-Western traditions. This is no less than we should expect, given the wholesale penetration of the globe by westernising ideologies and institutions. With the possible exception of the Iranian Revolution – though even here strong claims in support of its 'modernity' have been made[44] – the impress of Western revolutionism can be found in practically every instance of Third World revolution. 'African socialism', 'Islamic socialism' or 'South Yemeni Marxism' do, after all, by their very names proclaim their kinship with Western revolutionary thought. There is also the opposite but equally relevant point: the importation of Third World revolutionary ideas and examples – Mao and China, Guevara and Cuba – into Western conceptions. None of this so far adds up to a coherent synthesis; but it does indicate the degree of overlap and convergence that is part of the complex picture of revolution in our own time.

About one thing however we may be clear. The further away we go in time and space from the Great French Revolution of 1789 – still for many purposes the 'model' revolution – the less we should expect revolution to resemble it. Kropotkin was certainly right to claim that 'whatsoever nation enters on the path of revolution in our own day, it will be heir to all our forefathers have done in France'.[45] The contribution of the French Revolution to the ideology of revolutionism, in Europe and the rest of the world, has been unmistakable and incontrovertible. But Kropotkin did not live to see the great wave of Third World revolutions that broke over the world, especially after 1945. In this development not only the French Revolution but increasingly the Russian came to be seen as remote and unhelpful models. They remained undoubtedly a great source of emotional inspiration – in revolution always a great thing. But as models for practical imitation they could be dangerously anachronistic.

This distancing from European models of revolution has affected not just how the Third World regards the West but increasingly how Western radicals regard the Third World. It used to be more or less taken for granted that Western radicals were enthusiastic supporters of Third World revolutions – the more so as they had none of their own to support. Mao, Ho, Castro, even Nasser and Sukarno were at various times the objects of admiration, verging sometimes on adulation. More recently Western radicals have found it less easy to warm to revolutionary movements in the Third World. The Sandanistas of Nicaragua pose relatively few problems; as also the socialist guerrilla movement in neighbouring El Salvador. But what of the Islamic Hezbollah of the Lebanon or the Mujahadin of Afghanistan? What of the Revolutionary Council of Ethiopia or, for that matter, the National Liberation Front of Eritrea? What of Hamas, the main Palestinian Islamicist movement? As even earlier heroes, such as Mao and Castro, are critically re-examined, a certain disillusionment about Third World revolutions seems to have come upon a sizeable portion of the Western radical intelligentsia. The

outcome of many of these revolutions – the Iranian Revolution in particular – makes them unattractive models to wish upon other Third
World societies. At the same time they have lost their capacity to inspire
– however bizarrely in some instances – revolutionary fervour in the
industrial societies. Taken with the absence of revolutionary initiatives
in these societies for much of this century, and the sense that their populations have lost interest in revolution, the revolutionary project in the
West might appear to languish as at no time since it was launched upon
the world in 1789.

1989/1991: the rebirth of revolution?

Have the 1989 and 1991 revolutions in East-Central Europe and the
USSR changed this perception? Do they signal the rebirth of the revolutionary idea in Europe? Some have certainly been prepared to see
them in this light. If the West, sunk in the torpor of affluence and 'post-
modernist' inertia, has lost the taste for revolution, in the East it still
seems capable of arousing popular passions. The 1989 revolutions,
writes Fred Halliday, 'have restated, in a dramatic form, the most neglected facet of political life, ... namely the capacity of the mass of the
population to take sudden, rapid and novel political action after long
periods of what appears to be indifference'.[46] Mass action is also the
phenomenon that strikes Jürgen Habermas, who further draws a direct
parallel with 1789: 'It was mass anger ... that was directed at the appa-
ratuses of state security, just as it had once been directed at the Bastille.
The destruction of the Party's monopoly on state power could similarly
be seen to resemble the execution of Louis XVI.'[47]

It is not just the manner but the matter of the change which causes
these thinkers to hark back to the revolutionary legacy of 1789. For
obvious reasons 1917, the Russian Revolution, might not be an inspiration to the 1989ers; but, argues François Furet, the 'universal principles
of 1789' were what animated the revolutions of 1989. 'The Bolsheviks
thought that with 1917 they had buried 1789. Here, at the end of our century, we see that the opposite is happening. It is 1917 that is being buried
in the name of 1789.'[48] The themes of 1989 are the great themes of 1789:
liberty, democracy, civil society, nationhood.

That the participants – the historically minded among them, at least –
in the 1989 revolutions were aware of the European revolutionary tradition is undoubted. To the young Slovak historian, Ewa Kowalska, the

events of 1989 were 'the culmination of the slow and continuous "general revolution" of the western world, of the process that began economically and politically with the English and French revolutions and that is coming to an end spiritually and nationally with the upheavals of central Europe'.[49] Bronislaw Geremek, one of the leading theoreticians of the Polish Solidarity movement, is fond of quoting de Tocqueville and offers *The Old Regime and the Revolution* as the best guide to both the causes and the animating spirit of the 1989 revolutions.[50] Again and again, before, during and after 1989, East European intellectuals paid homage to the French Revolution, as the parent of their hopes and aspirations. For many intellectuals, the declaration that the revolutions represented the 'return to Europe' meant precisely the recovery of the lost revolutionary inheritance.[51]

At the same time we recall Ewa Kowalska's remark that 1989 marked the *end* of the long European revolution. There have been repeated comments in a similar vein. Observers have been struck by the backward-looking nature of the 1989 revolutions, their unwillingness to announce anything new. Habermas calls them 'rectifying revolutions', revolutions that seek to retrieve or restore, not to announce any new principles of state and society. The 1989 revolutions desire no more than 'to connect up constitutionally with the inheritance of the bourgeois revolutions....'[52] If, as Hannah Arendt once said, revolutions are distinguished by 'the pathos of novelty', then the 1989 revolutions are most unrevolutionary. In turning their back on the new, in wishing to do no more than 'return to their history' and catch up with the process of Western constitutional and commercial development, they almost seem to aspire to recall the old pre-modern sense of revolution, as a return or a restoration.

The singularity of the 1989/1991 revolutions appears in another way. Unlike most earlier revolutions, 'the people', despite appearances, played a relatively minor role. There were indeed courageous dissidents in the region; Solidarity, the Polish workers' movement that swept to power in the summer of 1989, was a powerful inspiration; there were mass demonstrations and some violent clashes in Leipzig, Prague, Budapest and Bucharest. But it is quite clear that on their own these would never have succeeded in toppling the Communist regimes. They seem scarcely to have been intended to. When attempts of a similar kind had been made before – in 1953, 1956, 1968 and 1980 – the use, or the threat, of Soviet tanks had been sufficient to crush them. Against Soviet resolve popular protests seemed futile, as Solidarity throughout accepted. In 1989 the unexpected and unhoped for happened. Mikhail

Gorbachev made it clear that Soviet troops would not be at the disposal of the Communist rulers of Eastern Europe. More daringly, Soviet influence was put to work to undermine the power and authority of thçe old hardliners at the top – Honecker, Kadar, Husak, Zhivkov, Ceauşescu. Deprived of Soviet backing their regimes crumbled one by one, usually through the machinations of reform-minded Communists within their own parties who were emboldened by Soviet support and encouragement. The 1989 revolutions, despite their undeniable significance, increasingly have the appearance of *frondes*, or palace revolutions.[53]

In this of course they are not so unusual. Nearly all revolutions, the French and Russian no less than more minor ones, begin from a split within the ruling class or ruling elite. The peculiar aspect of the 1989 revolutions was the high degree of control exercised by the ruling *nomenklaturas* throughout the period of transition to democracy and market society. Except in Romania, there was remarkably little violence, and even in Romania the violence was to a good extent deliberately provoked by dissident members of the ruling group.[54] It is this, coupled with the well-known success of old members of the *nomenklatura* in retaining their elevated positions within the new market dispensation, that has made some people question whether what happened in 1989 and 1991 can properly be called a revolution.[55]

Such definitional disputes can be the bugbear of all discussions of revolution; and this is not the place to engage in them, at least not in the formal sense. The important question may be not so much whether the events of 1989/91 fit conventional notions of revolution as what they may tell us about the future of revolution. Assuming that the momentousness and the speed of the change – nothing less than the sudden and sweeping end to an *ancien régime* – sufficiently justify the epithet 'revolutionary', does 1989/91 signal a renewal of revolution in Europe, after nearly a century of quiescence? Is revolution now once more on the agenda of advanced industrial societies? Or does this in some way confirm the 'sense of an ending', the feeling that it has merely completed some unfinished business, merely restored one section of Europe to the modernising path taken by most other industrial societies, from which it had unfortunately deviated? If so, that might suggest that, to the extent that Central and Eastern European societies develop democratic institutions and achieve a reasonable standard of living for the bulk of their populations, they too, as with the more affluent West, may make themselves relatively safe from revolution.

'Relative' is the crucial word here. The 1989 revolutions at least remind us of one important thing, that no society, the most developed no less than the least developed, is immune from revolution. No one is in a position to write off revolution as a mode of transformation of society, now or in the future. Observers and participants alike were caught by surprise in 1989 – at the speed and success of events, at the fact, disbelieved almost up to the day, that fundamental change was possible. Revolutions have always had this capacity for surprise – one remembers Lenin's famous remark in 1917, only a month before the February Revolution that brought down the Tsarist regime, that 'we, the old, may not live to see the decisive battles of the coming revolution'.[56] Revolution, as an idea and a practice, has become firmly lodged in the fabric of modern societies. No matter how long its absence, no matter how apparently unpromising the circumstances for its occurrence, it remains capable of convulsing society. And, as in the past, it is likely to happen when least expected, either by its enemies or its friends.

This is a different matter from saying that it is unaffected by social and historical changes. The virtual absence of revolution in the West in the twentieth century is clear testimony to the fact that the conditions that made it relatively common in the nineteenth century no longer exist, or exist in much modified form. Revolution is still always possible; it is simply less likely to happen, at least in its familiar forms.[57] The result has been that conceptual inflation that we have noted. Revolution as a concept has come to be filled to the bursting point with projects for human liberation on a vast scale. Not just the external but the internal forms of life are to be renewed. Human instincts must be redirected and freed from repression; a mentality of dependence and inferiority must be transformed into one of self-respect and daring in the face of the future. Transformation must be total or it will be nothing, the replacement of one form of tyranny by another.

As a concept, revolution has achieved a sort of theoretical completion and closure. It now embraces all aspects of the human condition, from politics to psychoanalysis, having taken in on the way economics and culture. It includes the 'politics of the nervous system' along with the politics of the social system. The cost of this theoretical filling-out has been to take revolution out of the sphere of political action and to place it in the realm of metaphysics. This is really what is meant by all the talk of the 'end of revolution'.[58] Revolution is no longer about changing the social order in any determinate time and place, by conscious, collective human action. It has been detached from history and 'universalised'. Revolution takes place in a timeless present. It now symbolises eternal protest against oppression and unfreedom as such, as more or less constant features of the human condition.

We return to Camus, with whom we started. For Camus, the revolutions of history stand condemned by their repeated consummation in murder and new forms of tyranny. Against revolution Camus counterposes the act of 'metaphysical rebellion'. 'It is metaphysical because it disputes the ends of man and creation....The metaphysical rebel protests against the human condition in general.'[59] Like many contemporary theorists of revolution, Camus follows a tradition of thinking that starts with Sade and continues with Baudelaire, Stirner, Nietzsche, Lautréamont and the Surrealists (all particular heroes of the revolutionaries of May 1968). Revolution, a historical invention that gave rise to a specific tradition of theory and practice, ends in rebellion, a metaphysics of protest against the arbitrary injustices and hypocrisies of social existence. Existential rebellion has its place, of course; but it is one alongside, rather than as a replacement for, revolution. If it has indeed substituted itself for revolution, then we may well feel that revolution has ceased to have any useful meaning, or to be in any real sense a programme of action.

It is too early to say whether the 1989 and 1991 revolutions in the East have fundamentally changed this situation, so marked in the West. Their outcomes are still uncertain, and reversals are by no means yet ruled out. Even their forms are, as we have noted, ambiguous, partaking both of the classic pattern of popular revolution and of the more familiar type of palace revolution. But enough is already clear to enable us to make some reasonable predictions. Once the inevitable disappointment and disillusionment with democracy and the market have set in, East Europeans are as likely as their Western counterparts to turn their backs on revolution – perhaps even, as seems increasingly to be the case in the West as well, on politics in general. In Eastern Europe the intellectual tradition of 'metaphysical rebellion', born of centuries of autocracy and empire, is if anything even stronger than in the more pragmatic West. On the other side is a tradition of detached irony and political passivity, both encouraged by the experience of Communist rule. If these traditions reassert themselves, no more in the East than in the West would there seem to be much room for revolution.

But it would, to repeat, be unwise to rest on such a conclusion. The end of revolution has been proclaimed on numerous occasions in the twentieth century, in the 1930s as well as the 1950s and the 1980s. In each case a surprise was in store. We will be surprised again; of that we can be sure.

Notes and References

1. THE DYNAMICS AND MEANING OF REVOLUTION IN TWENTIETH-CENTURY EUROPE
Tim Rees with Moira Donald

1. J. Dunn, *Modern Revolutions: an Introduction to the Analysis of a Political Phenomenon* (Cambridge, 1972), pp. 11–12. A revised edition of this book appeared in 1989 with few substantial changes made to it.
2. This point is also strongly made in a recent book, F. Halliday, *Revolution and World Politics: the Rise and Fall of the Sixth Great Power* (London, 1999), esp. pp. 234–60. One of the most ambitious attempts to interpret history in terms of the impact of revolutions is the comparative study by Barrington Moore, *Social Origins of Dictatorship and Democracy* (London, 1966). Two different comments upon it are provided by L. Stone, *The Past and the Present Revisited*, 2nd edn (London, 1987), pp. 154–65 and T. Skocpol *et al.* (eds), *Democracy, Revolution and History* (New York, 1998), esp. pp. 1–25. A recent volume reproducing articles on revolution, with an interesting introduction and bibliographical survey, is provided by A. J. Groth (ed.), *Revolution and Revolutionary Change* (Aldershot, 1996), esp. pp. xiii–xl.
3. E. Hobsbawm, *The Age of Revolution, 1789–1848* (London, 1962) narrows the period even further. Interestingly a recent textbook by A. Todd, *Revolutions, 1789–1917* (Cambridge, 1998), presents just this classical conception of European revolution.
4. Crane Brinton, *The Anatomy of Revolution* (London, 1953), pp. 2–3. There were two further editions of this book, the last published in 1965, but with few alterations from the original.
5. Dunn, *Modern Revolutions*, p. 2.
6. Compare, for instance, F. Fukuyama, *The End of History and the Last Man* (London, 1992) and J. Lucacs, *The End of the Twentieth Century and the End of the Modern Age* (1993). C. Tilly, *European Revolutions, 1492–1992* (Oxford, 1993), pp. 1–4 recognises that the revolutions of 1989–91 showed that revolution was not at an end in Europe.
7. Dunn, *Modern Revolutions*, p. 22.
8. K. Kumar, *Revolution: the Theory and Practice of a European Idea* (London, 1971), p. 7.
9. Kumar, *Revolution*, p. 18 and J. De Fronzo, *Revolutions and Revolutionary Movements*, 2nd edn (Boulder, Colo., 1996), p. 8. Similar points are made in D. Close and C. Bridge, *Revolution: a History of the Idea* (London, 1985).
10. See R. Porter and M. Teich (eds), *Revolution in History* (Cambridge, 1986).
11. Kumar, *Revolution*, pp. 15–16.
12. Comment on this can be found in J. Goldstone (ed.), *Revolutions: Theoretical, Comparative and Historical Studies*, 2nd edn (San Diego, Calif., 1996).

13. T. Skocpol, *States and Social Revolution* (Cambridge, 1979) and De Fronzo, *Revolutions*, pp. 22–3. Halliday, *Revolution and World Politics* specifically sees revolution as an international phenomenon in terms of its origins and impact. Other recent examples include T. Skocpol, *Social Revolution in the Modern World* (Cambridge, 1994); J. Goldstone *et al.* (eds), *Revolutions of the Late Twentieth Century* (Oxford, 1991); M. S. Kimmel, *Revolution: a Sociological Interpretation* (Cambridge, 1990).

14. Tilly, *European Revolutions*, pp. 10–14.

15. A still interesting study of the origins of revolutions is provided by T. Gurr, *Why Men Rebel* (Princeton, 1970). See also Halliday, *Revolution and World Politics*, pp. 161–91 on international factors in revolution.

16. See for instance the comments of De Fronzo, *Revolutions and Revolutionary Movements*, p. 8.

17. Skocpol, *States and Social Revolution*, p. 1.

18. De Fronzo, *Revolutions and Revolutionary Movements*, p. 9 also makes this point.

19. M. N. Katz, *Revolutions and Revolutionary Waves* (New York, 1997) and Halliday, *Revolution and World Politics*, esp. pp. 56–132.

20. For recent overviews of the Comintern see K. McDermott with J. Agnew, *The Comintern: International Communism from Lenin to Stalin* (London, 1996) and T. Rees and A. Thorpe (eds), *International Communism and the Communist International, 1919–1943* (Manchester, 1998). The extent to which revolutions can be exported is explored in detail in Halliday, *Revolution and World Politics*.

21. Tilly, *European Revolutions*, pp. 14–16.

22. Kumar, *Revolution*, pp. 24–5.

23. See P. Pilbeam, *The Middle Classes in Europe, 1789–1914* (London, 1990), pp. 235–93.

24. See also the comments of T. Kimer, 'The Inevitability of Future Revolutionary Surprises', *American Journal of Sociology*, 100 (1995), pp. 1528–51.

2. CHASING RAINBOWS: THE NINETEENTH-CENTURY REVOLUTIONARY LEGACY   *Pamela Pilbeam*

1. Useful summaries in J. Sperber, *The European Revolutions 1848–1851* (Cambridge, 1994), B. Waller (ed.), *Themes in Modern European History 1830–1890* (London, 1990), J. J. Sheehan, *German History 1770–1866* (Oxford, 1994), pp. 654–729, L. Riall, *The Italian Risorgimento* (London, 1994). The work of historians of France which have influenced recent thinking include M. Agulhon, *La république au village*, trans. *The Republic in the Village* (Cambridge, 1970); E. Berenson, *Populist Religion and Left-Wing Politics in France 1830–1852* (Princeton, 1984); T. W. Margadant, *French Peasants in Revolt. The Insurrection of 1851* (Princeton, 1979) and W. Sewell, *Work and Revolution in France: the Language of Labour from the Old Regime to 1848* (Cambridge, 1980).

2. J. de Maistre, *Considérations sur la France* (Geneva, 1796), p. 69.

3. A. de Tocqueville, *The Old Regime and the French Revolution*, trans. S. Gilbert (New York, 1955), pp. 88–203.

4. F. P. G. Guizot, *Mémoires pour servir à l'histoire de mon temps*, vol. 2 (Paris, 1858–67), p. 3.

5. M. Ozouf, 'Revolution', in F. Furet and M. Ozouf, *A Critical Dictionary of the French Revolution* (Cambridge, Mass., 1989), p. 817.

6. K. Marx, *The Class Struggles in France 1848 to 1850* in Marx, *Surveys from Exile. Political Writings*, vol. 2, D. Fernbach (ed.) (Penguin, 1992), pp. 35–142. K. Marx, *The Civil War in France*, in Marx, *The First International and After. Political Writings*, vol. 3 (Penguin, 1992), pp. 187–268.

7. G. Weill, *Histoire du parti républicain en France de 1814 à 1870* (Paris, 1900).

8. E. J. Hobsbawm, 'Revolution' in R. Porter and M. Teich (eds), *Revolution in History* (Cambridge, 1987), p. 14.

9. J. B. Landes, *Women and the Public Sphere in the Age of the French Revolution* (Ithaca, 1989). S. Melzer and L. Rabine, *Rebel Daughters. Women and the French Revolution* (Oxford, 1992).

10. M. Agulhon, *La république au village*, trans. *The Republic in the Village* (Cambridge, 1970).

11. J. Sperber, *The European Revolutions 1848–1851* (Cambridge, 1994).

12. F. Furet, *La Révolution de Turgot à Jules Ferry 1770–1880* (Paris 1988), trans. *Revolutionary France 1770–1880* (Oxford, 1992).

13. C. H. Church, *Europe in 1830* (London, 1983).

14. M. Agulhon, *Marianne. Les visages de la République* (Paris, new edn 1992), first edn trans. *Marianne into Battle. Republican Imagery and Symbolism in France 1789–1880* (Cambridge, 1981) pp. 30–7.

15. M.-C. Chaudonneret, *La Figure de la République. Le concours de 1848* (Paris, 1987), p. 30.

16. Chaudonneret, *La Figure de la République*, pp. 103, 227.

17. Words for these three songs taken from *History of the Soviet Union*. Vol. 1. *Revolution and Civil War*. Folkways Records Album no. FH 5420 (New York, 1964).

18. P. M. Jones, *Politics and Rural Society. The Southern Massif Central c. 1750–1880* (Cambridge, 1985). P. McPhee, *The Politics of Rural Life. Political Mobilization in the French Countryside 1846–1852* (Oxford, 1992). P. M. Pilbeam, *The 1830 Revolution in France* (London, 1991). P. Sahlins, *Forest Rites* (Cambridge, Mass., 1994).

19. J. R. Gillis, *The Prussian Bureaucracy in Crisis 1840–60* (Stanford, 1971).

20. B. Constant, 'De la liberté des anciens comparée à celle des modernes', lecture given in 1819 and published in E. Laboulage, *Cours de Politique constitutionnelle* (1861); reprinted in A. Bayet and F. Albert, *Les Ecrivains politiques du XIXe siécle* (Paris, 1924), p. 146.

21. F. Guizot, *The History of Civilisation, from the Fall of the Roman Empire to the French Revolution*, vol. 1 (London, 1887), p. 20.

22. Guizot, *History of Civilisation*, p. 284.

23. T. S. Hamerow, *Social Foundations of German Unification, 1858–71: Ideas and Institutions* (Princeton, 1970), pp. 181–2.

24. S. Woolf, *A History of Italy 1700–1860. The Social Constraints of Political Change* (London, 1979).

25. G. M. Trevelyan, *Garibaldi and the Thousand* (London, 1916).

26. J. Breuilly, *Nationalism and the State* (Manchester, 1995).

27. J. L Homme, *La grande bourgeoisie au pouvoir 1830–1880* (Paris, 1960).

28. D. C. Higgs, *Nobles in Nineteenth Century France. The Practice of Inegalitarianism* (Baltimore, 1987).

29. P. Buonarroti, *Conspiration pour l'égalité dite de Babeuf, suivie du procès auquel elle donna lieu* (Brussels, 1828).

30. P. M. Pilbeam, *Republicanism in Nineteenth-Century France* (London, 1995), pp. 131–9.

31. L. R. Villermé, *Tableau de l'état physique et moral des ouvriers employés dans les manufactures*, 2 vols (Paris, 1840).

32. M. Traugott (ed.), *The French Worker. Autobiographies from the Early Industrial Era* (University of California, Berkeley, Calif., 1993).

33. M. D. Sibalis, 'The Evolution of the Parisian Labour Movement 1789–1834' in *Proceedings of the 10th Annual Meeting of the Western Society for French History* (Winnipeg, 1984).

34. M. P. Driskel, 'The Proletarian's Body. Charlet's Representation of Social Class during the July Monarchy' in P. T. D. Chu and G. P. Weisberg (eds), *The Popularization of Images. Visual Culture under the July Monarchy* (Princeton, 1994), pp. 58–89.

35. M. Agulhon, *1848 ou l'apprentissage de la république 1848–1852* (Paris, 1973); rather misleadingly trans. *The Republican Experiment* (Cambridge, 1983), p. 84.

36. M. Traugott, *Armies of the Poor* (Princeton, 1985).

37. R. Tombs, 'L'année terrible 1870–1871', *Historical Journal*, 35 (1992), pp. 713–24.

38. J.Whittam, *The Politics of the Italian Army* (London, 1977), p. 28.

39. P. M. Pilbeam, *The Middle Classes in Europe 1789–1914* (London, 1990), pp. 156–7.

40. M. Kitchen, *The German Officer Corps, 1890–1914* (Oxford, 1968).

3. RUSSIA, 1905: THE FORGOTTEN REVOLUTION *Moira Donald*

1. A. Ascher, *The Revolution of 1905. Russia in Disarray* (Stanford, 1988), p. 6.

2. Ascher, *Revolution of 1905,* p. 94.

3. L. Ia. Gurevich, 'Narodnoe dvizhenie v Peterburge 9-go ianvaria 1905g.' *Byloe* 1 (1906), pp. 200–229, cited in Ascher, *Revolution of 1905*, p. 101.

4. E. D. Chermenskii, *Burzhuaziia i tsarizm v pervoi russkoi revoliutsii*, 2nd edn, Moscow, 1970), p. 58, cited in Ascher, *Revolution of 1905*, p. 112.

5. O. Figes, *A People's Tragedy. The Russian Revolution 1891–1924* (London, 1996), p. 189.

6. M. Perrie, 'The Russian Peasant Movement of 1905–07: its Social Composition and Revolutionary Significance', in B. Eklof and S. P. Frank (eds), *The World of the Russian Peasant: Post-Emancipation Culture and Society* (London, 1990), pp. 193–218 (p. 199).

7. Perrie, 'Russian Peasant Movement', pp. 199–206.

8. Perrie, 'Russian Peasant Movement', p. 214.

9. K. C. Chorley, *Armies and the Art of Revolution*, p. 20, cited in P. Calvert, *Revolution* (London, 1970), p. 98.

10. Chorley, *Armies*, p. 20.
11. K. Kautsky, *Die Soziale Revolution* (Berlin, 1902) p. 58.
12. Figes, *A People's Tragedy*, pp. 311–12.
13. Figes, *A People's Tragedy*, p. 315.
14. I. Deutscher, 'The Russian Revolution', *New Cambridge Modern History*, 2nd edn, vol. 12 (Cambridge, 1968), p. 403, cited in T. Skocpol, *States and Social Revolutions* (Cambridge, 1979), p. 95.
15. Skocpol, *States*, p. 95.
16. The distribution of publication dates of books which I found to be relevant to a conceptual study of revolution is as follows: 1938 (1), 1960–9 (0), 1970–9 (5), 1980–9 (1). For full details of these publications, see bibliography. S. Taylor in his work, *Social Science and Revolutions* (London, 1984), pp. 3–8 has argued that there have been three waves of writing on revolutions: the first wave being the classic analyses by post-Enlightenment social and political theorists including Locke, Burke, de Tocqueville, Hegel and Marx, the second wave encompassing pre-1960s academic publications such as those by Pitirim Sorokin and Crane Brinton, and the third wave, the work of the post-1960s generation of academics.
17. C. Brinton, *The Anatomy of Revolution* (London, 1953), pp. 16–17.
18. Brinton, *Anatomy*, p. 24.
19. Brinton, *Anatomy*, pp. 41, 74.
20. Calvert, *Revolution*, p. 15.
21. Calvert, *Revolution*, pp. 86, 90.
22. J. Baechler, *Revolution* (Paris, 1970) (trans. J. Vickers, Oxford, 1975), pp. 24, 32.
23. Baechler, *Revolution*, p. 35.
24. Baechler, *Revolution*, p. 36.
25. Dan to Kautsky, 27 October 1905, in B. Sapir (ed.), *Theodore Dan – Letters 1899–1946* (Amsterdam, 1985), p. 165.
26. L. Trotsky, *The History of the Russian Revolution*, trans. M. Eastman, vol. 1 (New York, 1967), pp. 87–8, reprinted in K. Kumar, *Revolution. The Theory and Practice of a European Idea* (London, 1971), p. 356.
27. Kumar, *Revolution*, p. 40.
28. Kumar, *Revolution*, pp. 40–1.
29. E. H. Carr, *A History of Soviet Russia*, vol. 1, *The Bolshevik Revolution* (London, 1960), p. 25, cited in Kumar, *Revolution*, p. 68.
30. Baechler, *Revolution*, pp. 64–5.

4. THE PARTING OF WAYS: COMPARING THE RUSSIAN
REVOLUTIONS OF 1917 AND 1991 *Edward Acton*

1. Alexander Herzen, *My Past and Thoughts*, vol. IV (London, 1968), p. 1678.
2. V. Bunce, 'Transforming Russia: a Comparison of Reforms under Alexander II and Mikhail Gorbachev', in M. Woo-Cunnings and M. Loriaux (eds), *Past as Prelude. History in the Making of a New World Order* (Boulder, Colo., 1993), pp. 111–36; W. Mosse, *Perestroika under the Tsars* (London, 1992).

3. R. Pipes, *Russia under the Old Regime*, 2nd edn (London, 1995).

4. A. Yanov, *The Origins of Autocracy. Ivan the Terrible in Russian History* (Berkeley, Calif., 1981); A. Yanov, 'Is Sovietology Reformable?', in R. O. Crummey (ed.), *Reform in Russia and the USSR* (Chicago, Ill., 1989), pp. 257–76.

5. R. Hellie, 'The Structure of Modern Russian History: towards a Dynamic Model', *Russian History*, IV (1977), pp. 1–22.

6. A. Ulam, *Russia's Failed Revolutions* (London, 1981).

7. G. Hosking, 'The Russian Myth: Empire and People', in P. J. S. Duncan and M. Rady (eds), *Towards a New Community: Culture and Politics in Post-Totalitarian Europe* (London, 1993), pp. 37–43. For the most recent general history whose central theme is Russia's failure to overcome authoritarian government, see J. Gooding, *Rulers and Subjects. Government and People in Russia, 1801–1991* (London, 1996).

8. Yegor Gaidar was Deputy Prime Minister for Economic Affairs from November 1991; Acting Prime Minister from June 1992 until December 1992; and returned to office as First Deputy Prime Minister in September 1993 before resigning after the elections of December 1993.

9. V. E. Bonnell, *Roots of Rebellion: Workers' Politics and Organisations in St Petersburg and Moscow, 1900–1914* (Berkeley, Calif., 1983); H. Hogan, *Forging Revolution: Metalworkers, Managers and the State in St Petersburg, 1890–1914* (Bloomington, Ind., 1993); D. Koenker, *Moscow Workers and the 1917 Revolution* (Princeton, NJ, 1981); D. Mandel, *The Petrograd Workers and the Fall of the Old Regime* (London, 1983); S. A. Smith, *Red Petrograd. Revolution in the Factories 1917–1918* (Cambridge, 1983).

10. T. Shanin, *The Roots of Otherness: Russia's Turn of Century*, vol. I (London, 1985); J. Brook, *When Russia Learned to Read. Literacy and Popular Literature, 1861–1917* (Princeton, NJ, 1985).

11. E. Clowes, S. Kassow and J. West (eds), *Between Tsar and People: Educated Society and the Quest for Public Identity in Late Imperial Russia* (Princeton, NJ, 1991); O. Crisp and L. Edmondson (eds), *Civil Rights in Imperial Russia* (Oxford, 1989); L. McReynolds, *The News under Russia's Old Regime: the Development of a Mass-Circulation Press* (Princeton, NJ, 1991).

12. L. H. Haimson (ed.), *The Politics of Rural Russia, 1905–1914* (Bloomington, Ind., 1979); R. T. Manning, *The Crisis of the Old Order in Russia: Gentry and Government* (Princeton, NJ, 1982).

13. See the brilliant survey by M. Lewin, *The Gorbachev Phenomenon. A Historical Interpretation* (London, 1988).

14. L. H. Siegelbaum, *The Politics of Industrial Mobilisation in Russia, 1914–1917. A Study of the War-Industry Committees* (London, 1983), p. 212. For a valuable synthesis of recent work, see T. McDaniel, *Autocracy, Capitalism and Revolution in Russia* (Berkeley, Calif., 1988).

15. E. D. J. Acton, 'Revolutionaries and Dissidents', in J. Jennings and A. Kemp-Welch (eds), *Intellectuals and Politics from the Dreyfus Affair to Salman Rushdie* (London, 1997).

16. The best account pinpointing the critical personal role of Gorbachev is A. Brown, *The Gorbachev Factor* (Oxford, 1996).

17. On the protracted debate over the prospects for reform under late-Tsarism, see E. D. J. Acton, *Rethinking the Russian Revolution* (London, 1990).

18. See Bonnell, *Roots of Rebellion*; R. Zelnik, 'Russian Bebels: an Introduction to the Memoirs of the Russian Workers Semen Kanatchikov and Matvei Fisher', *Russian Review*, 35 (1976), pp. 249–89, 417–47.

19. L. J. Cook, *The Soviet Social Contract and Why it Failed: Welfare Policy and Workers' Politics from Brezhnev to Yeltsin* (Cambridge, Mass., 1993).

20. V. Zaslavsky, *The Neo-Stalinist State: Class, Ethnicity and Consensus in Soviet Society* (New York, 1982).

21. D. R. Jones, 'The Soviet Defence Burden through the Prism of History', and A. Nove, 'The Defence Burden – Some General Observations', in C. J. Jacobsen (ed.), *The Soviet Defence Enigma. Estimating Costs and Burden* (Oxford, 1987), pp. 151–74; 175–86.

22. For a classic statement, see A. Gerschenkron, 'Problems and Patterns of Russian Economic Development', in C. E. Black (ed.), *The Transformation of Russian Society* (Cambridge, Mass., 1960), pp. 42–72.

23. W. C. Fuller, *Civil–Military Conflict in Imperial Russia, 1881–1914* (Princeton, NJ, 1985); A. K. Wildman, *The End of the Russian Imperial Army. The Old Army and the Soldiers' Revolt (March–April 1917)* (Princeton, NJ, 1980).

24. See for example M. Lewin, *Political Undercurrents in Soviet Economic Debates: From Bukharin to the Modern Reformers* (London, 1975); Lewin, *The Gorbachev Phenomenon*; R. D. Marwick, 'Catalyst of Historiography, Marxism and Dissidence', *Europe-Asia Studies*, 46 (1994), pp. 579–96; J. Gooding, 'Perestroika as Revolution from Within', *Russian Review*, 51 (1992), pp. 36–57; M. S. Shatz, *Soviet Dissent in Historical Perspective* (Cambridge, 1980).

25. But note the point carefully argued in Brown, *The Gorbachev Factor*, pp. 225–30, that Reagan's raising of the stakes in the arms race had done nothing to change the policy of Gorbachev's predecessors and had no part in bringing Gorbachev to power.

26. D. C. B. Lieven, *Russia and the Origins of the First World War* (London, 1983), p. 83.

27. From early in his leadership, Gorbachev made abundantly clear his own confidence in Soviet security, *Perestroika. New Thinking for Our Country and the World* (London, 1987), Part Two.

28. Brown, *The Gorbachev Factor*, p. 181; R. V. Daniels, *The End of the Communist Revolution* (London, 1993), pp. 34–5.

29. S. White, G. Gill and D. Slider, *The Politics of Transition: Shaping a Post-Soviet Future* (Cambridge, 1993), pp. 60–78.

30. See T. Hasegawa, *The February Revolution: Petrograd 1917* (Seattle and London, 1981) for the most authoritative account of the formation of the first Provisional Government.

31. H. J. White, 'The Ministry of Internal Affairs and Revolution in the Provinces', unpublished research seminar paper (CREES, Birmingham, 1988); White *et al.*, *Politics of Transition*, pp. 212–29.

32. S. White, *Gorbachev and After* (Cambridge, 1992), pp. 68–9.

33. L. Kochan, 'Kadet Policy in 1917 and the Constitutional Assembly', *Slavonic and East European Review*, XLV (1967), pp. 83–92; Brown, *The Gorbachev Factor*, pp. 202–5.

34. For the best recent portrait, see C. Read, *From Tsar to Soviets. The Russian People and their Revolution, 1917–1921* (London, 1996).

35. White *et al.*, *Politics of Transition*, pp. 79–97.

36. For the *apologia* of the two leaders, see A. F. Kerensky, *The Prelude to Bolshevism. The Kornilov Rebellion* (London, 1919) and M. S. Gorbachev, *The August Coup: the Truth and the Lessons* (London, 1991).

37. O. Figes, *Peasant Russia, Civil War. The Volga Countryside in Revolution (1917–1921)* (Oxford, 1989); Smith, *Red Petrograd*; A. K. Wildman, *The End of the Russian Imperial Army: the Road to Soviet Power and Peace* (Princeton, NJ, 1987).

38. On opinion polls in the period, see White *et al.*, *Politics of Transition*, pp. 178–92.

39. The argument is explored in O. N. Znamenskii, *Vserossiiskoe Uchreditel'noe sobranie: istoriia sozyva i politicheskogo krusheniia* (Leningrad, 1976). For the best Western treatment, see O. Radkey, *The Elections to the Russian Constituent Assembly of 1917*, 2nd edn (Ithaca, 1989).

40. For a lively evocation of the mood after the August *putsch*, see J. H. Billington, *Russia Transformed: Breakthrough to Hope. Moscow, August 1991* (New York, Oxford, 1992).

41. For a guide to the development of Lenin's approach to the economy in the revolutionary period, see N. Harding, *Lenin's Political Thought*, vol. II (London, 1981), pp. 1–200.

42. For Gaidar's own retrospective account of his approach, see Y. Gaidar and K. Otto Pohl, *Russian Reform/International Money* (Cambridge, Mass., 1995), pp. 1–54.

43. See S. Malle, *The Economic Organisation of War Communism, 1918–1921* (Cambridge, 1985).

44. W. Maley, 'The Shape of the Russian Macroeconomy', in A. Saikal and W. Maley (eds), *Russia in Search of its Future* (Cambridge, 1995), pp. 48–65; R. E. Ericson, 'The Russian Economy since Independence', in G. W. Lapidus (ed.), *The New Russia. Troubled Transformation* (Boulder, Colo., 1995), pp. 37–77.

45. W. G. Rosenberg (ed.), *Bolshevik Visions: First Phase of the Cultural Revolution in Soviet Russia* (Ann Arbor, Mich., 1984); D. P. Koenker, W. G. Rosenberg and R. G. Suny (eds), *Party, State and Society in the Russian Civil War: Explorations in Social History* (Bloomington, Ind., 1989); R. Stites, *Revolutionary Dreams: Utopian Vision and Experimental Life in the Russian Revolution* (Oxford, 1989).

46. See J. Richter, 'Russian Foreign Policy and the Politics of National Identity', in C. A. Wallander (ed.), *The Sources of Russian Foreign Policy after the Cold War* (Boulder, Colo., 1996), pp. 69–93.

47. On workers after October, see the discussion in L. H. Siegelbaum, *Soviet State and Society between Revolutions, 1918–1929* (Cambridge, 1992), pp. 8–38; on peasants, see Figes, *Peasant Russia, Civil War*, pp. 184–245.

48. W. G. Rosenberg, 'Russian Labor and Bolshevik Power after October', *Slavic Review*, 44 (1985), pp. 213–38; S. Whitefield and G. Evans, 'The Russian Election of 1993: Public Opinion and the Transition Experience', *Post-Soviet Affairs*, 10 (1994), pp. 38–60.

49. O. Anweiler, *The Soviets: the Russian Workers, Soldiers' and Peasants' Councils 1905–1921* (New York, 1974); R. Service, *The Bolshevik Party in Revolution: a Study in Organisational Change* (London, 1979).

50. For a useful account of the high politics of these two years, see L. Shevtsova, 'Russia's Post-Communist Politics: Revolution or Continuity?', in G. W. Lapidus (ed.), *The New Russia. Troubled Transformation* (Boulder, Colo., 1995), pp. 5–36.

5.	STALIN'S GREAT TURN: A REVOLUTION WITHOUT
	FOOTSOLDIERS?	*Catherine Merridale*

1.	For an excellent discussion of the 'revolution from above', see
R. Tucker (ed.), *Stalinism: Essays in Historical Interpretation* (New York,
1977).
2.	T. Skocpol, *States and Social Revolutions* (Cambridge, Mass., 1979),
p. 4.
3.	The best account of this in English remains R. W. Davies, *The Socialist
Offensive: the Collectivisation of Soviet Agriculture, 1929–1930* (London and
Cambridge, Mass., 1980).
4.	See R. Conquest, *The Harvest of Sorrow: Soviet Collectivisation and the
Terror-Famine* (London, 1986).
5.	Skocpol, *States and Social Revolutions*, p. 4.
6.	*XVI moskovskaya gubernskaya konferentsiya VKP(b)* (Moscow, 1927),
bulletin no. 10, p. 88.
7.	See A. M. Ball, *Russia's Last Capitalists, the Nepmen, 1921–1929*
(Berkeley and Los Angeles, 1987) especially Chapter 3.
8.	R. W. Davies, *The Soviet Economy in Turmoil, 1929–1930* (London and
Cambridge, Mass., 1989).
9.	J. Stalin, Speech to the Conference of Business Executives, 23 June 1931
(*Pravda*, 5 July 1931), and see S. Fitzpatrick, *Education and Social Mobility in
the Soviet Union, 1921–34* (Cambridge, 1979).
10.	For the 'Industrial Party' trial, see H. Kuromiya, *Stalin's Industrial
Revolution* (Cambridge, 1988), pp. 167–72.
11.	These changes are discussed in C. Merridale, *Moscow Politics and the
Rise of Stalin* (London, 1990), Chapters 4 and 9.
12.	The division within the Party between 'Russians' and *émigrés* is dis-
cussed by R. McKean, *St. Petersburg between the Revolutions* (New Haven and
London, 1990).
13.	On Kamenev's political style and its contrast with the 'Russian'
Stalinists, see C. Merridale, 'The Making of a Moderate Bolshevik: an
Introduction to L. B. Kamenev's Political Biography', in J. Cooper, M. Perrie
and E. A. Rees (eds), *Soviet History, 1917–1953, Essays in Honour of
R. W. Davies* (London, 1995).
14.	The simplest, starkest exposition of this is the Communist Party's own
History of the Communist Party of the Soviet Union (Bolsheviks): Short Course
(Moscow, 1939).
15.	See P. A. Ginsborg, 'Gramsci and the Era of Bourgeois Revolutions', in
J. Davies (ed.), *Gramsci and Italy's Passive Revolution* (London, 1978).
16.	For an example, see R. Medvedev, *Let History Judge* (New York, 1972
and 1989).
17.	*Polnoe sobranie sochinenii*, 5th edn, vol. 39, pp. 183–4.
18.	On this remark, and the literature about it, see Ger P. van den Berg, 'The
Soviet Union and the Death Penalty', *Soviet Studies*, vol. XXXV, no. 2 (April
1983), pp. 156 and 168.
19.	For Lenin's last years, see R. Service, *Lenin: a Political Life*, vol. III
(London, 1995).
20.	Tucker's work has been voluminous, and includes a stimulating and per-
ceptive biography of Stalin, yet to be completed. The first volume of this, *Stalin*

as Revolutionary, 1879–1929 (London, 1974) includes an exposition of this basic view.

21. Some examples would include the work of R. W. Davies cited earlier, and, in very different veins, A. Nove's *Economic History of the USSR* (London, 1969) and H. Kuromiya's *Stalin's Industrial Revolution*. Many other excellent studies of aspects of Soviet industrialisation could be cited; it is one of the most carefully researched episodes in Soviet history, and has attracted scholars of exceptional calibre since the 1950s.

22. Again, a very large number of writers might be cited. Rather than taking the risk of leaving one out of an exhaustive list, I shall cite the classic statement of the theory from a British-based scholar (the majority were in the USA), which is L. Schapiro's *Totalitarianism* (London, 1970).

23. M. Fainsod, *Smolensk under Soviet Rule* (Cambridge, Mass., 1958 and 1989).

24. For examples of both 'revisionist' and anti-revisionist positions, see the debate between S. Fitzpatrick *et al.*, 'New Perspectives on Stalinism', *Russian Review*, 46 (1985).

25. The accusation was made by Alfred G. Meyer in his contribution to the above debate in *Russian Review*, 404.

26. See J. Habermas, 'Vom öffentlichen Gebrauch der Historie', *Die Zeit*, 7 November 1986.

27. As a Russian historian and sociologist insisted to me recently (1994), 'You [the West] were right and we were wrong. And to know how wrong, you would have to have lived, as I have lived, under a totalitarian regime.'

28. This emphasis on the elite also in part explains why the initial focus of *glasnost* history within the USSR was on personalities, the 'return of the repressed', rather than on the social and economic history of the Stalin period.

29. Because of the Terror of 1919 and reactions to it, the Kremlin car pool was eventually moved to the Manege (September 1919). From then on, the Kremlin elite had almost no reason to set foot outside their walled stronghold, and very powerful incentives to avoid personal exposure to life on the streets. O. Yu. Danilov, 'Gosudarstvennaya deyatel'nost' L. B. Kameneva 1917–1923 gg.' Rossiskii gosudarstvennyi gumanitarnyi universitet istoriko-arkhivnyi institut, diplomnaya rabota (1993), p. 64.

30. For an example, see C. Merridale, 'The 1937 Census and the Limits of Stalinist Rule', *Historical Journal*, 39, 1 (1996), pp. 225–40.

31. Stalin collected information in advance of the great turn using a number of channels, including secret police informers at factory level (see Merridale, *Moscow Politics*, pp. 58–67), but without a reliable Civil Service and advisors, even these detailed pieces of information cannot have furnished him with a complete or reliable picture, either of the economy or of the country's political mood.

32. Numerous recent works document this view. For an example, see E. A. Rees, *Stalinism and Soviet Rail Transport, 1928–41* (London, 1995).

33. See Merridale, *Moscow Politics*, Chapter 3.

34. Merridale, *Moscow Politics*, p. 75.

35. For examples, see Merridale, *Moscow Politics*, pp. 75–7.

36. For examples of low-level protest, see D. Filtzer, *Soviet Workers and Stalinist Industrialization* (London, 1986), pp. 130–51. Mutual protection among groups of ex-peasants within Moscow industry is discussed by David

Hofman, *Peasant Metropolis: Social Identities in Moscow, 1929–1941* (Ithaca and London, 1994), pp. 85–91.

37. For the organised opposition of religious groups to the 1937 Census, see Merridale, 'The 1937 Census'. Reports of religious believers allying themselves with fascists or wearing fascist insignia were frequent, although their propaganda value, for the Communist leadership, may have increased the frequency of reporting.

38. S. Kotkin, *Magnetic Mountain: Stalinism as a Civilization* (Berkeley and Los Angeles, 1995), p. 228.

39. Merridale, *Moscow Politics*, pp. 59–67. As G. Bordyugov and V. Kozlov explained in 1988, 'Dissatisfaction with the New Economic Policy grew among cadre workers. By 1928, many were already psychologically prepared for its breakup.' '1929 povorot i al'ternativa Bukharina', *Voprosy istorii KPSS*, 8 (1988).

40. Semenov, cited by G. A. Bordyugov and V. A. Kozlov in *Literaturnaya Gazeta*, 12 October 1988, p. 11.

41. A study of this phenomenon was made in the 1920s by the Bolshevik Party itself. N. Semenov, *Litso fabrichnykh rabochikh prozhivayushchikh v derevnyakh i politprosvetrabota sredi nikh* (Moscow–Leningrad, 1929). See also D. Hofman, *Peasant Metropolis*, especially Chapters 2 and 3.

42. Merridale, *Moscow Politics*, p. 77.

43. See Hofman, *Peasant Metropolis* and Kotkin, *Magnetic Mountain* especially Chapter 2.

44. David Hofman speaks of 'a struggle for hegemony in the workplace': *Peasant Metropolis*, p. 108.

45. Hofman, *Peasant Metropolis*, pp. 88–91.

46. S. Merl, 'Socio-economic Differentiation of the Peasantry', in R. W. Davies (ed.), *From Tsarism to the New Economic Policy* (Basingstoke and London, 1990).

47. See L. A. and L. M. Vasil'evskii, *Kniga o golode* (Petrograd, 1920).

48. Interview with famine survivor, Moscow, April 1994.

49. See Hofman, *Peasant Metropolis*, p. 124, for routine racism at work. For complaints about the organised repression of believers, see the petition to Kalinin of 1930 which cited incidents of suicide by believers faced with repression and uncertainty. Gosudarstvennyi Arkhiv Russkoi Federatsii (GARF), 5263/1/7.

50. Among these are included the cited works of David Hofman, Stephen Kotkin and Hiroaki Kuromiya.

51. The most important work here is the book on popular culture by S. Davies, *Popular Opinion in Stalin's Russia: Terror, Propaganda and Dissent, 1934–41* (Cambridge, 1997).

52. Kotkin makes this point himself. As he puts it, 'despite the energies that went into my study of Magnitogorsk and its inhabitants, I come away with the feeling that I have only managed to scratch the surface', *Magnetic Mountain*, p. 373.

53. This is the approach adopted by Sarah Davies in her study of the language of Leningrad workers in the 1930s.

54. For a discussion of this aspect of worker acculturation, see Kotkin, *Magnetic Mountain*, Chapter 5, 'Speaking Bolshevik'.

55. The suggestion that it is more than indulgent, and even morally questionable, to focus on such topics 'as if the Soviet government were just like any

other government operating in difficult circumstances' was made by Peter Kenez in the debate in *Russian Review* cited above (pp. 397–9).

56. See R. Tucker's 'What Time is it in Russia's History?' in C. Merridale and C. Ward (eds), *Perestroika: the Historical Perspective* (Sevenoaks, 1991).

57. This range of topics was selected by glancing at the programme of the V World Congress of Slavic and East European Studies, which was held in Warsaw in August 1995.

6. THE NAZI REVOLUTION   *Jeremy Noakes*

1. On the question of Nazism and social revolution, useful overviews are: T. Saunders, 'Nazism and Social Revolution' in G. Martel, *Modern Germany Reconsidered 1870–1945* (London, 1992) and I. Kershaw, 'The Third Reich: "Social Reaction" or "Social Revolution"?' in I. Kershaw, *The Nazi Dictatorship*, 3rd edn (London, 1993), pp. 131–49.

2. On the question of the revolutionary nature of the Nazi 'seizure of power' see H. Möller, 'Die nationalsozialistische Machtergreifung: Konterrevolution oder Revolution?' in *Vierteljahrshefte für Zeitgeschichte*, XXXI (1983), pp. 25–51.

3. For a very useful, though controversial, discussion of Hitler's revolutionary self-image and aims see R. Zitelmann, *Hitler. Selbstverständnis eines Revolutionärs*, 2nd edn (Stuttgart, 1989). For a penetrating and judicious assessment of Hitler see I. Kershaw, *Hitler 1889–1936. Hubris* (London, 1998), especially pp. xix–xxx.

4. E. Jaeckel, *Hitler, Sämtliche Aufzeichnungen 1905–1924* (Stuttgart, 1980), pp. 652, 670.

5. Ibid., p. 938.

6. A. Hitler, *Mein Kampf* (London, 1969), p. 485.

7. M. Domarus, *Hitler, Reden 1932 bis 1945* (Wiesbaden, 1973), p. 371.

8. For the following see, above all, Hitler, *Mein Kampf*. See also E. Jaeckel, *Hitler's World View: a Blueprint for Power* (Cambridge, Mass., 1981), which focuses in particular on the ideological background of Hitler's foreign policy.

9. E. Fröhlich (ed.), *Die Tagebücher von Joseph Goebbels. Sämtliche Fragmente*, Teil 1, *Aufzeichungen 1924–1941*, vol. 3 (Munich, 1987) p. 55.

10. *Akten der Reichskanzlei*, Reg. Hitler, Teil I, vol. 1, p. 630.

11. On the 'power vacuum' and on the collapse of the Weimar Republic in general see the classic study by Karl Dietrich Bracher, *Die Auflösung der Weimarer Republik. Eine Studie zum Problem des Machtverfalls in der Demokratie* (Villingen, 1955). For more recent assessments see Hans Mommsen, *Die verspielte Freiheit. Der Weg der Republik von Weimar in den Untergang 1918 bis 1933* (Frankfurt am Main, 1989), pp. 275ff; G. Schulz, *Von Brüning zu Hitler. Der Wandel des politischen Systems in Deutschland 1930–1933* (Berlin, 1992); H. A. Winkler (ed.), *Die Deutsche Staatskrise 1930–33* (Munich, 1992), idem., *Weimar 1918–1933. Die Geschichte der Ersten Deutschen Demokratie* (Munich, 1993), pp. 375ff; H. A. Turner, *Hitler's Thirty Days to Power January 1933* (London, 1996). For a useful brief introduction see E. Kolb, *The Weimar Republic* (London, 1988), pp. 96–126, 179–96. For a valuable discussion of recent research approaches to the collapse of the Weimar see I. Kershaw (ed.), *Weimar: Why did German Democracy Fail?* (London, 1990).

12.   See H. Mommsen, 'Die nationalsozialistische Machtergreifung und die deutsche Gesellschaft' in W. Michalka (ed.), *Die nationalsozialistische Machtergreifung* (Paderborn, 1984), p. 42.

13.   On this see R. Bessel, *Germany after the First World War* (Oxford, 1993), pp. 254ff.

14.   On this point see in particular L. E. Jones, ' "The Dying Middle": Weimar Germany and the Fragmentation of Bourgeois Politics', *Central European History*, XII (1979), pp. 143–68 and L. E. Jones, *German Liberalism and the Dissolution of the Weimar Party System 1918–1933* (Chapel Hill, 1988).

15.   E. Fröhlich (ed.), *Die Tagebücher von Joseph Goebbels, Sämtliche Fragmente*. Teil 1 *Aufzeichnungen 1924–1941*, vol. 2 (Munich, 1987), p. 397.

16.   On the Nazi takeover of power see above all the classic study by K. D. Bracher, W. Sauer and G. Schulz, *Die nationalsozialistische Machtergreifung. Studien zur Errichtung des totalitären Herrschaftssystems in Deutschland 1933/34* (Cologne, 1960). See also M. Broszat *et al.* (eds), *Deutschlands Weg in die Diktatur* (Berlin, 1983); V. Rittberger (ed.), *1933. Wie die Republik der Diktatur erlag* (Stuttgart, 1983); Michalka (ed.), *Die nationalsozialistische Machtergreifung*; P. Stachura (ed.), *The Nazi Machtergreifung* (London, 1984); M. Broszat, *Hitler and the Collapse of Weimar Germany* (London, 1987).

17.   On this see M. Broszat, 'Soziale Motivation und Führer-Bindung des Nationalsozialismus', *Vierteljahrshefte für Zeitgeschichte*, 18, 197 (1970), pp. 392–409 and P. Fritzsche, *Germans into Nazis* (Cambridge, Mass., 1998).

18.   On German youth in this period see the brief but penetrating comments in D. J. K. Peukert, *The Weimar Republic* (London, 1991), pp. 86ff. On university students and Nazism see M. H. Kater, *Studentenschaft und Rechtsradikalismus in Deutschland 1918–1933* (Hamburg, 1975); M. S. Steinberg, *Sabers and Brown Shirts. The German Students' Path to National Socialism 1918–1935* (Chicago, 1977); K. H. Jarausch, *Deutsche Studenten 1800–1970* (Frankfurt am Main, 1984); G. J. Giles, *Students and National Socialism in Germany* (Princeton, 1985); M. Grüttner, *Studenten im Dritten Reich* (Paderborn, 1995).

19.   On the 'spirit of 1914' see K. Schwabe, *Wissenschaft und Kriegsmoral. Die deutschen Hochschullehrer und die politischen Grundfragen des Ersten Weltkrieges* (Göttingen, 1969), pp. 21–45; W. J. Mommsen, 'Der Geist von 1914: Das Programm eines politischen Sonderwegs der Deutschen' in *idem., Der autoritäre Nationalstaat. Verfassung, Gesellschaft und Kultur im deutschen Kaiserreich* (Frankfurt am Main, 1990), pp. 407–21.

20.   See T. W. Mason, *Sozialpolitik im Dritten Reich. Arbeiterklasse und Volksgemeinschaft* (Cologne, 1977), p. 26. For the relevance of the 'spirit of 1914' to Nazism see Fritsche, *Germans into Nazis*, pp. 13ff. and *passim*.

21.   See T. Mann, *Tagebücher 1933–1934* (Frankfurt am Main, 1977), pp. 22, 43.

22.   See J. Noakes and G. Pridham (eds), *Nazism 1919–1945*, vol. 1, *The Rise to Power 1919–1934* (Exeter, 1983), pp. 131–4.

23.   *Völkischer Beobachter*, 67, 8 March 1933.

24.   This statement was in fact made in 1934, when a section of the Protestant Church was already beginning to resist the encroachment of Nazism on the Church. It was more typical of the attitude of many Protestant Germans during the previous year. See R. P. Ericsen, *Theologians under Hitler* (New Haven, 1985), p. 87.

25.   *Reichsgesetzblatt* I (1933), p. 586.

26. On 'Potsdam Day' see Bracher *et al.*, *Die Nationalsozialistische Machtergreifung*, pp. 149–52 and above all W. Freitag, 'Nationale Mythen und kirchliches Heil: Der "Tag von Potsdam" ', *Westfälische Forschungen*, 41 (1991), pp. 380–430.

27. See Freitag, 'Nationale Mythen', p. 400.

28. Ibid., pp. 417ff.

29. See Bracher, *Die Auflösung der Weimarer Republik*, pp. 181–3.

30. On May Day in Gelsenkirchen see H-J. Priamus and S. Goch, *Macht der Propaganda oder Propaganda der Macht? Inszenierung nationalsozialistischer Politik im 'Dritten Reich' am Beispiel der Stadt Gelsenkirchen* (Essen, 1992), pp. 68–9.

31. See Bracher *et al.*, *Die Nationalsozialistische Machtergreifung*, p. 183, fn. 63.

32. See E. Heuel, *Der umworbene Stand. Die ideologische Integration der Arbeiter im Nationalsozialismus 1933–1935* (Frankfurt am Main, 1989), pp. 42–187 and A. Lüdtke, 'Wo blieb die "rote Glut"? Arbeitererfahrungen und deutscher Faschismus', in A. Lüdtke (ed.), *'Alltagsgeschichte'. Zur Rekonstruktion historischer Erfahrungen und Lebensweisen* (Frankfurt, 1989), pp. 230ff.

33. On the SA see P. Merkl, *The Making of a Stormtrooper* (Princeton, 1980); C. Fischer, *Stormtroopers. A Social, Economic and Ideological Analysis 1929–35* (London, 1983); R. Bessel, *Political Violence and the Rise of Nazism: the Storm Troopers in Eastern Germany 1925–1934* (New Haven, 1984); M. Jamin, *Zwischen den Klassen. Zur Sozialstruktur der SA-Führerschaft* (Wuppertal, 1984).

34. On clashes between Communists and Nazis see E. Rosenhaft, *Beating the Fascists?* (Cambridge, 1983).

35. On the SS agenda see the first part of B. Wegner, *Hitler's Political Soldiers: the Waffen SS 1933–1945* (London, 1990).

36. See C. Graf, *Politische Polizei zwischen Demokratie und Diktatur* (Berlin, 1983).

37. See Noakes and Pridham, *Nazism*, p. 136.

38. *The Times*, 24 February 1933.

39. For the following see Bracher *et al.*, *Die Nationalsozialistische Machtergreifung*, pp. 136ff and numerous local studies such as W. S. Allen, *The Nazi Seizure of Power. The Experience of a Single German Town 1922–1945* (London, 1989). For a discussion of the Nazi seizure of power at local level see J. Noakes, 'Nationalsozialismus in der Provinz. Kleine und mittlere Städte im Dritten Reich', in H. Möller *et al.*, *Nationalsozialismus in der Region. Beiträge zur regionalen und lokalen Forschung und zum internationalen Vergleich* (Munich, 1996), pp. 238–45.

40. See M. Broszat, E. Fröhlich and F. Wiesemann, *Bayern in der NS-Zeit. Soziale Lage und politisches Verhalten der Bevölkerung* (Munich, 1977), pp. 56–7.

41. For examples see *The Brown Book of the Hitler Terror and the Burning of the Reichstag* (London, 1933).

42. For the following see M. Broszat, 'The Concentration Camps 1933–1945', in H. Krausnick and M. Broszat, *Anatomy of the SS State* (London, 1968), pp. 146ff.

43. On the 'co-ordination' (*Gleichschaltung*) of societies see local studies such as Allen, *The Nazi Seizure* and Noakes, 'Nationalsozialismus'.

44. On the SA crisis of 1934 see Bracher *et al.*, *Die Nationalsozialistische Machtergreifung*, pp. 897ff.

45. For a comparison of Hitler's and Röhm's notions of revolution see H. Mau, 'Die "Zweite Revolution" – Der 30 Juni 1934', *Vierteljahrshefte für Zeitgeschichte*, I (1953), pp. 121ff.

46. Noakes and Pridham, *Nazism*, pp. 167–8.

47. See fn. 45.

48. Noakes and Pridham, *Nazism*, pp. 170–2.

49. Domarus, *Hitler*, p. 371.

50. See D. Schoenbaum, *Hitler's Social Revolution. Class and Status in Nazi Germany 1933–1939* (London, 1966).

51. A good introduction is M. Burleigh and W. Wippermann, *The Racial State: Germany 1933–1945* (London, 1991).

52. Hitler's proclamation of 7 September 1937 in Domarus, *Hitler*, p. 717.

53. See in particular the work of D. Peukert, for example 'The Genesis of the "Final Solution" from the Spirit of Science', in D. Crew (ed.), *Nazism and German Society 1933–1945* (London, 1994), pp. 274–99 and of G. Aly, for example, G. Aly and S. Heim, *Vordenker der Vernichtung* (Hamburg, 1991).

54. For a discussion of this aspect of the Nazi Revolution see J. Noakes, 'Nazism and Revolution', in N. O'Sullivan (ed.), *Revolutionary Theory and Political Reality* (London, 1983), pp. 93ff.

7. BATTLEGROUND OF THE REVOLUTIONARIES: THE REPUBLIC AND CIVIL WAR IN SPAIN, 1931–39. *Tim Rees*

1. G. Orwell, *Homage to Catalonia* (London, 1938).

2. Perhaps the closest attempt to do this is S. Payne, *The Spanish Revolution* (New York, 1970), though revolution is identified wholly with the political left. See also J. Tusell, *Los intelectuales y la República* (Madrid, 1990); A. Garosci, *Los intelectuales y la guerra de España* (Madrid, 1981) and P. Preston, 'War of Words: the Spanish Civil War and the Historians', in P. Preston (ed.), *Revolution and War in Spain, 1931–1939* (London, 1984).

3. On republicanism see N. Townson (ed.), *El republicanismo en España* (1830–1977) (Madrid, 1994) and S. Ben-Ami, *The Origins of the Second Republic in Spain* (Oxford, 1978), chap. 1. Lower case republican is used here to indicate the supporters and ideology of the liberal parties, as opposed to upper case Republican indicating all the supporters of the regime.

4. Useful overviews include E. Ucelay Da Cal, 'The Nationalisms of the Periphery: Culture and Politics in the Construction of National Identity', in H. Graham and J. Labanyi (eds), *Spanish Cultural Studies: an Introduction* (Oxford, 1995); D. Conversi, *The Basques, the Catalans and Spain: Alternative Routes to Nationalist Mobilization* (London, 1997); A. Balcells, *Catalan Nationalism* (London, 1996) esp. chap. 8 and S. Payne, *Basque Nationalism* (Reno, Nevada, 1975), esp. chap. 4.

5. There was also a 'centrist' faction around Julián Besteiro. P. Heywood, *Marxism and the Failure of Organised Socialism in Spain, 1879–1936* (Cambridge, 1990); R. Gillespie, *The Spanish Socialist Party: a History of*

Factionalism (Oxford, 1989); S. Juliá, *Los socialistas en la política española, 1879–1982* (Madrid, 1997). J. C. Gibaja Velázquez, *Indalecio Prieto y el socialismo español* (Madrid, 1995); E. Cornide Fervant, *Indalecio Prieto: socialista a fuera del liberal* (Sada A Coruña, 1995); J. Aróstegui, *Francisco Largo Caballero: la última etapa de un líder obrero* (Madrid, 1990); Unión General de Trabajadores, *Francisco Largo Caballero, 1869–1946* (Madrid, 1996).

6. Ben-Ami, *Origins of the Second Republic*, pp. 76–83, 127–53; Heywood, *Marxism*, pp. 100–9; Juliá, *Los socialistas*, chap. 4.

7. M. Aragón, 'Manuel Azaña y su ideal de la República', in V. A. Serrano and J. M. San Luciano (eds), *Azaña* (Madrid, 1980), pp. 225–52; M. Suárez Cortina, 'La quiebra del republicanismo histórico, 1898–1931' and S. Juliá, 'La experiencia del poder: la Izquierda Republicana, 1931–33', pp. 165–7 both in Townsen (ed.), *El republicanismo en España*; P. Preston, *The Coming of the Spanish Civil War*, 2nd edn (London, 1994), pp. 35–7; M. Contreras, *El PSOE en la II República: organización y ideología* (Madrid, 1981), pp. 209–18.

8. For instance the leading republican, Manuel Azaña, described it as such in a speech to a republican rally on 29 September 1930: 'La revolución en marcha', *Obras completas*, vol. 2 (Mexico, 1966), pp. 13–18. For further examples see S. Juliá, *Manuel Azaña: una biografía política* (Madrid, 1990), pp. 55–137.

9. Ben-Ami, *Origins*, pp. 93–9.

10. Ben-Ami, *Origins*, pp. 238–52 and S. Ben-Ami, 'The Crisis of the Dynastic Elite in the Transition from Monarchy to Republic, 1929–1931', in F. Lannon and P. Preston (eds), *Elites and Power in Twentieth Century Spain* (Oxford, 1990).

11. J. Tusell *et al.*, *Las Constituyentes de 1931: unas elecciones de transición* (Madrid, 1982).

12. Azaña, 'Acción Republicana ante la revolución y ante las Cortes', *Obras completas*, vol 2, pp. 19–28.

13. The fortunes of this reforming project are a central theme of the literature on the Second Republic. Contrasting interpretations can be found in S. Payne, *Spain's First Democracy. The Second Republic, 1931–1936* (Madison, Wis., 1993), esp. pp. 81–124; Preston, *The Coming* and J. Gil Pecharromán, *La segunda República* (Madrid, 1989). See also E. Montero, 'Reform Idealized: the Intellectual and Ideological Origins of the Second Republic', in Graham and Labanyi (eds), *Spanish Cultural Studies* and N. Jones, 'Regionalism and Revolution in Catalonia', in Preston (ed.), *Revolution and War*.

14. O. Ruiz Manjón, *El Partido Republicano Radical (1908–1936)* (Madrid, 1976) and for background J. Alvarez Junco, *El emperador del paralelo. Lerroux y la demogogia populista* (Madrid, 1990).

15. Juliá, *Los socialistas*, chap. 5; Heywood, *Marxism*, pp. 110–32; Preston, *The Coming*, chap. 3.

16. J. R. Montero, *La CEDA: el catolicismo social y político en la II República*, 2 vols (Madrid, 1977); M. Vincent, *Catholicism in the Second Spanish Republic: Religion and Politics in Salamanca, 1930–36* (Oxford, 1996), esp. chap. 9 and L. M. Moreno Fernández, *Acción Popular Murciana* (Murcia, 1987). Preston, *The Coming* and R. Robinson, *The Origins of Franco's Spain* (Newton Abbot, 1970) also offer rival interpretations of the nature of CEDA.

17. In addition to the general works on the Republic see N. Townson, 'Una República para todos los españoles: el Partido Radical en el poder, 1933–1935', in Townsen (ed.), *El republicanismo* and 'Algunas consideraciones sobre el proyecto "republicano" del Partido Radical', in J. L. García Delgado (ed.), *La II República española: bienio rectificador y Frente Popular, 1934–36* (Madrid, 1988).

18. M. Blinkhorn, 'Spain', in S. Salter and J. Stevenson (eds), *The Working Class and Politics in Europe and America, 1929–1945* (London, 1990); G. Meaker, *The Revolutionary Left in Spain, 1914–1923* (Stanford, Calif., 1974); B. Martin, *The Agony of Modernization: Labor and Industrialization in Spain* (Ithaca, 1990).

19. J. Casanova, *De la calle al frente. El anarcosindicalismo en España (1931–39)* (Barcelona, 1997); A. Elorza, *La utopía anarquista bajo la segunda República española* (Madrid, 1973); J. Alvarez Junco, *Ideología y política del anarquismo español, 1880–1910* (Madrid, 1988); M. Bookchin, *The Spanish Anarchists: the Heroic Years, 1868–1936* (New York, 1977) and R. Gómez Casas, *Anarchist Organisation: the History of the FAI* (Montreal, 1986).

20. R. Cruz, *El Partido Comunista de España en la segunda República* (Madrid, 1987); V. Alba, *The Communist Party in Spain* (New Brunswick, NJ, 1983); P. Pagès, *Historia del Partido Comunista de España* (Barcelona, 1978); A. Elorza, 'In the Shadow of God: the Formation of the Comintern's Spanish Policy', in M. Narinsky and J. Rojahn (eds), *Centre and Periphery: the History of the Comintern in the Light of New Documents* (Amsterdam, 1996) and 'Stalinisme et Internationalisme en Espagne, 1931–39', in S. Wolokow and M. Cordillot (eds), *Prolétaires de tous les pays, unissez-vous? Les difficiles chemins de l'internationalisme (1848–1956)* (Dijon, 1993).

21. The BOC was itself an amalgamation of the original Catalan section of the PCE, which had been expelled in 1928 for failing to follow the Comintern line, and a small dissident Catalan Communist group, the Partit Comunista Català. It was by far the largest of the two parties, as the ICE had literally only a handful of members. See A. Durgan, *BOC 1930–1936: El Bloque Obrero y Campesino* (Barcelona, 1996) and 'The Catalan Federation and the International Communist Movement', in Centenaire Jules Humbert-Droz, *Colloque sur l'Internationale Communiste. Actes* (Geneva, 1992); V. Alba and S. Schwartz, *Spanish Marxism Versus Soviet Communism: a History of the POUM* (New Brunswick, NJ, 1988) and Y. Riottot, *Joaquín Maurín: de l'anarcho-syndicalisme au communisme (1919–1936)* (Paris, 1997).

22. In addition to works cited above see J. Mintz, *The Anarchists of Casas Viejas* (Chicago, 1982); A. Barrio Alonso, *Anarquismo y anarcosindicalismo en Asturias (1890–1936)* (Madrid, 1988), pp. 313–422; C. Ealham, 'Anarchism and Illegality in Barcelona, 1931–1937', *Contemporary European History*, 4, 2 (1995), pp. 133–52; G. Kelsey, *Anarchosyndicalism, Libertarian Communism and the State: the CNT in Zaragoza and Aragón, 1930–1937* (Amsterdam, 1992) and S. Juliá, *Madrid, 1931–1934: de la fiesta popular a la lucha de clases* (Madrid, 1984), pp. 147–265.

23. Luis Araquistáin, 'Tres años de la República', *Leviatán* no. 1 (March 1934).

24. On the growth of discontent see G. A. Collier, *Socialists of Rural Andalusia. Unacknowledged Revolutionaries of the Second Republic* (Stanford, Calif., 1987), pp. 88–130; A. Shubert, *The Road to Revolution in Spain. The Coal Miners of Asturias, 1860–1934* (Chicago, 1987), pp. 141–62; P. Biglino, *El*

socialismo español y la cuestion agraria, 1890–1936 (Madrid, 1986), pp. 383–441. On developments within the PSOE leadership see Juliá, *Los socialistas*, chap. 6 and Preston, *The Coming*, pp. 120–60.
    25. On attempts at unity see V. Alba, *La Alianza Obrera* (Madrid, 1978); S. Juliá, *Orígenes del Frente Popular en España (1934–1936)* (Madrid, 1979), pp. 12–26.
    26. G. Jackson *et al.*, *Octubre 1934* (Madrid, 1985); A. Shubert, 'The Epic Failure: the Asturian Revolution of October 1934', in Preston (ed.) *Revolution and War*.
    27. See Juliá, *Orígenes* and 'The Origins and Nature of the Spanish Popular Front', in M. Alexander and H. Graham (eds), *The French and Spanish Popular Fronts: Comparative Perspectives* (Cambridge, 1989); P. Preston, 'The Creation of the Popular Front in Spain', in H. Graham and P. Preston (eds), *The Popular Front in Europe* (London, 1987) and J. Tusell, *Las elecciones del Frente Popular*, 2 vols (Madrid, 1971).
    28. R. Viñas, *La formación de las Juventudes Socialistas Unificadas (1934–1936)* (Madrid, 1978); H. Graham, *Socialism and War. The Spanish Socialist Party in Power and Crisis, 1936–1939* (Cambridge, 1991), pp. 15–52; S. Juliá, *La izquierda del PSOE (1935–1936)* (Madrid, 1977) and Heywood, *Marxism*, pp. 171–9.
    29. J. Gil Pecharromán, *Conservadores subversivos: la derecha autoritaria alfonsina (1913–1936)* (Madrid, 1994); R. Morodo, *Los origenes ideológicos del franquismo: Acción Española* (Madrid, 1985); P. C. Gonález Cuevas, *Acción Española: teología política y nacionalismo autoritario en España (1913–1936)* (Madrid, 1998); M. Blinkhorn, *Carlism and Crisis in Spain, 1931–1939* (Cambridge, 1975).
    30. On the role of religion see F. Lannon, *Privilege, Persecution and Prophecy. The Catholic Church in Spain, 1875–1975* (Oxford, 1987), pp. 179–97 and 'The Church's Crusade against the Republic' in Preston (ed.), *Revolution and War*; M. Vincent, 'Spain', in T. Buchanan and M. Conway (eds), *Political Catholicism in Europe, 1918–1965* (Oxford, 1996). On the right as a whole see M. Blinkhorn, 'Conservatism, Traditionalism and Fascism in Spain, 1898–1937', in M. Blinkhorn (ed.), *Fascists and Conservatives* (London, 1990).
    31. S. Ellwood, *Prietas las filas. Historia de Falange Española, 1933–1983* (Barcelona, 1984); S. Payne, *Falange: a History of Spanish Fascism* (Stanford, Calif., 1962); J. Jiménez Campo, *El fascismo en la crisis de la II República* (Madrid, 1979); P. Preston, 'The Myths of José Antonio Primo de Rivera', in R. A. Stradling *et al.* (eds), *Conflict and Coexistence* (Cardiff, 1996); J. Gil Pecharromán, *José Antonio Primo de Rivera: retrato de un visionario* (Madrid, 1996); J. L. Mínguez Goyanes, *Onésimo Redondo, 1905–1936: precursor sindicalista* (Madrid, 1990).
    32. Quoted in Lannon, *Privilege, Power and Prophecy*, p. 200.
    33. *JONS* 2 June 1933; reproduced in R. Ledesma Ramos, *Escritos políticos 1933–34* (Madrid, 1985), p. 76.
    34. *JONS* 8 January 1934; *Escritos políticos*, p. 7.
    35. H. Thomas (ed.), *José Antonio Primo de Rivera. Selected Writings* (London, 1972), pp. 132–7.
    36. The extent to which the right was united in practice has been a matter of some debate. Paul Preston has interestingly suggested that the right as a whole can be seen as essentially fascist if it is compared with the coalition of support behind, for instance, Italian fascism. In this sense the Falange could be seen as

the radical fringe, much like similar movements within fascism elsewhere: P. Preston, 'Spain', in S. Woolf (ed.), *Fascism in Europe* (London, 1981) and 'Resisting Modernity: Fascism and the Military in Twentieth Century Spain', in P. Preston, *The Politics of Revenge* (London, 1995). See also Blinkhorn, 'Conservatism, Traditionalism and Fascism' and R. Griffin, *The Nature of Fascism* (London, 1991), esp. pp. 49–50.

37. Montero, *La CEDA*, vol 1, pp. 582–655.

38. Preston, *The Coming*, pp. 239–75; Payne, *Spain's First Democracy*, pp. 321–70.

39. A. Reig Tapia, 'La justificación ideológica del "alzamiento" de 1936', in García Delgado (ed.), *La II República*.

40. The bibliography on the war is vast and unrepeatable here. For good recent introductions and bibliographies see P. Preston, *A Concise History of the Spanish Civil War*, 2nd edn (London, 1996); G. Esenwein and A. Shubert, *Spain at War. The Spanish Civil War in Context, 1931–1939* (London, 1995) and M. Tuñón de Lara *et al.*, *La guerra civil española: 50 años después* (Madrid, 1985).

41. J. Aróstegui, 'Manuel Azaña y la guerra civil como tragedia', in A. Alted *et al.* (eds), *Manuel Azaña: pensamiento y acción* (Madrid, 1996); Gibaja Velázquez, *Indalecio Prieto*, chap. 8; Graham, *Socialism and War*, pp. 60–1, 138–9, 148.

42. At the centre of the debate is the anti-Communist view of Burnett Bolloten, best expressed in his *The Spanish Civil War: Revolution and Counter-revolution* (Hemel Hempstead, 1991). For a critique and persuasive alternative views see H. R. Southworth, ' "The Grand Camouflage": Julián Gorkin, Burnett Bolloten and the Spanish Civil War' and H. Graham, 'War, Modernity and Reform: the Premiership of Juan Negrín, 1937–1939', both in P. Preston and A. Mackensie (eds), *The Republic Besieged. Civil War in Spain, 1936–1939* (Edinburgh, 1996); H. Graham, 'Spain, 1936. Resistance and Revolution: the Flaws in the Front', in T. Kirk and T. McElligott (eds), *Opposing Fascism: Community, Authority and Resistance in Europe* (Cambridge, 1999).

43. W. Bernecker, *Colectividades y revolución social. El anarquismo en la guerra civil española, 1936–1939* (Barcelona, 1982); A. Castells, *Les collectivitzaciones a Barcelona (1936–1939)* (Barcelona, 1993); Kelsey, *Anarchosyndicalism*; M. Seidman, *Workers against Work. Labor in Paris and Barcelona during the Popular Fronts* (Berkeley, Calif., 1991); J. Casanova, *Anarquismo y revolución en la sociedad rural aragonesa, 1936–1938* (Madrid, 1985); M. A. Ackelsberg, *Free Women of Spain. Anarchism and the Struggle for the Emancipation of Women* (Bloomington, Ill., 1992); L. Garrido González, *Colectividades agrarias en Andalucía: Jaén (1931–1939)* (Madrid, 1979); and N. Rodrigo González, *Las colectividades agrarias en Castilla-La Mancha* (Toledo, 1985). In addition to the general works, Anarchist and POUM views can be followed in J. Peirats, *La CNT en la revolución española*, 3 vols (Toulouse, 1951–3); R. Tostorff, *Die POUM im Spanischen Burgerkrieg* (Frankfurt, 1987) and Alba and Schwartz, *Spanish Marxism*, pp. 111–71.

44. See C. Ealham, ' "From the Summit to the Abyss": the Contradictions of Individualism and Collectivism in Spanish Anarchism', in Preston and Mackensie (eds), *The Republic Besieged*, pp. 135–62. A. Montero Montero, *Historia de la persecución religiosa en España, 1936–1939* (Madrid, 1961) is the most reliable account of the religious persecution. See also J. M. Sánchez, *The Spanish Civil War as a Religious Tragedy* (Notre Dame, 1987).

45. Graham, *Socialism and War*, p. 89; T. Rees, 'The Highpoint of Comintern Influence? The Communist Party and the Civil War in Spain', in T. Rees and A. Thorpe (eds), *International Communism and the Communist International, 1919–1943* (Manchester, 1998), p. 153; Garrido González, *Colectividades agrarias* and Rodrigo González, *Las colectividades agrarias*

46. Juliá, *Los socialistas*, chap. 8; Graham, *Socialism and War*, pp. 53–85 and 'War, Modernity and Reform', pp. 167–9.

47. Juliá, *Los socialistas*, chap. 8 and Graham, *Socialism and War*, pp. 53–85; B. Bolloten and G. Esenwein, 'Anarchists in Government: a Paradox of the Spanish Civil War, 1936–1939', in Lannon and Preston (eds), *Elites and Power*.

48. Bolloten, *The Spanish Civil War* is the classic account from this perspective. See also E. H. Carr, *The Comintern and the Spanish Civil War* (London, 1984); D. Smyth, ' "We Are With You": Solidarity and Self-interest in Soviet Policy towards Republican Spain, 1936–1939', in Preston and Mackensie (eds), *The Republic Besieged*; Elorza, 'In the Shadow of God' and P. Broue, *Staline et la Révolution: Le cas espagnol* (Paris, 1993).

49. See Rees, 'The Highpoint of Comintern Influence?' 'Corrective' views of the revolution include Seidman, *Workers against Work* and J. Casanova, 'Social History and Spanish Anarchists during the Civil War', *International Review of Social History*, 37, 3 (1992–3), pp. 398–404.

50. See, for instance, the official history: D. Ibárruri *et al. Guerra y revolución en España, 1936–1939*, 4 vols (Moscow, 1966–77).

51. See Rees, The Highpoint of Comintern Influence'.

52. See Graham, 'Spain 1936' and 'War, Modernity and Reform' for excellent explanations.

53. R. Fraser, 'The Popular Experience of War and Revolution, 1936–1939', in Preston (ed.), *Revolution and War*, p. 231 makes the same point.

54. See A. Castells Duran, *El proceso estatizador en la experiencia colectivista catalana (1936–1939)* (Madrid, 1996).

55. F. Borkenau, 'State and Revolution in the Paris Commune, the Russian Revolution and the Spanish Civil War', *Sociological Review*, xxxix (1937), pp. 41–75.

56. H. Graham, 'The Eclipse of the Socialist Left, 1934–1937' in Lannon and Preston (eds), *Elites and Power*; 'War, Modernity and Reform' and *Socialism and War*, pp. 94–103.

57. Influential in creating this rhetoric was Palmiro Togliatti, Comintern advisor in Spain in the later part of the war: P. Togliatti, *Opere* 4, 1 (Rome, 1979), pp. 152–3 reproduces his speech 'Un tipo nuovo di repubblica democratica'. See also A. Elorza, 'Storia di un manifesto: Ercoli e la definizione del Frente Populare in Spagna', *Studi Storici*, 36 (1995), pp. 353–62.

58. For an overview of conditions in the Nationalist zone see J. Grugel and T. Rees, *Franco's Spain* (London, 1987), chap. 1 and Blinkhorn, *Carlism*, pp. 256–8.

59. S. Ellwood, 'Falange Española, 1933–39: from Fascism to Francoism', in M. Blinkhorn (ed.), *Spain in Conflict, 1931–1939* (London, 1986) and *Prietas*, esp. pp. 78–82; R. Chueca, *El fascismo en los comienzos del régimen de Franco* (Madrid, 1983).

60. This was best represented in the notion of a 'Crusade' against the Republic: H. Southworth, *El mito de la Cruzada de Franco* (Paris, 1963). On the role of repression in tying together the Nationalists see M. Richards, *A Time of*

Silence: Civil War and the Culture of Repression in Franco's Spain, 1936–1945
(Cambridge, 1998) and 'Civil War, Violence and the Construction of
Francoism', in Preston and Mackensie (eds), *The Republic Besieged*.
 61. P. Preston, *Franco* (London, 1993), pp. 144–83.
 62. M. García Venero, *Historia de la Unificación. Falange y Requeté en
1937* (Madrid, 1970); H. Southworth, *Antifalange* (Paris, 1967) and Ellwood,
Prietas, pp. 99–100.
 63. See Ellwood, *Prietas* and Chueca, *El fascismo*.
 64. Ellwood, 'Falange Española'; Chueca, *El fascismo*, pp. 233–64; M.
Aparicio, *El sindicalismo vertical y la formación del Estado franquist*a
(Barcelona, 1980) and A. de Miguel, *Sociología del franquismo* (Barcelona,
1975).
 65. J. Tusell, *Franco en la Guerra Civil* (Madrid, 1992), pp. 223–37;
S. Payne, *The Franco Regime* (Madison, 1987), pp. 180–2.
 66. R. Chueca, 'FET y de las JONS: la paradójica víctima de un fascismo
fracasado', in J. Fontana (ed.), *España bajo el franquismo* (Barcelona, 1986)
and *El fascismo*; Ellwood, *Prietas*, esp. pp. 128–30 and 'Falange Española';
P. Preston, 'Populism and Parasitism: the Falange and the Spanish
Establishment, 1939–75', in Blinkhorn (ed.), *Fascists and Conservatives*;
Grugel and Rees, *Franco's Spain*, pp. 30–43. The extent to which the regime
was still 'fascist' is a debate that lies outside this article.
 67. See Ellwood, *Prietas*; Preston, 'Populism' and Grugel and Rees,
Franco's Spain.
 68. For a recent example of the continued vitality of this debate see the spe-
cial issue of *Revolutionary History*, 4, 1/2 (1992) on 'The Spanish Civil War: the
View from the Left'.

8. YET ANOTHER FAILED GERMAN REVOLUTION?
THE GERMAN DEMOCRATIC REPUBLIC 1989–90   *Jonathan Osmond*

 1. This appeared as a spurious mathematical formula (Multiple dysfunction
+ Elite intransigence + X = Revolution) by Chalmers Johnson, cited in
A. S. Cohan, *Theories of Revolution: an Introduction* (London, 1975), p. 128.
 2. For example, H. Joas and M. Kohli (eds), *Der Zusammenbruch der DDR:
Soziologische Analysen* (Frankfurt am Main, 1993) pp. 9 and 49–50.
 3. See their respective memoirs: E. Krenz, *Wenn Mauern fallen: Die
friedliche Revolution: Vorgeschichte–Ablauf–Auswirkungen* (Vienna, 1990); G.
Schabowski, *Der Absturz* (Berlin, 1991).
 4. The Economist Intelligence Unit, *Country Report: East Germany* 4
(London, 1988), pp. 3–4.
 5. The Economist Intelligence Unit, *Country Report: East Germany* 1
(London, 1989), pp. 3–4.
 6. G. Schabowksi, *Das Politbüro: Ende eines Mythos: Eine Befragung*, F.
Sieren and L. Koehne (eds) (Reinbek, 1990); H. Modrow, *Aufbruch und Ende*
(Hamburg, 1991); H. Modrow, *Ich wollte ein neues Deutschland* (Munich,
1999). More recalcitrant are: G. Mittag, *Um Jeden Preis: Im Spannungsfeld
zweier Systeme* (Berlin, 1991) and Honecker himself in R. Andert and
W. Herzberg, *Der Sturz: Erich Honecker im Kreuzverhör* (Berlin, 1990).

7. A. Mitter and S. Wolle (eds.), *Ich liebe euch doch alle! Befehle und Lageberichte des MfS Januar-November 1989* (Berlin, 1990).

8. J. Kopstein, *The Politics of Economic Decline in East Germany, 1945–1989* (Chapel Hill, NC, 1997), pp. 78, 87–8; Schabowksi, *Absturz*, pp. 121–4.

9. See further comments in J. Osmond, 'The End of the GDR: Revolution and Voluntary Annexation' in M. Fulbrook (ed.), *German History since 1800* (London, 1997), pp. 456–7.

10. Probably the best currently in English are: K. H. Jarausch, *The Rush to German Unity* (Oxford, 1994); and C. S. Maier, *Dissolution: the Crisis of Communism and the End of East Germany* (Princeton, 1997). For overviews of the literature, see: J. Osmond, 'From Tubby and Biffy to Honecker and Kohl', *Times Higher Education Supplement*, 1220 (22 March 1996), 26–7; J. Osmond, review in *German History*, 15 (1997), pp. 173–6; M. Fulbrook, 'Re-Reading Recent (East) German History', *German History*, 17 (1999), pp. 271–84. For a chronology, a directory of people, places and organisations, and political and economic tables, see J. Osmond, *German Reunification: a Reference Guide and Commentary* (Harlow, 1992), pp. 3–14 and 201–55.

11. A few of many are: S. Meuschel, *Legitimation und Parteiherrschaft: Zum Paradox von Stabilität und Revolution in der DDR* (Frankfurt am Main, 1992); Joas and Kohli, *Zusammenbruch der DDR*; M. D. Hancock and H. A. Welsh (eds), *German Unification: Process and Outcomes* (Boulder, 1994); and J. Habermas, *A Berlin Republic: Writings on Germany* (Lincoln, 1997).

12. For example H.-J. Maaz, *Behind the Wall: the Inner Life of Communist Germany* (New York, 1995); Kopstein, *Politics of Economic Decline*; S. Meuschel, 'Revolution in der DDR. Versuch einer sozialwissenschaftlichen Interpretation', in Joas and Kohli, *Zusammenbruch der DDR*, pp. 93–114; G. Rein, *Die protestantische Revolution 1987–1990: Ein deutsches Lesebuch* (Berlin, 1990).

13. Maier, *Dissolution*, p. 167; G.-J. Glaessner, 'Am Ende des Staatssozialismus – Zu den Ursachen des Umbruchs in der DDR', in Joas and Kohli, *Zusammenbruch der DDR*, p. 74; M. Fulbrook, unpublished paper at the Cardiff conference on 'Ulbricht's Germany: State and Society in the SBZ/DDR 1945–1971', March 1999.

14. Maaz, *Behind the Wall* and *Das Gestürzte Volk: Die Verunglückte Einheit* (Berlin, 1991).

15. J. Gauck, *Die Stasi-Akten: Das unheimliche Erbe der DDR* (Reinbek, 1991), p. 25.

16. Maier, *Dissolution*, pp. 135 and 168ff.

17. See R. Collins and D. Waller, 'Der Zusammenbruch von Staaten und die Revolutionen im sowjetischen Block: Welche Theorien machten zutreffende Voraussagen?', in Joas and Kohli, *Zusammenbruch der DDR*, pp. 309–11.

18. See Hancock and Welsh, *German Unification: Process and Outcomes*, pp. 75 and 299. The portentous capital letters are in the original.

19. 'Change' or 'turn'; 'breakdown' or 'collapse'; 'upheaval' or 'radical change'; 'decline' or 'downfall'. In English Maier contributes 'dissolution' as the title of his book.

20. A. Mitter and S. Wolle, *Untergang auf Raten: Unbekannte Kapitel der DDR-Geschichte* (Munich, 1993). This work – 'Downfall in Instalments' – has met with criticism for its episodic concentration upon crises in the GDR from

the early years and its teleology of collapse. The difficulty in highlighting 1953, 1956, 1961 and 1968, as Mitter and Wolle do, is that these were crisis years which the GDR evidently survived.

21. C. Offe, 'Wohlstand, Nation, Republik: Aspekte des deutschen Sonderweges vom Sozialismus zum Kapitalismus', in Joas and Kohli, *Zusammenbruch der DDR*, p. 296.

22. K. Marx, *The Class Struggles in France* and *The Eighteenth Brumaire of Louis Bonaparte*.

23. Offe, 'Wohlstand, Nation, Republik', p. 296.

24. H. Bude, 'Das Ende einer tragischen Gesellschaft', in Joas and Kohli, *Zusammenbruch der DDR*, p. 278.

25. This point underlies much of the argument in Kopstein, *Politics of Economic Decline*.

26. For an elaboration of this East–West economic dimension, see Maier, *Dissolution*, especially pp. 102ff.

27. Modrow, *Ich wollte ein neues Deutschland*, p. 172.

28. A recurrent theme in Schabowski, *Das Politbüro* and in Modrow, *Ich wollte ein neues Deutschland*.

29. Modrow, *Ich wollte ein neues Deutschland*, p. 282.

30. See for example, Bärbel Bohley's distrust of Wolfgang Schnur and Rainer Eppelmann as conveyed in D. Philipsen, *We Were the People: Voices from East Germany's Revolutionary Autumn of 1989* (Durham, NC, 1993), pp. 297–9.

31. Cf. D. Pollack, 'Religion und gesellschaftlicher Wandel: Zur Rolle der evangelischen Kirche im Prozess des gesellschaftlichen Umbruchs in der DDR', in Joas and Kohli, *Zusammenbruch der DDR*, pp. 255–6.

32. Modrow, *Ich wollte ein neues Deutschland*, p. 244. In relation to the Dresden area Modrow writes of popular perception of 'the unjust advantaging of the capital'.

33. Modrow, *Ich wollte ein neues Deutschland*, pp. 152–257: 'Bezirk. Dresden', here particularly p. 175.

34. Cf. K.-D. Opp, 'DDR '89: Zu den Ursachen einer spontanen Revolution', in Joas and Kohli, *Zusammenbruch der DDR*, pp. 214–15.

35. Modrow, *Ich wollte ein neues Deutschland*, p. 272; P. Robinson, *Ludwig van Beethoven: Fidelio* (Cambridge, 1996), pp. 77–8.

36. This is a process under investigation in local studies. The issue is discussed in the review article by J. Grix, '1989 Revisited: Getting to the Bottom of the GDR's Demise', *German Politics*, 6, 2 (1997), pp. 190–8.

37. Cf. Gauck, *Die Stasi-Akten*, p. 13.

38. Modrow's attitude to the Federal Republic from his younger days is given expression in Modrow, *Ich wollte ein neues Deutschland, passim*. His trenchant view of Kohl's allegedly arrogant behaviour in February 1990 is to be found on pp. 420–1.

39. Cf. W. Zapf, 'Die DDR 1989/1990 – Zusammenbruch einer Sozialstruktur', in Joas and Kohli, *Zusammenbruch der DDR*, pp. 33–4.

40. For a detailed account of the meetings of the round table, see U. Thaysen, *Der Runde Tisch. Oder: Wo blieb das Volk?* (Opladen, 1990).

41. Modrow, *Ich wollte ein neues Deutschland*, p. 400.

42. Malcolm Lowry to Downie Kirk, 13 December 1950, quoted in G. Bowker, *Pursued by Furies: a Life of Malcolm Lowry* (London, 1993), p. 477.

9. THE AGE OF PARADOX: THE ANTI-REVOLUTIONARY REVOLUTIONS OF 1989–91 *Richard Sakwa*

1. Ivan Turgenev, 'On Belinsky', in G. Gibian (ed.), *The Portable Nineteenth-Century Russian Reader* (London, 1993), p. 390.

2. F. Halliday, 'Revolutions and the International', *Millennium: Journal of International Studies*, 24, 2 (1995), p. 279.

3. John Gray notes that 'It is in the common origins in the secular faith of the Enlightenment that the affinity of the two revolutions [the French and the Russian] is most plainly seen', including such notions as 'a self-consciously planned society' and of 'a universal civilisation grounded in scientific knowledge', *Post-Liberalism: Studies in Political Thought* (London, 1993), pp. 194–5.

4. R. Koselleck, *Critique and Crisis: Enlightenment and the Pathogenesis of Modern Society* (Oxford, 1988).

5. Contrary to the common view of Rousseau as the ideologue of the French Revolution, Koselleck notes, paradoxically, that Rousseau frequently warned of the dangers 'because the evils of a revolution were greater than the evils it wished to eradicate', *Critique and Crisis*, p. 161, fn. 7. Rousseau thus emerges as the first great anti-revolutionary, insisting on the unity of morality and politics.

6. The major works of these authors include: C. Brinton, *The Anatomy of Revolution*, revised edn (New York, 1965); T. R. Gurr, *Why Men Rebel* (Princeton, NJ, 1970); S. P. Huntington, *Political Order in Changing Societies* (New Haven, Conn., 1968); B. Moore, Jr, *Social Origins of Dictatorship and Democracy* (London, 1969); C. Tilly, *From Mobilization to Revolution* (New York, 1978); T. Skocpol, *States and Social Revolutions* (Cambridge, 1979); M. S. Kimmel, *Revolution: a Sociological Interpretation* (Cambridge, 1990); and J. A. Goldstone, *Revolution and Rebellion in the Early Modern World* (Berkeley, Calif., 1991).

7. C. Tilly, *European Revolutions, 1492–1992* (Oxford, 1993).

8. Cf. A. Giddens, *The Consequences of Modernity* (Oxford, 1990).

9. The characterization is by E. Voegelin, *From Enlightenment to Revolution* (Durham, NC, 1975), p. 167.

10. K. Marx, *The German Ideology*.

11. A. Walicki, *Marxism and the Leap to the Kingdom of Freedom: the Rise and Fall of the Communist Utopia* (Stanford, Calif., 1995).

12. Letter to Vera Zasulich, 23 April 1885, quoted in R. V. Daniels, *The End of the Communist Revolution* (London, 1993), p. 101.

13. Daniels, *The End of the Communist Revolution*.

14. N. Harding, The Marxist-Leninist Detour', in J. Dunn (ed.), *Democracy: the Unfinished Journey, 508 BC to AD 1993* (Oxford, 1993), pp. 155–88.

15. R. H. Dix, 'Eastern Europe's Implications for Revolutionary Theory', *Polity*, 24, 2 (Winter 1991), pp. 227–42.

16. Andrew Arato, 'Interpreting 1989', *Social Research*, 60, 3 (Fall 1993), p. 611.

17. For a contrary view, which suggests that even the apparently most anti-Enlightenment revolution of them all, the Iranian Revolution, in practice adopted European themes, see E. Abrahamian, *Khomeinism* (London, 1994).

18. E. Bernstein, *The Preconditions for Socialism*, edited by H. Tudor (Cambridge, 1993), p. 6.

19. M. Gorbachev, *Perestroika: New Thinking for our Country and the World* (London, 1987), pp. 55–9.

20. T. Garton Ash, ' Reform or Revolution?', *New York Review of Books*, 27 October 1988, pp. 47–56; 'Refolution in Hungary and Poland', *New York Review of Books*, 17 August 1989, pp. 9–15; see also his 'Refolution', in *The Uses of Adversity* (Cambridge, 1989), pp. 276–88.

21. R. Dahrendorf, *Reflections on the Revolution in Europe* (London, 1990), p. 22.

22. See M. Forsyth, *Reason and Revolution: the Political Thought of the Abbé Sieyès* (Leicester, 1987), pp. 98–102.

23. Arato, 'Interpreting 1989', p. 616.

24. The Meiji restoration has often been compared with the 'great' revolutions, giving rise, despite the traditionalist rhetoric, to profound processes of social, political and economic transformation, but failing to generate new patterns of autonomous political organisation, see S. N. Eisenstadt, 'Frameworks of the Great Revolutions: Culture, Social Structure, History and Human Agency', *International Social Science Journal*, 133 (August 1992), p. 389.

25. Eisenstadt, 'Frameworks of the Great Revolutions', p. 390; see also H. Webb, *The Japanese Imperial Institution in the Tokugawa Period* (New York, 1968).

26. C. Barker and C. Mooers, 'Marxism and the 1989 Revolution', paper presented to the PSA conference, University of Swansea, April 1994, collected papers, pp. 987–1001, at p. 999.

27. J. Habermas, 'What Does Socialism Mean Today? The Rectifying Revolution and the Need for New Thinking on the Left', *New Left Review*, 183 (September/October 1993), pp. 3–21; the description is from Arato, 'Interpreting 1989', p. 610.

28. On peasant revolutions, see the classic work by E. Wolf, *Peasant Wars of the Twentieth Century* (London, 1971).

29. For example, J. M. Colomer and M. Pascual, 'The Polish Games of Transition', *Communist and Post-Communist Studies*, 27, 3 (September 1994), pp. 275–94.

30. A. Michnik, 'A New Evolutionism', in *Letters from Prison and Other Essays* (Berkeley, 1985), pp. 135–48.

31. G. Konrád, *Antipolitics: an Essay* (San Diego, 1984).

32. D. Selbourne, *Death of the Dark Hero: Eastern Europe, 1987–90* (London, 1990), p. 236.

33. G. Konrád, *Antipolitics* (San Diego, 1984), p. 129.

34. Konrád, *Antipolitics*, p. 118.

35. Konrád, *Antipolitics*, p. 199.

36. Arato, 'Interpreting 1989', p. 613.

37. T. Garton Ash, 'Does Central Europe Exist?', in G. Schopflin and N. Wood (eds), *In Search of Central Europe* (Oxford, 1989), pp. 200–1.

38. T. Skocpol, *Social Revolutions in the Modern World* (Cambridge, 1994), p. 203.

39. The concept is discussed by K. Kumar (ed.), in his 'Introduction' to *Revolution: the Theory and Practice of a European Idea* (London, 1971), p. 2.

40. J. de Maistre, 'Supposed Dangers of Counter-Revolution', in *Considerations on France* (Cambridge, 1994), pp. 83–105 at p. 105.

41. A. Horváth and A. Szakolczai, *The Dissolution of Communist Power: the Case of Hungary* (London, 1992); Dmitrii Furman notes also how the Soviet

regime consistently sapped the viability of its own ideology by suppressing all sources of internal renewal, 'Revolyutsionnye tsikly Rossii', *Svobodnaya mysl'*, 1 (1994), p. 9.

42. R. Khasbulatov, *The Struggle for Russia* (London, 1993), p. 181.

43. M. Weber, *The Russian Revolutions*, translated and edited by G. C. Wells and P. Baehr (Oxford, 1995), pp. 23–4.

44. M. Kundera, 'The Tragedy of Central Europe', *New York Review of Books*, 26 April 1984. The latter point, and the italics, are from T. Garton Ash, 'Does Central Europe Exist?', in Schöpflin and Wood (eds), *In Search of Central Europe*, p. 195.

45. See in particular S. M. Frank, 'Etika nigilizma', in *Vekhi: sbornik statei o russkoi intelligentsii* (Moscow, 1909; reprinted Frankfurt, 1967), pp. 175–210.

46. *Iz glubiny: sbornik statei o russkoi revolyutsii* (Moscow, 1989).

47. A. Solzhenitsyn *et al.*, *From Under the Rubble* (London, 1974).

48. An argument made by Voegelin, *From Enlightenment to Revolution*, p. 252.

49. The distinction between stability and order is discussed in my 'The Fall of the USSR: a Structural Approach', in M. Cox (ed.), *Rethinking the Soviet Collapse. Sovietology, the Death of Communism and the New Russia* (London, 1999).

50. For an updated version of her arguments covering *perestroika*, see G. E. Schroeder, 'The Soviet Economy on a Treadmill of Perestroika: Gorbachev's First Five Years', in A. Dallin and G. W. Lapidus (eds), *The Soviet System in Crisis: a Reader of Western and Soviet Views* (Boulder/Oxford, 1991), pp. 376–82.

51. O. Rumyantsev, *Osnovy konstitutsionnogo stroya Rossii* (Moscow, 1994), pp. 159–60.

52. F. D. Colburn, *The Vogue of Revolution in Poor Countries* (Princeton, NJ, 1994).

53. Capitalism, of course, is still prone to crises, but the immediate prospects of an ideology based on the abolition of private property and the market would appear to be slim. For an excellent debate on the subject, see A. Shtromas (ed.), *The End of 'isms'? Reflections on the Fate of Ideological Politics after Communism's Collapse* (Oxford, 1994).

54. K. Vladina, 'Ded epokhi', *Nezavisimaya gazeta*, 10 August 1994, p. 5.

55. *Le Débat*, November–December 1990.

56. L. Holmes, *The End of Communist Power* (Oxford, 1993), p. xi and *passim*.

57. N. Ascherson, '1989 in Eastern Europe: Constitutional Representative Government as a "Return to Normality"?', in Dunn (ed.), *Democracy: the Unfinished Journey*, pp. 221–38.

58. M. Glenny, *The Rebirth of History: Eastern Europe in the Age of Democracy* (London, 1990).

59. Cf. Daniels, *The End of the Communist Revolution*, p. 108.

60. Arato, 'Interpreting 1989', p. 629.

61. D. Shlapentokh warns that the analogy also serves as a warning, noting in particular the rapid breakdown of governability in 1917 and 1991, 'Two Revolutions', *Current Politics and Economics of Russia*, 3, 1/2 (1992), pp. 133–5.

62. Cf. John Gray's view that 'Soviet totalitarianism is at war with the most fundamental institutions of the modern world', in 'Totalitarianism, Reform and

Civil Society', in *Post-Liberalism: Studies in Political Thought* (London, 1993), p. 195.

63. See R. Sakwa, 'The Revolution of 1991 in Russia: Interpretations of the Moscow Coup', *Coexistence*, 29, 4 (December 1992), pp. 27–67.

64. F. Fukuyama, 'The End of History?', *The National Interest* (Summer 1989), pp. 3–18.

65. Cf. Michael Oakeshott's approach to these problems, e.g. *On Human Conduct* (Oxford, 1975), and *Morality and Politics in Modern Europe* (New Haven, 1993).

66. L. A. Gordon and A. K. Nazimova, 'Perestroika in Historical Perspective: Possible Scenarios', *Government and Opposition*, 25, 1 (Winter 1990), pp. 16–29.

67. For example B. Kagarlitsky, *Restoration in Russia: Why Capitalism Failed*, translated by R. Clarke (London, 1995).

68. D. Erebon, *Michel Foucault* (London, 1991), p. 284.

69. K. Kumar, 'Introduction', in Kumar (ed.), *Revolution: the Theory and Practice of a European Idea*, p. 1.

70. More positively, in contrast to his thesis on 'the boredom at the end of history', Fukuyama describes a type of post-modern politics in which Marxist class politics is replaced by Nietzschean concerns for authenticity and autonomy (*thymos*), F. Fukuyama, *The End of History and the Last Man* (London, 1992).

71. Tamás, 'Civil Society', p. 213.

72. *The Observer*, 7 May 1995.

73. P. Wagner, *A Sociology of Modernity: Liberty and Discipline* (London, 1993).

74. H. G. Liddell and R. Scott, *A Greek–English Lexicon*, 7th edn (Oxford, 1983), p. 847, outline a number of meanings: we here use the term more in the sense suggested by Hippocrates and Demosthenes. I am grateful to David McLellan for an illuminating discussion on the issue, although he bears no responsibility for the views presented here.

10. THE REVOLUTIONARY IDEA IN THE TWENTIETH-CENTURY WORLD   *Krishan Kumar*

1. On the distinctly cool French response to the bicentenary, see E. Hobsbawm, *Echoes of the Marseillaise* (London, 1990), pp. ix–x, 96–113.

2. Richard Cobb's remark, from a talk of 21 July 1981, is quoted in the *Times Literary Supplement*, 7 August 1981, p. 919.

3. R. Lowenthal, 'The "Missing Revolution" of Our Times: Reflections on New Post-Marxist Fundamentals of Social Change', *Encounter*, June (1981), p. 18.

4. And not just in Eastern Europe, but even further east. The Chinese students who constructed the 'Goddess of Democracy' in Tiananmen Square in May 1989 paid explicit homage to the French Revolution in their struggle to achieve democratic rights.

5. A. Camus, 'Neither Victim nor Executioner' (1946), in K. Kumar (ed.), *Revolution: the Theory and Practice of a European Idea* (London, 1971), pp. 302–3.

6. Quincy Wright, quoted in S. Neumann, 'The International Civil War', *World Politics*, 1 (1949), p. 334, note 2.

7. Neumann, 'The International Civil War'.

8. On the Russian Revolution of 1917 as the model for Third World revolutions, see T. H. Von Laue, *Why Lenin? Why Stalin? A Reappraisal of the Russian Revolution. 1900–1930*, 2nd edn (Philadelphia, 1971).

9. Thus John Dunn, in seeking to explain the relatively high number of revolutions in the twentieth century, puts this down to 'the dramatic intensification in the economic relations between human populations across the globe', leading to an 'increasingly direct and hectic interaction of state powers across the globe'. *Modern Revolutions*, 2nd edn (Cambridge, 1989), p. xix.

10. On the play of international forces, specifically Portugal's NATO allies, in the Portuguese Revolution of 1974, see M. Kayman, *Revolution and Counter-Revolution in Portugal* (London, 1987). For the 1989 revolutions, see below.

11. F. Engels, 'Introduction' (1895) to K. Marx, 'The Class Struggles in France 1848–50', in K. Marx and F. Engels, *Selected Works in Two Volumes*, vol. 1 (Moscow, 1962), pp. 118–38.

12. Though the ingenious use of laptop computers and the Internet by some contemporary insurgents, such as the reborn Zapatistas of southern Mexico and the Shining Path guerrillas of Peru, should be noted. For Castro's remark, see R. Debray, *Revolution in the Revolution?* Trans. B. Ortiz (Harmondsworth, 1968), p. 67.

13. Debray, *Revolution in the Revolution?* p. 24.

14. For an example of Comintern thinking of the 1920s, see *Armed Insurrection* published in 1928 and attributed to the pseudonymous 'A.Neuberg' (London, 1970).

15. See e.g. E. Hermassi, 'Toward a Comparative Study of Revolution', *Comparative Studies in Society and History,* 18 (1976), pp. 211–35.

16. See further on this my 'Twentieth Century Revolutions in Historical Perspective', in K. Kumar, *The Rise of Modern Society: Aspects of the Social and Political Development of the West* (Oxford, 1988), pp. 177–83.

17. See J. H. Billington, *Fire in the Minds of Men: Origins of the Revolutionary Faith* (London, 1980); also M. Lasky, *Utopia and Revolution* (Chicago, 1976), Part One.

18. K. Marx, 'Contribution to the Critique of Hegel's Philosophy of Right', in T. B. Bottomore (trans. and ed.), *Karl Marx: Early Writings* (London, 1963), p. 55.

19. Lenin is quoted by C. B. A. Behrens, 'The Spirit of the Terror', *New York Review of Books*, 27 February 1969.

20. See especially L. Trotsky, *The Revolution Betrayed* (1936) (London, 1967), pp. 86–114.

21. The debates on these issues among Russian intellectuals in the early years of the revolution are discussed in J. Burbank, *Intelligentsia and Revolution: Russian Views of Bolshevism, 1917–22* (New York, 1986).

22. For these developments, see the characteristically incisive discussion in P. Anderson, *Considerations on Western Marxism* (London, 1976).

23. For Mao's attempt to 'transform a whole culture' through the 'Great Proletarian Cultural Revolution', and the relevance of this attempt to Western radicals, see the sympathetic account by R. M. Pfeffer, 'The Pursuit of Purity:

Mao's Cultural Revolution', in B. Mazlish, A. D. Kaledin and D. B. Ralston (eds), *Revolution: a Reader* (New York, 1971), pp. 338–57.

24. A. Huxley, 'Foreword' (1946) to *Brave New World* (Harmondsworth, 1964), p. 10.

25. Herbert Marcuse's most important work in this respect is *Eros and Civilization: a Philosophical Inquiry into Freud* (New York, 1962).

26. R. Vaneigem, *The Revolution of Everyday Life*, trans. J. Fullerton and P. Sieveking (London, 1973), p. 11.

27. The best account of the thinking behind the May events is A. Willener, *The Action-image of Society: On Cultural Politicization*, trans. A. M. Sheridan Smith (London, 1970); the most balanced account of the events themselves is B. E. Brown, *Protest in Paris: Anatomy of a Revolt* (Morristown, NJ, 1974).

28. See my 'Twentieth Century Revolutions in Historical Perspective', pp. 190–9.

29. L. Kolakowski, *New Statesman*, 27 July 1973, p. 119.

30. It is probably true to say that all serious conceptions of revolution have been 'totalistic', in the general sense that – at least since the French Revolution of 1789 – they have aimed at the creation of a new species of humanity in a totally transformed social environment. For the intellectual sources of such a conception of revolution, see B. Yack, *The Longing for Total Revolution: Philosophic Sources of Social Discontent from Rousseau to Marx and Nietzsche* (Berkeley, Calif., 1992). But up to the Russian Revolution, it was possible to some extent to separate 'the revolution' – the taking of state power on some more or less realistic model – from the creation of the 'new man' at some fairly unspecified date after the revolution. This was still, for instance, Trotsky's view in the 1920s. What has changed in the West in the period since is the fusion of these two phases or episodes. The revolution is, and must be, the making of the new man. These are virtually synonymous concepts and occur within a simultaneous process. The recoil in particular from the Russian Revolution has made it appear dangerous to separate the two.

31. See T. J. Clark, *The Absolute Bourgeois: Artists and Politics in France 1848–51* (Princeton, 1982), pp. 9–30.

32. See J. Berger, *Art and Revolution: Ernst Neizvestny and the Role of the Artist in the USSR* (Harmondsworth, 1967), pp. 31–48; S. White, *The Bolshevik Poster* (New Haven and London, 1988).

33. F. Halliday, 'Revolution in the Third World: 1945 and After', in E. E. Rice (ed.), *Revolution and Counter Revolution* (Oxford, 1991), p. 136. To the examples in the text we might want to add Turkey in 1919, Yugoslavia in 1945, Egypt in 1952, Mozambique and Angola in 1975, perhaps Afghanistan in 1978 – and even Russia in 1917, which has good claim to be considered, among other things, a Third World revolution.

34. See E. Kedourie, 'The Third World: the Idea of Revolution', in Rice (ed.), *Revolution and Counter Revolution*, p. 196.

35. F. Castro, *History Will Absolve Me* (London, 1968), pp. 95ff.

36. J-P. Sartre, 'Preface' to F. Fanon, *The Wretched of the Earth*, trans. C. Farrington (Harmondsworth, 1967), pp. 18–19. For Fanon's influence among Third World liberation theorists, see E. W. Said, *Culture and Imperialism* (London, 1994), pp. 322–36.

37. See D. Caute, *Fanon* (London, 1970), p. 94.

38. On the role of the middle stratum of the peasantry in Third World revolutions, see especially E. Wolf, *Peasant Wars of the Twentieth Century* (New York, 1969), pp. 276–302.

39. Fanon, *The Wretched of the Earth*, p. 254.
40. Caute, *Fanon*, p. 97.
41. For some examples see H. Munson, Jr, *Islam and Revolution in the Middle East* (New Haven and London, 1988).
42. Marquis de Condorcet, 'Sur Le Sens Du Mot Révolutionnaire' (1793), in Kumar (ed.), *Revolution*, p. 93 (my translation). In my 'Introduction' to this volume I tried to defend such a concept of revolution; today I would do so still, but differently.
43. See, for interesting discussions of some of these examples, E. Weber, 'Revolution? Counter-Revolution? What Revolution?', in W. Laqueur (ed.), *Fascism: a Reader's Guide* (Harmondsworth, 1979), pp. 488–531; R. H. Dir, 'The Varieties of Revolution', *Comparative Politics*, 15 (1983), pp. 281–93; E. K. Trimberger, *Revolution From Above: Military Bureaucrats and Development in Japan, Turkey, Egypt and Peru* (New Brunswick, NJ, 1978).
44. See especially Halliday, 'Revolution in the Third World', pp. 148–50.
45. P. Kropotkin, *The Great French Revolution 1789–1793*, trans. N. F. Dryhurst (London, 1909), p. 582.
46. F. Halliday, 'The Ends of the Cold War', *New Left Review*, 180 (1990), p. 5.
47. J. Habermas, 'What Does Socialism Mean Today? The Revolutions of Recuperation and the Need for New Thinking', in R. Blackburn (ed.), *After the Fall: the Failure of Communism and the Future of Socialism* (London, 1991), p. 27.
48. F. Furet, 'From 1789 to 1917 to 1989: Looking Backward at Revolutionary Traditions', *Encounter*, September (1990), p. 5.
49. Quoted in R. Darnton, 'Runes of the New Revolutions', *The Times Higher Education Supplement*, September 6 (1991), p. 17.
50. B. Geremek, 'Between Hope and Despair', *Daedalus*, Winter (1990), p. 99.
51. See my 'The 1989 Revolutions and the Idea of Europe', *Political Studies*, 40 (1992), pp. 439–61.
52. Habermas, 'What Does Socialism Mean Today?', p. 26.
53. See further on this my 'The Revolutions of 1989: Socialism, Capitalism, and Democracy', *Theory and Society*, 21 (1992), pp. 309–56; and 'The Revolutions of 1989 in East-Central Europe and the Idea of Revolution', in R. Kilminster and I. Varcoe (eds), *Culture, Modernity and Revolution* (London, 1996), pp. 127–53.
54. See especially M. Frankland, *The Patriots' Revolution* (Chicago, 1992), pp. 318–33.
55. See, for example, T. Garton Ash, *We, the People: the Revolution of '89* (Cambridge, 1990), p. 14.
56. Lenin, 'Lecture on the 1905 Revolution' (January 1917), in *Selected Works in Three Volumes*, vol. 1 (Moscow, n.d.), p. 842.
57. For the changes that have made revolution less likely in twentieth-century industrial societies, see my 'Twentieth Century Revolutions in Historical Perspective', esp. pp. 183–90.
58. See, for example, Octavio Pat, 'Twilight of Revolution', in I. Howe (ed.), *Twenty-Five Years of Dissent* (New York and London, 1979), pp. 314–25.
59. A. Camus, *The Rebel*, trans. A. Bower (Harmondsworth, 1962), p. 29.

Notes on Contributors

EDWARD ACTON is Professor of Modern European History at the University of East Anglia. He has published *Alexander Herzen and the Role of the Intellectual Revolutionary* (1979), *Rethinking the Russian Revolution* (1990), *Russia: the Tsarist and Soviet Legacy* 2nd edn (1995) and *A Critical Companion to the Russian Revolution, 1914–1921* (1997).

MOIRA DONALD is Senior Lecturer in History at the University of Exeter. Her publications include *Marxism and Revolution: Karl Kautsky and the Russian Marxists, 1900–1924* (1993) and *Gender and Material Culture*, 3 vols (1999).

KRISHAN KUMAR is Professor of Sociology at the University of Virginia. His publications include *Revolution: the Theory and Practice of a European Idea* (1971), *Prophecy and Progress: the Sociology of Industrial and Post-Industrial Society* (1978), *Utopia and Anti-Utopia in Modern Times* (1986), *Utopias and the Millennium* (1993), *From Post-Industrial to Postmodern Society: New Theories of the Contemporary World* (1995).

CATHERINE MERRIDALE is Senior Lecturer in European History at the University of Bristol. She has published *Moscow Politics and the Rise of Stalin: the Communist Party in the Capital, 1925–1932* (1990) and *Perestroika: the Historical Perspective* (1991).

JEREMY NOAKES is Professor of History at the University of Exeter. Among his publications are *The Nazi Party in Lower Saxony, 1921–1933* (1971), *Intelligence and International Relations, 1900–1945* (1987), *The Civilian in War: the Home Front in Europe, Japan and the USA in World War Two* (1992) and *Nazism, 1919–1945: a Documentary Reader*, 4 vols (1983–98).

JONATHAN OSMOND is Professor of Modern European History at the University of Wales, Cardiff. He has published *Rural Protest in the Weimar Republic: the Free Peasantry in the Rhineland and Bavaria* (1993) and *German Reunification: a Reference Guide and Commentary* (1992).

PAMELA PILBEAM is Professor of French History at Royal Holloway College, University of London. Her publications include *The French Revolution of 1830* (1991), *The Middle Classes in Europe, 1789–1914: France, Germany, Italy and Russia* (1990), *Republicanism in Nineteenth Century France, 1814–1871* (1995), *The Constitutional Monarchy in France, 1814–48* (1999) and *French Socialists before Marx: Workers, Women and the Social Question, 1796–1852* (2000).

230   *Notes on Contributors*

TIM REES is Lecturer in History at the University of Exeter. His publications include *Franco's Spain* (1997) and *International Communism and the Communist International, 1919–1943* (1998).

RICHARD SAKWA is Professor of Politics at the University of Kent at Canterbury. Among his publications are *Soviet Communists in Power. A Study of Moscow During the Civil War, 1918–21* (1988), *Soviet Politics: an Introduction* (1989), *Gorbachev and his Reforms, 1985–1990* (1990), *Russian Politics and Society* 2nd edn (1996) and *The Rise and Fall of the Soviet Union, 1917–1991* (1999).

Index

Index